75 Years of

GREYHOUND
CANADA 🍁

EVE HARRIS

GREYHOUND
CANADA 🍁
75th
1929   2004
Going Places for 75 Years

Library and Archives Canada Cataloguing in Publication

Harris, Eve, 1970-
        75 years of Greyhound Canada : a corporate history of
        Greyhound Canada Transportation Corp., 1929-2004 / by Eve Harris.

        Includes index.
        ISBN 1-55383-051-2

        1. Greyhound Canada Transportation Corp.–History.
        I. Greyhound Canada Transportation Corp. II. Title.
        III. Title: Seventy-five years of Greyhound Canada.

HE5635.Z7G74 2004   388.3'22'0971   C2004-906708-7

Design/Compostion: *Mad Dog Design Connection, Toronto*
Printed in Canada by *Friesens, Altona, Manitoba*

Available from:
Greyhound Canada Transportation Corp.
Attn: Dennis Tillotson
877 Greyhound Way S.W.
Calgary, Alberta T3C 3V8

CONTENTS

FOREWORD

As Greyhound Canada celebrates its 75th anniversary, I am very proud to share with you this account of our history.

Greyhound Canada has been an integral part of Canada's transportation landscape since 1929. From small beginnings in Nelson, B.C., our network has grown to encompass British Columbia and the Territories through the Prairies to Ontario and Quebec. Today we serve more than 1,200 communities across Canada, and provide interline connections throughout North America.

This anniversary marks an important stage in the continual process of upgrading our fleet and our facilities. We recently completed renovations to our Calgary terminal, opened our new Coquitlam terminal, and are embarking on a program to enhance our Southern Ontario commuter services in the Golden Horseshoe. At the same time we are making dramatic changes in our courier business, including adding a new pup trailer fleet and implementing new hardware and software applications to track and trace our shipments.

Since before the Great Depression, through World War II, the prosperous 50's, the computer age and into the new millennium, Greyhound Canada has been carrying people and packages safely, comfortably and reliably. We are committed to providing a quality, safe and affordable means of travel that is accessible to all Canadians; to offering new technologies that fulfill travel and shipping needs; to implementing intermodal terminals that provide true interregional connectivity; and to continually focussing our services in harmony with our customers' needs. Greyhound Canada is reinventing George Fay's spirit of innovation.

My thanks and congratulations to all Greyhound Canada employees, agents and partners who have helped us achieve our 75th anniversary. You're going places. Go Greyhound.

Dave Leach
Senior Vice President, Canada

A "Y" coach in front of Greyhound's Calgary head office and depot, 1932

CHAPTER ONE

OUR FOUNDERS

The creation of what would become Greyhound Canada Transportation Corp. began, very quietly, with a trip to Canada in the mid 1920s by George Fay, a sales manager for General Motors' Yellow Coach and Truck Division. During this sales trip Fay would meet Barney Olson, a taxi and sightseeing operator, his brother R.S. "Speed" Olson and John Learmonth, who operated a Nelson bus service.

Over the next five years, George Fay would bring the separate enterprises of these individuals together to form Canadian Greyhound Coaches Ltd., B.C. He would go on to bind together first large and small prairie and interior B.C. centres, and eventually the greater part of western Canada, to build the premier intercity bus company in the country.

George Fay at his office desk in the Southam Building

George Fay

George Black Fay was born on October 17, 1897 at Austin, Illinois, a suburb of Chicago, the son of a printer. As a boy he demonstrated an aptitude for mechanics and electrical work and became interested in airplanes, then in their early stage of development. When Fay was nineteen, the United States entered the First World War and he enlisted in the Army, where he quickly received his Master Electrician papers. Transferring to the 12th Aero Squadron, he was sent overseas and served in England, France and Germany. He advanced quickly and by war's end was a Master Signal Electrician, the first in the United States.

After serving in the army of occupation he was honourably discharged in June 1919 and upon his return to the United States went to work for the Curtis Aircraft Company. An ambitious young man, seeing little chance for advancement, he left Curtis in the early twenties to join General Motors' sales force, initially selling taxicabs for the company. At the time the White Motor Company was beginning to build buses and GM decided to get into this business as well. It created its Yellow Coach and Truck Division and Fay began selling motor coaches, initially working out of Chicago. He worked in a number of sales territories, including Virginia and the Carolinas, and at one point was sales manager for the state of Texas.

Sometime in the mid-twenties, the exact date is unclear, Fay became sales manager for Yellow in Seattle, working the Pacific Northwest. His territory included Washington and Idaho, and the Canadian provinces British Columbia and Alberta, new territory that he was instructed to open up. He was provided with the name of Barney Olson as a contact in Victoria, B.C., a man who was rapidly making a reputation for himself in the bus industry.

R.S. "Speed" Olson at the wheel of a Kootenay Valley Transportation Yellow "W" coach, 1929

Barney Olson

Harold B. Olson was born in 1895 near Milltown in northern Wisconsin. Of Danish descent, he was the third of four boys whose father farmed and ran a feed and flour mill until he met an early death. The family went through hard times and Harold was forced to leave school at fifteen and work in the lumber camps in the winter and on the railroad in the summer. He also spent two summers working in North Dakota as a farm labourer and eventually saved enough money to study his first love, automobile mechanics, at a school in Minneapolis.

By the time Harold graduated, his older brother Henry was working in British Columbia. Because he longed to travel and wanted to see the coast, Harold decided to head west. As he later remembered it: "I bought my ticket by day coach. My mother packed me a lunch. I arrived in Victoria October 5, 1912, with $4 in my pocket and my first long-pants suit paid for." He found his brother driving a truck hauling ties for the B.C. Electric Company Railway to Deep Cove, and took on a similar job. Soon he responded to an advertisement for a chauffeur for Charles Spratt, manager of the Victoria Machinery Depot, and got the job with his automobile school diploma. Spratt owned a large under-slung car. As automobiles were rare at the time, Olson was soon known around town as "Barney", from the famous race car driver Barney Oldfield.

Barney worked as Spratt's chauffeur for six years, saving his money with hopes of establishing a business of his own. His opportunity came in 1918 when he and two friends each bought a one-third interest in a taxicab. The three took turns driving, operating the cab around the clock, and within a year Barney was able to buy his partners out. At first he drove eighteen hours a day by himself, but soon became so successful that he was able to buy more cabs and hire other drivers. His big break came in 1921 when he gained the franchise for the taxi service at the CPR's luxurious Empress Hotel.

From then on, as the Empress Taxi and Sightseeing Company, he grew rapidly. About 1922 he purchased a Pierce Arrow from the Dunsmuir Estate and stretched it, making it into the first sightseeing bus on the island. Around the same time he joined with J.S.H. Matson, owner of the Victoria *Colonist*, in a company known as Circle Tours. This company took its name from the fact that it ran excursion buses on a circle route to Butchart

Barney Olson's stretched car, ca. 1925

Gardens, by ferry to the Malahat and then back to Victoria.

To assist him in this venture Barney brought out his younger brother, Roosevelt, from Wisconsin, who soon acquired a nickname of his own – "Speed" – a tribute to being pinched for driving a car thirty-five m.p.h. up the Yates Street hill. The sightseeing business also proved successful and in 1926 Barney took his next step, obtaining licences to run regularly scheduled bus service from Victoria to Nanaimo and return.

The Trip

When Fay first met Olson he found a man who, like himself, had great ambitions in the bus industry, and the two quickly became friends and associates. Olson gave Fay the names of several potential customers. There were already several small bus lines on Vancouver Island in addition to Olson's, such as Gorge Motor Bus Company, Union Stage & Taxi Company, and Motor Transport, Ltd. In Vancouver Fay paid a call on the B.C. Rapid Transit Company in an attempt to convince it to use Yellow coaches on its New Westminster route, rather than the White buses it had in service. Moving inland to the province's second most populous area, the Kootenays, he contacted John Learmonth, who had been operating a small bus business out of Nelson since 1922 using vehicles he had built himself.

Fay then visited Calgary, Alberta. He tried unsuccessfully to sell some buses for transit use to Bob Brown, the superintendent of the city's street railway system. But his main target in Alberta was a sightseeing company in Banff, the Brewster Transport Company, which was quickly becoming one of the major bus companies in Canada, and would in future play a significant part in the Greyhound Canada story. Unfortunately, his first sales contact with Brewster was unsuccessful, as the company had recently purchased several White buses, the sightseeing transportation standard in U.S. parks.

Despite the futility of this first B.C. – Alberta sales swing, the trip was important for Fay. Travelling over the rudimentary road system of the two provinces, he recognized the clear need for an extensive intercity bus system to tie together the growing communities, which were not adequately served by the railways. He put the idea in the back of his mind for future reference.

Inter-State Coach Company

Fay's friendship with Olson grew while B.C. and Alberta were a part of his sales territory. By 1929 Olson was experiencing legal difficulties with his partner Matson in the Circle Tours company and decided to sell instead of going to court, receiving $325,000 for his interest. Matson would later go on to develop the company into Vancouver Island Coach Lines.

This was just the opening Fay had been waiting for and he quickly approached his friend with a proposal. Fay knew of a small bus line operating between Spokane, Washington and Lewiston, Idaho, the Inter-State Coach Company. Fay's contacts in the bus business told him that the company had great potential and was available at a rock bottom price, as the owner was a recently widowed lady who wanted to sell. Olson was easily convinced and they purchased the company, with Barney providing most of the capital. Each partner held half the stock. Although he continued to sell for Yellow for the time being, Fay became secretary and treasurer of Inter-State.

The purchase could not have come at a better time. Unlike Canada, in the United States the railroad companies had quickly recognized the threat posed by intercity stage lines. Rather than try to fight by building expensive branch lines, most major railroad companies acquired bus holdings themselves. This was the case with Inter-State Coach. No sooner had Fay and Olson bought it than they began to negotiate with the Union Pacific Railroad for its sale. Ninety days after the acquisition they closed a deal with Union Pacific Stages, the railroad's bus subsidiary, netting a very quick and handsome profit.

After the sale, Barney Olson became involved in a transportation venture in Seattle with the Gray Line franchise. Meanwhile, with the profit from the sale, Fay felt ready to pursue his ideas about bus lines in the British Columbia interior and on the Alberta prairies.

John Learmonth

In 1922 John Learmonth began a bus service in the Kootenay Lake area with buses he had built himself on truck chassis. Like the captain of a ship, Learmonth gave his vehicles female names. He named his first one "Miss Balfour" after his first run between Nelson and Balfour, which he operated under the name of Learmonth's Motor Bus Lines. Later, when an additional service to Nakusp was added, he named his second bus "Miss Nakusp."

John Learmonth in his first bus, 1922

The original Nelson-Balfour run was a hair-raising, time-consuming adventure. The "Miss Balfour" left Nelson at 3:50 in the afternoon and made its way over the zigzag track through the numerous rock cuts that passed as a road, stopping at McDonald and Long Beach en route. At 6 p.m. the bus pulled into Balfour – two hours and ten minutes to cover roughly twenty miles.

"The Marjorie" at Trail, B.C., 1925

4

Learmonth, an excellent body man, bought a large Packard touring car in 1925 and stretched it to increase its passenger capacity. He called it "The Marjorie" and used it on his new daily service between Trail and Nelson. Jolted to pieces on the rough road, the car had to be rebuilt twice over the next few years when the frame broke. Each time the design changed and "The Marjorie" went through a number of transformations.

Kootenay Valley Transportation Company, Ltd.

Learmonth soon had competition in the Kootenays. Because the CPR lines ran more or less east and west across the area, there were many opportunities for north-south connections along the valley. Two other pioneer operators were Herb Harum, who ran between Nelson and Kaslo, and Adam Cruickshank, who served Nelson-Slocan. In November 1928 Harum joined with Learmonth and another operator, H. Fields, to incorporate their interests under a single operating name, the Kootenay Valley Transportation Company, Ltd.

This merger made the business into a saleable going concern and they soon attracted a buyer, Speed Olson. In early 1929 Olson bought the company, probably with money from his brother Barney, and John Learmonth took a job in a Nelson body shop.

This purchase provided the springboard for Fay's plan. It seems likely that Fay had convinced Barney Olson his idea of expansion was viable when Speed acquired the company. However, Fay did not initially have an interest in the company and it was only after the Inter-State sale that he came into the business as a partner with a nominal single share.

Canadian Greyhound Coaches Ltd., B.C.

On November 30, 1929 the Kootenay Valley Transportation Company was reincorporated under B.C. law as Canadian Greyhound Coaches Ltd., B.C. Using four buses and some 7-passenger touring cars, its operations were consolidated to Nelson-Trail, Nelson-Kaslo and Nelson-Nakusp. The decision to use the word "Greyhound" in the new company's name was to be significant and controversial, resulting in a protracted dispute in the years ahead.

This was only preliminary work for Fay's intended move east into Alberta, where he felt the real potential lay. He and Speed had already made several trips to the Calgary area to scout out the bus business, taking passenger counts at the various railroad stations at every opportunity.

Foothills Transportation Company, Ltd.

The first step Fay and Speed Olson took was contacting W.L. Watson, owner and manager of the Foothills Transportation Company, Ltd., who ran a one bus line from Calgary to Nanton. Securing an option to purchase Foothills, Fay went to Edmonton where he had some contacts. Through their influence he obtained an interview with O.L. McPherson, Minister of Public Works, whose department was responsible for regulating the infant provincial bus industry through the Public Vehicles Act of 1927.

As there were less than a dozen licensed operators in the entire province and as the government was anxious to improve public services, Fay had no difficulty in convincing the minister to extend the franchise. On November 29th the deputy minister wrote:

> Your application filed today between Calgary and McLeod, McLeod and Lethbridge and McLeod and Cardston has been accepted subject to the following conditions; that the rates be subject to the approval of the Public Utilities Commissioners, and that the Foothills Transportation Company withdraw the service they are now giving from Calgary south.

On November 30th, the same day as Canadian Greyhound Coaches Ltd., B.C. was incorporated, Fay and Olson purchased Watson's franchise and his interest in a Reo motor bus for the sum of $1,500. Fay made a down-payment of $5,000 and agreed to pay an additional $1,000 and take over responsibility for a $2,300 mortgage on the bus by January 15, 1930, the day on which the pair were to take over the business.

Canadian Greyhound Coaches Limited, Alberta

Agreement and licence in hand, Fay and Olson now had the foothold they needed to begin establishing the major operation they envisioned. On January 14, 1930, Canadian Greyhound Coaches Limited was incorporated under Alberta law with headquarters in Calgary. Among its objects were "to carry on the business of omnibuses, cab-dray, taxicab, motor-bus, auto-dray, motor truck, aeroplane, boats including motor boats and canoes, or other private or public conveyance . . ."

Fay and Olson each purchased one share for $100 to get the new company, Greyhound Coaches, underway. Once Fay was elected as president and managing director and Olson as secretary and treasurer, they began to acquire more shares. First, Fay subscribed to purchase 149 shares of common stock in

A Canadian Greyhound Coaches bus on a rudimentary road in the Kootenays, ca. 1930

the company with a par value of $100 each for cash. He had already advanced $6,300 as part of this cash to pay Watson for Foothills Transportation, some as a deposit on three buses being bought from General Motors and some to cover current accounts and loans of the B.C. operation.

As well, Fay was given an additional 100 common shares in return for turning over his option-agreement with Foothills Transportation and the extended franchise he had been able to acquire from the Minister of Public Works. Secondly, Speed Olson traded his 248 shares in Canadian Greyhound Coaches Ltd., B.C. for 249 shares in the Alberta company. This left each partner equally with 250 common shares in the new company.

Canadian Yelloway Lines, Ltd.

While Fay and Speed Olson were setting up Canadian Greyhound Coaches Ltd., Alberta, Barney Olson was establishing a second company in Calgary, Canadian Yelloway Lines, Ltd. Yelloway was created to operate service between Calgary and Edmonton, although the actual service would be handled by Fay and Speed Olson in conjunction with Greyhound Coaches. The "Yelloway" name had been borrowed from the United States where Yelloway was a transcontinental affiliation of independent lines.

The original rights on the Calgary-Edmonton run had been granted in 1927 to the Brewster Transport Company. However, since Brewster's service on the route had been very spotty, the Department of Public Works decided to let Yelloway have a go and see if it could be more dependable. This challenge to Brewster Transport on the Calgary-Edmonton run was the first of many times that Fay and the Olsons would find themselves locked in combat with this company.

On May 5, 1930, Greyhound Coaches created a new class of 7% preference shares valued at $100 each. Fay immediately purchased fifty of these shares for $5,000. At a subsequent directors meeting on July 8, 1930, Speed Olson transferred half of his 250 common shares to his brother Barney, who was then elected as a third director. The shareholders meeting which followed decided that the directors of the company should remain at three during the lifetime of the present shareholders, and also passed a resolution altering the Memorandum of Association to allow for the capital to be increased to $100,000 by the addition of 250 Class B non-voting shares valued at $100 each.

Next, the shareholders tidied up the matter of the associated Yelloway company. Payment of 250 Class B shares and fifty Greyhound Coaches preferred shares were tendered to Canadian Yelloway Lines as payment for the purchase of the assets, franchise and goodwill of the company. Barney Olson then immediately turned over half of the Class B shares he had thus obtained to his brother Speed. These manipulations effectively divided the control of Greyhound

Yellow Coach model No. 22. Parked outside the Calgary depot on Seventh Avenue SW in 1932, about to load for the 200 mile trip to Edmonton. The coaches were parked on the street until Greyhound purchased a small store beside the depot and built a canopied loading area

Coaches equally between Fay as one party and the Olsons as the other, each party owning 125 shares of the original voting stock, now known as Class A shares.

Finally, the shareholders agreed to buy partnership life insurance so that if any of them died the surviving shareholders could purchase his interest from the estate.

These arrangements complete, Fay and Olson faced the task of getting the company through its first summer of operation. It was now employing about twenty people and had twenty commission agents, with Fay acting as general manager and Speed Olson as operations manager. They hired a young Calgary accountant, Duncan Robertson, to take care of the finances. Chief mechanic Jack Deagon supervised the garage and made sure that the company's buses were in good running condition with the help of two Danish mechanics.

On September 16, 1930, Greyhound Coaches, Alberta began a new newspaper advertising campaign in the *Calgary Herald* under the slogan "Ride the Greyhounds." It listed the cost of round-trip fares to Edmonton, Lethbridge, Cranbrook, Spokane and Seattle, and highlighted connections at Spokane for Portland, San Francisco, and Vancouver, B.C.

Shortly afterwards, on November 19, 1930, the shareholders of Greyhound Coaches held a special meeting to consider a suggestion by Fay "that in view of the fact that the operations of the Company were being carried on in Alberta and westward into the Province of British Columbia as far as Nelson, and in view of the further fact that a possible amalgamation or merger might be made with the company incorporated under the laws of British Columbia under practically the same name, namely Canadian Greyhound Coaches (B.C.) Limited, under a name somewhat more descriptive of the scope of the company's operations as 'Central Canadian Greyhound Lines Limited', it would be advisable to change the name of the company accordingly."

The resolution passed unanimously and the B.C. and Alberta companies became one. However, the British Columbia operation continued to function as a separate branch, and by 1931 it was back under the direction of John Learmonth, whom Fay had been forced to buy out a second time when Learmonth began a small line in opposition to Greyhound Coaches, B.C. between Nelson and Nakusp. With its new name and rationalized organization, Central Canadian Greyhound went into its first winter of operation in Alberta.

CHAPTER TWO

MANAGEMENT AND OWNERSHIP
The Depression Years

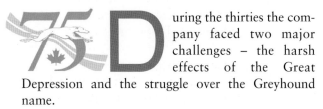

During the thirties the company faced two major challenges – the harsh effects of the Great Depression and the struggle over the Greyhound name.

The Great Depression
At the end of their first year of operation, Fay and the Olsons could take pride in what they had accomplished in such a short period of time. However, by the spring of 1931 the country was deep in the depression. As times got worse people had less money for travel, a luxury most had to do without. The only bright spot for the company was that, as fewer people could afford to own automobiles, their only choice was public transportation. Nevertheless, cash flow often slowed to a trickle, making it hard to pay for and maintain the equipment the company needed to provide the service.

Another fiscal concern during the depression was the amount of money the company was paying in road and gasoline taxes to the provincial governments. Fay recognized that Greyhound should pay its fair share for the exclusive right to provide public transportation over certain provincial roads, but felt that the amount charged was severe, particularly in Alberta. The application to license a motor bus in Alberta included an agreement "to pay to the Minister of Public Works 1/10th of a cent per passenger mile of travel, over or along Class A highways, and 1/15th of a cent per passenger mile of travel over or along Class B highways." Additionally, gasoline was taxed at .5 cents per gallon.

In a letter written to the minister in December 1930, Fay pointed out that the basic costs of operating a motor coach were 20% higher in Canada than in the United States before taxes were even considered. When taxes were added in, the cost became even greater. Using figures taken from Greyhound's first ten months of service, he calculated highway and gasoline taxes were $2,076 per annum per vehicle, plus a $36 licence fee, making a total of $2,112. This was four and a half times more than the average $475 paid in similar taxes per coach in the United States.

Fay said that he objected to the highway tax principally because it was applied to every seat in the coach, whether or not it was occupied. He then closed his appeal with two paragraphs that summed up very succinctly the importance of the new motor coach industry to the economy:

The Motor Coach Industry is a Public Utility. A good Motor Coach System furnishes an artery of commerce through the community and speeds up the heart beat of industry. With Public support and co-operation, the usefulness of Motor Coach Transportation may be developed to the highest point consistent with Public Welfare and Public Service. Every dollar of revenue received with the exception of equipment purchases and replacement parts remains in circulation in the community, represented by payrolls, purchases of supplies etc., and adds in a measure of that stabilizing quality that is necessary for general good business. We are personally desirous of giving to Alberta a Motor Coach System that is second to none, that will stand the test of any comparison.

We therefore urge that the matter of taxation be given your sincere consideration. We firmly believe that the present basis of taxation will materially retard the progress of this industry.

Despite the logic of his argument, it fell on the deaf ears of a provincial government that needed every dollar it could muster in its Depression-ridden treasury.

In the worsening economic situation and with high operating costs, the company lost money for the next few years even though its operating mileage increased. From 1930 to 1934 it lost an average of $1,600 a year on an average total operational mileage of 871,000. During these four years, company administrative salaries, including the salaries of Fay and Speed Olson, averaged $4,700 total per annum. Fay sometimes did not even cash his pay cheques.

An employee who joined the company in 1934 recalled that during his interview with Fay the president told him he could not pay very much – $60 per month was all he could afford. To emphasize the point, he pulled a handful of his own uncashed pay cheques out of his desk drawer. The job seeker got the point and was pleased to be offered a job at any salary in the circumstances. Drivers were paid at the rate of 1.5 cents per mile. One unfortunate driver pulled a very short haul with a 3-cent cheque that he framed and kept as a conversation piece.

The Greyhound Name

Money problems, although severe, were not the only difficulties Greyhound faced as the Depression continued. Equally ominous was a legal situation that threatened the very existence of the company. This arose from Fay's initial decision to use the word "Greyhound" in its name.

The problem first appeared in 1932 when the company expanded into interline transportation. Through Greyhound Coaches, B.C., it had two agreements with American companies. In order to offer service all the way to California it sought to extend its interline agreements beyond Spokane, first with Union Pacific Stages and Washington Motor Coaches to Portland and then with Pacific Greyhound Lines from there to San Francisco. In working out the last agreement the problem arose.

Mesaba Transportation Company

In the 1920s small bus lines were springing up like weeds all over the United States. Bus companies appeared literally by the thousands every year (there were 6,500 of them by 1925), most of them running only one or two buses over short routes. The most significant of these traced its origins to Carl Eric Wickman, a Swedish immigrant miner. In 1914 Wickman had been talked into opening a sales agency

for a popular automobile, the Hupmobile, at Hibbing in the heart of the rugged Mesaba Iron Ore Range in Minnesota. Wickman found little market for his product and ended up using his Hupmobile for a jitney service.

Because some miners wanted to visit a neighbouring town four miles away called Alice, the location of a popular saloon and bordello, he soon found it profitable to run a regular service between the two points. With the help of his friend Andrew Anderson, a blacksmith, he stretched the Hupmobile from a 7- to a 10-passenger capacity. Wickman began hourly departures from Hibbing to Alice. The fare was 15 cents one way or 25 cents for the round trip.

Wickman and Anderson drove the car in shifts virtually day and night and soon needed more equipment to expand the service. They purchased more cars, stretched them, and began serving other mining towns as well as carrying children to school. Consolidating their interests into the Hibbing Transportation Company, they approached Ralph Bogan, another jitney driver who had begun a similar service to Duluth, ninety miles distant. Bogan agreed to merge his operation with Wickman's and Anderson's, and in 1916 two additional partners and their fresh capital were brought in. The venture was reincorporated as the Mesaba Transportation Company, the embryo from which the Greyhound Corporation would eventually grow.

Each partner served as an officer and director of the company, as well as helping to drive the five bus fleet. The company did well and within two years the Mesaba Company had acquired eighteen buses and built its first garage. In 1922 Wickman decided to sell his interest and strike out on his own, purchasing the White Lines of Duluth, Minnesota and extending it to Minneapolis. His former partners also expanded, developing bus lines in Michigan, Wisconsin and Indiana.

In 1925 Carl Wickman combined his White Bus Lines with another company, Superior White Company, operated by Orville S. Caesar of Superior, Wisconsin, to form a new company, Northland Transportation Company. Like Wickman, Caesar had started as a frustrated automobile dealer unable to sell two new White buses. Using them as his initial fleet, he had begun Superior White's service between Superior and Duluth and later extended it to Ashland, Wisconsin. The new Northland company was large enough to attract the railroad and within a short time the Great Northern Railway bought a majority interest. Armed with substantial capital, the company, under Wickman's direction, began to integrate a number of smaller bus lines in the region, including the old Mesaba company.

This new integrated company was christened Motor Transit Management in 1926 and by 1928 was acquiring interests at an unbelievable rate. Shortly after Minneapolis banker Glenn Traer took over the company finances in 1928, he acquired over sixty bus lines in a matter of weeks. Expansion spread east from Detroit and west to the lucrative markets of California where several important bus companies had also begun in the late teens and early twenties. Two of the most notable were the Pickwick Stages, begun by J.T. Hayes using Model T Fords at a pick-up point in front of San Diego's Pickwick Theatre, and the Pioneer Yelloway System, originally an early family stagecoach business owned by W.E. "Buck" Travis. The purchase of Pioneer Yelloway cost Motor Transit $6 million in 1930, a tremendous investment considering the times.

Capital for major investments again came mainly from the railroads, including the Southern Pacific and the Pennsylvania and New York Central, allowing for such acquisitions as Southland Greyhound Company in Texas and for the formation of other subsidiaries such as Eastern Greyhound Lines on the Atlantic coast.

The Greyhound Corporation

In 1930 the name of Motor Transit Management was legally changed to the Greyhound Corporation, and the running greyhound dog was adopted as its trademark. The name in the United States had originally been used by Safety Motor Coach Lines of Muskegon, Michigan, which began to use the slogan "Ride the Greyhounds" in 1922, having bought some Fageol coaches painted grey.

Eventually Safety Motor Coach was absorbed by Motor Transit, which decided to capitalize on the advertising possibilities of the greyhound theme. By the early thirties, the Greyhound Corporation was serving 40,000 route miles and operating twenty-nine companies in seven divisions. It intended to protect the name.

Protection of the name was a concern not only in the United States but also in Canada where the Greyhound Corporation had established a presence. Seeing that the shortest, best route between Detroit and Buffalo lay through southern Ontario, the Corporation applied for and obtained running rights from the Ontario government and incorporated Canadian Greyhound Lines, Ltd. on January 14, 1930.

By pure coincidence, this was exactly the same date that Canadian Greyhound Coaches Ltd. was incorporated in Alberta by Fay and Olson. Canadian Greyhound Lines began its services in January 1931. Later the same year Canadian Greyhound acquired Arrow Coach Lines, which served Detroit and Toronto once daily as well as running frequent services between Windsor, Essex, Harrow and Leamington.

Considering his background in the United States and his industry connections, Fay must have been aware of the importance of the Greyhound name in North America and was capitalizing on it when he chose the name for his company. He had even borrowed the original Greyhound slogan "Ride the Greyhounds" and incorporated it into his advertising and stationery. Initially he must have given little thought to a conflict with the Greyhound Corporation, as it was still legally known as Motor Transit Management when Greyhound Coaches, B.C. was incorporated.

However, by 1931 he was having some concerns about the name and asked his lawyer, P.L. Sanford of the well-known Calgary firm of Bennett, Nolan, Chambers and Might, to do some investigation. In January 1931 Sanford reported on a recent case involving the Brewster Transport Company's dispute with an affiliation of sightseeing companies known as the Royal Blue Line. Brewster had used the Royal Blue Line name for some years on its stage services to southern Alberta, but had discontinued using it when Greyhound Coaches took away that business. Royal Blue Line (Massachusetts) then granted the use of the name to Brewster's competitor, Rocky Mountain Tours and Transport Company.

The case was argued all the way to the Supreme Court of Canada and the judgement went against Brewster Transport, the majority ruling that the company had not established sufficient use of the name to prevent other bona fide operators from using it as well. In fact, the judgement went further and expressed doubt as to whether any company could establish in a particular locality the exclusive right to the use of a name that had a wide reputation in other parts of the world.

This helped to set Fay's mind somewhat at ease regarding his company's use of the Greyhound name,

Fay's buses incorporated American insignia and markings from the outset

but Sanford pointed out a possible pitfall: if the Greyhound Corporation decided to open up branches in the Province of Alberta it too could legally use the name Greyhound. In light of this Sanford offered the advice that "in order to avoid any litigation on the question of the name, that you use every endeavour to come to some understanding with the Greyhound Lines Corporation of the States whereby you either become their agents in the Province of Alberta and British Columbia, or get their permission to use the name in the Province without interference by them." This advice was to temper Fay's actions for the next four years.

Fay's desire to make his first interline agreement with a Greyhound Corporation company, Pacific Greyhound Lines, brought the matter to a head. T.B. Wilson, president of Pacific Greyhound, recognized the value of the proposed agreement. The route was a logical one from the prairies to California, and he believed many Alberta residents would use it to come south to California for the winter and return home in the spring.

The Lawsuit

An informal arrangement allowed Central Canadian Greyhound to use the name of United States destinations on its buses and Pacific Greyhound to publish Central Canadian schedules and fares in its literature. But once copies of the correspondence between Fay

and Wilson reached the desks of officials of Greyhound Management Company, the arm of the Greyhound Corporation managing its eastern interests, including Canadian Greyhound Lines, matters took an ugly turn. In September 1931, Greyhound Management brought suit against Central Canadian Greyhound asking the court to award $5,000 damages and to restrain Central Canadian from using the word "Greyhound."

Fay expressed his feelings about the situation in a letter to Wilson, hoping for a sympathetic ear: "Personally, I regret very much that this situation has developed. At the time we first started operations in Canada there was no other company in Canada, or had we any knowledge or thought that the Eastern groups would ever have any desire to come into Canada. It seems rather unfair that an action should be started at this late date after we have spent considerable time and effort in establishing the name of our company."

On seeing a copy of this letter, O.S. Caesar, president of Greyhound Management in Chicago, wrote to his lawyer, C.P. McTague in Windsor, Ontario, informing him that he would contact Wilson "suggesting that if Central Canadian had developed into an important carrier for Mr. Wilson, they enter into an interline trip agreement for the use of the name, provided that they pay the costs which we have been put in this suit. They must also agree that if, or in the event that this agreement is ever cancelled, they will peaceably agree to give up the name of 'Greyhound' in that territory and for their company. In any event we must insist that the name 'Greyhound' can be used only as a trade name, and they are not to be allowed to use the name 'Greyhound' in their corporate set-up."

In his reply, McTague pointed out that Central Canadian was already using the word 'Greyhound' in its corporate name and he advised that it should continue to be allowed to do so "provided they admit that they derive the right from us, and that on our demand, as may be outlined in the agreement, they will agree to delete it from their corporate title." Of course, Fay was not prepared to do any such thing and, knowing the Supreme Court's Royal Blue Line decision, decided to let the suit proceed.

Matters dragged on with proposals and counter-proposals and Fay did not appear for examination for discovery in the Supreme Court of Alberta until October 17, 1932. Meanwhile, he gathered information from contacts he made in England with The Greyhound Motors Ltd. of Bristol that it had incorporated the Greyhound name in 1921. Furthermore, he learned that stagecoach services in England had used the name for many decades before that.

Fay's Examination for Discovery

At his appearance, Fay testified on a number of matters. He stated that when he incorporated in B.C. and Alberta he had no knowledge of any Greyhound operations in Canada, pointing out that Canadian Greyhound Lines had been incorporated on the same date as his Alberta company. He did admit that he had seen American Greyhound literature prior to incorporation and that his buses carried American destinations printed on their sides as well as a running greyhound dog. These, he maintained, were features "of any bus in the motor coach transportation business."

When pressed by the plaintiff's lawyer about the running dog symbol and in particular how it appeared on an insignia shield underneath the words "Greyhound Lines" as did the Greyhound Corporation's, Fay did admit that he had given a rough idea of what he wanted to the artist who had drawn it up. Among other things, he told the artist that he wanted the insignia to show mountains, because the company operated through the mountainous territory of B.C., to show the wheatfields of Alberta and to incorporate the slogan "Through the bread basket of the world" which he had formerly used while running Inter-State Coach. On further questioning, despite saying he couldn't remember the exact details, he did allow that he had probably told the artist where to put the running greyhound.

Fay's testimony went on to deal with the historic use of the name "Greyhound," pointing out its long usage in England and also drawing in its use in connection with "Ocean Greyhounds," blockade runners during the American Civil War. He finished his appearance by reiterating that when the partners started the business "we knew that there was no Greyhound operation within 1000 miles of our particular territory" and they therefore felt "there could be no possible connection between the two companies." The hearing concluded with his promising to provide the court with copies of all the company's tickets, advertising, schedules and baggage claim forms.

The Portland Conference

After the completion of examination for discovery, the Greyhound Corporation apparently became convinced that it was going to be very difficult to win its suit. Accordingly, it began to seek an accommodation, the first step being the holding of a conference in Portland. Representing Central Canadian Greyhound were Fay and Barney Olson, while Caesar, Wilson and B.W. Lemen acted for the Greyhound Corporation. The subject was two-fold: an interline agreement between Central Canadian and Pacific Greyhound; and a licence agreement to allow Central Canadian the right to use the word "Greyhound."

There was no disagreement on the first item, but its success was obviously contingent on the resolution of the second. Caesar presented a draft licence agreement that, with the exception of a few points that needed adjustment, was basically acceptable. One was the term of the agreement. It was decided to make the term for at least ten years with provision for renewal for similar periods thereafter provided the terms were carried out by both parties. The other item was the basis on which the Greyhound Corporation could cancel the agreement.

It was decided that the agreement would only be cancelled if the Canadian company created one of three conditions: 1) invading Greyhound's territory competitively; 2) permanently ceasing and abandoning the service; or 3) definitely and knowingly violating traffic agreements.

It was also decided that the two parties' attorneys should meet to consider a "side agreement" that would release Central Canadian from the licence agreement if the "highest court holds that the rights and exclusive use of the word 'Greyhound' is not subject to license nor owned or controlled by either Greyhound or the Canadian Company."

The meeting seemed to provide the consensus necessary for agreement, but several matters intervened to delay a final resolution. Primary was Fay's decision to back away for a time on the advice of his lawyers. They felt that the so-called "side agreement" should form a part of the actual licence agreement and that, in any event, "the Greyhound Corporation cannot restrain your use of the name 'Greyhound' in Alberta and B.C."

Also, the proposed interline traffic agreement became more complicated when it was suggested that two other American lines, Washington Motor Coach Company and Northland Greyhound, be included in it. Ultimately C.E. Wickman became frustrated with the lack of an agreement and led his lawyer to believe he "was willing to give the Central Canadian Greyhound Company the perpetual use of the name in exchange for traffic agreements and the admission that they were entitled to control the name."

In a further meeting in Seattle on December 22, 1934, Fay and Olson ironed out the differences. They agreed that the initial licence would be for ten years but that there would be a series of renewals for an additional fifteen or twenty years and that there would be an arbitration clause to settle disputes.

The licence issued was to cover "the territory east of a line from Trail, British Columbia to Tête Jaune Cache, British Columbia, via Vernon, British Columbia, also the entire Province of Alberta: also territory in Saskatchewan west of a line drawn from Orkney, Saskatchewan to Canwood, Saskatchewan via Swift Current, Saskatchewan and Saskatoon, not to include the licensing of an operation to any company between Saskatoon and Prince Albert, Saskatchewan."

"Greyhound" Licence Application

On March 7, 1935, pursuant to a resolution of the directors of the company, Fay signed the licence application. Its preamble read: "Recognizing the value and benefits of the name 'Greyhound' and/or 'Greyhound Lines' and the identifying insignia and colours which have been or may be adopted and are owned by The Greyhound Corporation as a trade name, the undersigned, engaged in business as a motor carrier of passengers for hire upon the public highways, being desirous of obtaining the right to the use of such trade name, trade-mark, insignia, and colours in said business, hereby makes application for license to adopt and carry such name on its motor coaches, advertising matter, schedules and tariffs and use the same as an identifying trade name in its business, and to use said identifying insignia in its business."

Wickman signed the licence on May 21, 1935. The same day, Central Canadian Greyhound, Pacific Greyhound, Northland Greyhound and Washington Motor Coach signed their interline traffic agreement.

The Greyhound Corporation may have won the battle over the use of the name "Greyhound," but Fay and Central Canadian had won the war. He had taken on the giant in North American bus transportation and had emerged unscathed. The claim for damages had been dropped, the company's name and all its routes were intact, and he had obtained even more American interline agreements than he had set out to.

Central Canadian Greyhound Lines

It was a feather in the cap for Fay and brought him to the attention of the decision-makers in the Greyhound Corporation, a fact that would have important future ramifications.

Temporary Halt to Expansion

Once the Saskatchewan boundary was reached in the east and the new U.S. connection inaugurated in the west, Central Canadian's expansion halted temporarily to regroup and build the resources necessary to continue. This was not surprising given that the company had continued to grow throughout five years of depression.

From small beginnings on the eve of the Depression, by 1935 Central Canadian had accumulated $282,640 worth of assets, the bulk of which ($253,500) were motor coaches. Almost all of these had been bought with operating funds, as banks were not inclined to lend money to anything so tenuous as a bus line during those difficult times. As witness, the company's liabilities showed only $1,500 in bank loans.

The profit and loss account showed total revenues of $399,000 based on 1,672,453 miles of operation for 1935. This included $366,800 in passenger revenue, $22,900 in express revenue, $11,100 in special revenue, such as charters, and a deficit of $3,000 on ferry tolls in its Kootenay Valley operations. Total operating costs were $329,000, the largest expenses being $62,000 for gasoline, $43,900 for bus repairs, $38,500 for drivers' wages and bonuses, $26,700 in garage salaries and $15,300 for road taxes and licences.

Profit in 1935

These figures produced a profit of $70,000 for 1935; an impressive showing since the cumulative profits to this point had been $2,300. In the circumstances, the shareholders decided that the company should accumulate enough profits to declare a dividend on the 7% cumulative preference shares. Considering the work that Fay and Speed Olson had put into the business to date for very little return, this was entirely appropriate.

Barney Olson's Return

Another factor that may have influenced the halt in the expansion drive concerned Barney Olson's situation. Olson, a silent partner in Central Canadian, initially spent his time developing his Gray Line operation in Seattle and running a bus service from Seattle to Spokane. His bus service went broke around 1932, forcing Barney to look for other sources of income. In 1933 he acquired the Robertson Scotch Whiskey distributorship on the West Coast and moved his family to Whittier, California, near Los Angeles. This new endeavour also had its problems and by 1935 he was pressing Fay for some sort of income from Central Canadian, offering to become actively involved in the business.

After five years of having his own way, Fay was not prepared to share the role of chief executive officer. He devised a solution that was acceptable to the two Olsons. Under the terms Barney Olson agreed to take no active part in the company other than "spreading goodwill" on its behalf in return for

Barney Olson with Seattle Gray Line coach

receiving a salary equivalent to five-ninths of the salary paid to either Fay or Speed Olson to a maximum of a $12,000 annual salary for the latter two.

With this security in hand, Barney once again became involved in a new business. The new company, called Trans Continental Coach Lines Limited, incorporated in Manitoba late in 1935 and established its headquarters in Winnipeg, where the Olson

Greyhound's mid-thirties advertising used a popular cliché, the Mountie

family had moved. The company began its operations on a route between Winnipeg and Virden, Manitoba that it acquired from Manitoba Motor Coach, owned by Fred Geiler of Brandon, one of the biggest bus concerns in the province.

Under Olson's direction Trans Continental soon began to challenge Manitoba Motor Coach and Manitoba's other major operator, Grey Goose Bus Lines of Winnipeg, as the pre-eminent company in the province. Fay and Central Canadian Greyhound had no direct interest in the company, all the shares being held by Barney Olson, but Fay likely loaned some of the capital to get the business started. Central Canadian also had a strong working relationship with Trans Continental and seemed content, for the time being, to let it develop Manitoba routes.

First Dividend

Meanwhile, things slowly improved in Central Canadian's own operation. By early 1937 it could address the dividend question and in April 1937 the company paid dividends on the preferred shares in the amount accumulated to January 1, 1937. This made such a dent in the company's coffers that Fay was forced to reduce salaries between April and the beginning of July.

The number of employees grew quite rapidly as the decade progressed and several smaller companies were acquired. As a result of these take-overs, a new position, general passenger agent, was created to oversee all ticket agents throughout the system. The first person to hold this position was Grant Smith, promoted from his position as depot manager in Edmonton in 1935. His successor was a man whose knowledge, experience and understanding of the bus industry would guide Greyhound into the complex modern era of bus transportation. His name was Robert L. "Bob" Borden.

Bob Borden

Robert L. Borden was born October 14, 1914 in Edmonton, the son of Willard Borden, originally from Pugwash, Nova Scotia. Willard Borden had fought in the Boer War and then worked as a mine manager in Coldsboro, Nova Scotia before going to New York to work as a steelworker. His wife contracted T.B. in New York and the doctors at the Mayo Clinic suggested a move to a drier climate in Arizona or Alberta.

As Willard was eligible for a soldier's land grant, the choice was easy. He took out the land grant near Saint Paul, northeast of Edmonton, staying just long

Robert L. "Bob" Borden

job was available he soon left and took on a position at Burns Packers for the winter. He was laid off the following spring. At loose ends, he accompanied the junior basketball team he was coaching to a tournament in Calgary. While there he heard he could get some training as a Greyhound ticket agent, and having been promised a position in the Edmonton depot as soon as one became available, he decided that it would be good experience.

Bob spent the next several months at the Calgary depot learning all aspects of the operation. George Fay spent a fair amount of time in the ticket area and Bob soon got to know him well. By the summer of 1935 he was back in Edmonton. That fall Grant Smith left to take on his new duties as general passenger agent, deWynter became depot manager, and Bob secured the position of ticket agent.

Edmonton Training Ground

The Edmonton depot proved an excellent training ground for Borden, as it had for several other individuals who went on to have notable careers with Greyhound, including our present Senior Vice President, Dave Leach. Grant Smith had been the first depot manager and had hired Jerry Brown as ticket agent. Jerry Brown later became traffic manager in Calgary and district superintendent in Vancouver. Similarly, Smith had hired Bill deWynter who would go on to other important positions in the company, acting as a district superintendent for many years and upon Lorne Frizzell's retirement succeeding him as vice president, transportation and labour relations.

The Union Bus Depot, as it was known, was opened by Greyhound on May 1, 1931 at the corner of 102nd Avenue and 102nd Street in a remodelled garage that once belonged to Eaton's department store. The Edmonton depot was busier than the headquarters depot in Calgary because it was shared by other bus lines such as Frizzell's Midland Bus Lines and J.V. Horner's Northland Rapid Transit. Because the Calgary office left the Edmonton operation entirely in the local manager's hands, often not contacting him for weeks on end, those working there received a more rounded education in solving the problems of bus line operation.

The work was hard and the hours were long at the Union Depot. When Borden started as ticket agent he made $60/month and deWynter, the depot manager, made $105/month. Jack Green was in charge of baggage and the steadily growing express department. The three of them kept the depot open

enough to prove up the land, while working as a steelworker on the building of the High Level Bridge and the construction of the Grand Trunk Pacific Railway. After the railway's completion, he went to work for its successor, Canadian National Railways, for the remainder of his career.

Bob Borden grew up in Edmonton and attended Alec Taylor School and Victoria High School, graduating in the spring of 1932. He spent three months at the University of Alberta, but decided that it was not for him. Through a friend he got a job at the Institute of Applied Arts copying and mailing out materials for the provincial correspondence school. Laid off at the end of the term, he was able to get a summer job through his father with the C.N.R. in Jasper National Park. Originally employed to maintain the line, he was soon promoted to the transportation department. There he sold tickets and provided information at the company's desk in the Jasper Park Lodge, gaining his first experience in the transportation business.

Upon his return from Jasper at the end of the summer, Bob was asked by a family neighbour, Bill deWynter, if he would like to help out at the Edmonton bus depot. Bill had gone there to work as a ticket agent in May 1931. Borden agreed and worked as a joe-boy for a while, but as no permanent eighteen hours a day, seven days a week, opening at 6 a.m. to prepare for the first bus out at 6:45 and closing at midnight, or later, after the last bus due at 11:30 p.m. had arrived. They also sold tickets and provided services for smaller lines. If any of the three employees was sick or took a day off, which they rarely did, the remaining two covered for him.

Fay must have been impressed with Borden's performance during his two and a half years in the Edmonton depot. When Smith was promoted to district superintendent, Fay appointed Bob "out of the ranks" to general passenger agent, a practice that became a hallmark of Greyhound operations. Borden left Edmonton on May 24, 1938 for Calgary to take on his new role, and was so busy he did not return to see his wife, Jerry Brown's sister whom he had married in 1933, until October.

In fall 1939 Borden was promoted to the position of district superintendent in Regina. This was short-lived, as Fay soon called him back to Calgary to assist at the head office on special assignments. At one point he was required to go to Winnipeg and assist Barney Olson with the management of Trans Continental Coach Lines, essentially giving him responsibility for its operations from Winnipeg to Swift Current.

Borden's star in the company was clearly on the rise as Fay began to rely on him more heavily to assist with the increasingly complex management of Greyhound. The same growth was leading Fay and the Olsons to think about other options open to them, which would soon lead to one of the most important events in the history of the company – its sale.

Partnership Troubles

On the eve of the Second World War, Fay and the Olsons had been building Greyhound for ten years. Their impressive success had come at a heavy cost. Seven-day weeks were the norm for Fay and Speed Olson throughout and for Barney Olson during his years with Trans Continental. Acquisitions had been paid in cash and by assuming existing debts, so the company, although strong on paper, made little profit for the shareholders.

There were also signs that the partnership had worn itself out. Observers noted that Fay constantly complained that he was doing all the work, Barney Olson was continually bragging that he was the money behind Greyhound, and Speed Olson's abrasive nature was irritating everyone. Speed's personality had effectively kept operations running in the

early days of the company, but as its interests expanded and its staff increased, his rough treatment of employees became a detriment. It made Fay's life more difficult and he finally took his concerns to Barney Olson.

The result was a settlement very similar to that which had been worked out in 1935 with Barney before he began Trans Continental. In July 1939 Speed agreed to resign and not to "interfere in any manner whatsoever with the management or business of the company", in return for a salary of 75% of the salary paid to either of the other two directors, and "to do anything he could to promote the interests of the Company at any time insofar as it did not interfere with any other activities in which he may be engaged, but only at the express instructions of either the President or H.B. Olson."

Fay and Barney accepted this offer and at the same meeting directed that a 7% dividend be declared in favour of the holders of the preferred stock of the company as soon as Fay felt the funds were available.

With this matter settled, things seemed to get better as Jerry Brown assumed most of Speed's responsibilities. The company entered two long term commitments, including an agreement between the directors that no one of them would have the right to sell his stock without the consent of the other two for a ten year period.

Up for Sale

Despite these commitments to the future, it was not long before the possibility of selling Central Canadian Greyhound was being actively discussed. Fay was probably aware that they had taken the company as far as it could go with the capital available. The future was clouded with the Second World War raging in Europe and Canada's involvement increasing.

Barney Olson appeared to be tired of living in Winnipeg and wanted to return to the coast, perhaps to pursue other business interests and increase his time with his family. Fay also had family concerns, as in August 1935 he married Irene Hill, the daughter of a Calgary real estate developer, and by 1940 the couple had two children, a son George Robert (Bob) and a daughter Marguerite Anne.

Whatever the motivation, by the summer of 1940 the partners were actively looking for a buyer.

War Time

With growing business uncertainty as World War II began, the forties opened with the historic sale of Greyhound. Business would soon be impacted by the war's restrictions on supplies, but the war would also bring perhaps Greyhound's finest moment – The North West Service Command.

Looking for a Buyer

Because many bus companies in the United States, including the Greyhound Corporation, were largely owned by railroad companies, the first approach was made to the Canadian Pacific Railway. This approach made sense, as in several areas Greyhound was their chief competitor. As well, Greyhound's package express services, begun as a convenience to its customers, had grown to the point where Greyhound was now competing with the railway on small freight.

Unfortunately, although some negotiations were held, the CPR was not prepared to make a serious offer. Fay and Olson then turned to the next potentially interested party, the Greyhound Corporation of Chicago, Illinois.

The Greyhound Corporation

Following the resolution of the Greyhound trademark issue, the relations between Central Canadian Greyhound and the Greyhound Corporation had been very cordial. The many Greyhound Corporation bus companies and affiliates had increasingly included Canada in their advertising. Almost every piece of literature featured a map which showed connecting lines in the two countries.

The interline agreements had also proven valuable for all concerned, particularly the connection that Trans Continental forged with Northland Greyhound Lines in Winnipeg. Northland

Greyhound operated routes out of Minneapolis west as far as Butte, Montana. As well, it ran north from Fargo, North Dakota through Emerson, Manitoba into Winnipeg.

This allowed for the first direct exchange of passengers between a Central Canadian Greyhound-controlled company and a major American Greyhound Corporation line. Through the Northland connection and those with other Greyhound companies, including Canadian Greyhound Lines, Ltd. in Ontario, passengers could travel all the way to southern Ontario from western Canada, although the route east of Winnipeg lay in the United States.

The potential of this route was not lost on Carl Wickman and other officers of the Greyhound Corporation, and the time was ripe to acquire more Canadian interests. Waging a cut-throat price war with other bus companies, the Corporation had survived the effects of the Depression, the intervention of the Interstate Commerce Commission and the imposition of a nation-wide Motor Carrier's Act in 1935. By the late thirties it had completed a reorganization streamlining its twenty-nine affiliated companies into seven operating divisions.

The Corporation was now a giant, owning over 2,500 buses, employing 9,500 people and operating over 200 million miles a year. At the time its officers began to look seriously at Central Canadian Greyhound, the Corporation's interests had grown so broad that it was also actively negotiating five other major acquisitions in the United States.

The Purchase

Details of the discussions leading up to the offer by the Greyhound Corporation to purchase Central Canadian Greyhound and Trans Continental Coach Lines are sketchy, but they seem to have been initiated by Fay and carried out on the Corporation's behalf by W.S. Moore and Merrill Buffington, comptroller and secretary respectively.

Agreement was reached by early October 1940. On October 14th, Buffington met with fellow attorney D.A. McNiven of Regina, Saskatchewan, on retainer with the Greyhound Corporation, to draw up the Memorandum of Association for a new company, Western Canadian Greyhound Lines, Ltd. Once completed, the two lawyers met in Calgary with Fay and Corporation executives W.S. Moore and R.E. Maxwell. On October 18th the five men formalized the sale of the stock of Central Canadian to Western Canadian Greyhound.

Barney Olson was paid $325,000 for his 125 Class A, 125 Class B and 600 preferred shares, while Speed Olson received $270,000 for his 125 Class A, 125 Class B and 50 preferred shares. In both cases part of the payment was in cash, $225,000 for Barney and $170,000 for Speed, and the balance was in the form of a debenture bearing 5.5% interest. As part of the agreement, the brothers both transferred their one remaining share of Trans Continental Coach Lines to the company.

With that, the Olsens were now completely out of the company they had helped to develop from a few old buses running short routes in the Kootenays into western Canada's major stage line. Both returned to Victoria and once more became involved in the city's business community, using the profits they made on the sale. Speed built the first motel in Victoria, the Windsor, and later acquired an automobile dealership on Yates Street, Olson Motors. In 1946 Barney bought one of the city's landmarks, the Strathcona Hotel on Douglas Street, and subsequently became very involved with bringing hockey to Victoria, renovating the old Willows Arena in the fairgrounds.

In contrast, Fay had no intention of cutting his Greyhound ties, and his agreement was slightly different, reflecting the fact that he would manage the new company and would remain a shareholder. For his 250 Class A and 100 preferred shares, Fay received $200,000 in cash, $50,000 in 5.5% debentures and 2,975 $50 shares of the capital stock of Western Canadian Greyhound. In addition, he purchased twenty-five shares for cash, giving him a total of 3,000 shares valued at $150,000.

The four Greyhound Corporation executives subscribed one share each and the Corporation itself purchased 11,996 shares. Of the 15,000 shares issued,

Fay now owned 20% while the Greyhound Corporation owned or controlled 80%. The agreement called for the Greyhound Corporation to buy out Fay's interest over a fifteen-year period at a price based on annual earnings.

After the creation of the company it became normal for the board to annually pass a resolution paying off $25,000 of capital plus accumulated interest on the outstanding debentures held by Fay and the Olsons.

Western Canadian Greyhound

After allocating shares, the meeting turned to transferring some shares to the chief executive officers of the Corporation and to electing officers for the new company. McNiven's share was transferred to C.E. Wickman and Merrill Buffington's to O.S. Caesar. The directors and officers were then elected, creating the following slate: chairman of the board, C.E. Wickman; president, G.B. Fay; vice president, O.S. Caesar; treasurer, R.E. Maxwell; comptroller, W.S. Moore; assistant comptroller, Duncan Robertson; secretary, D.A. McNiven; assistant secretaries, Merrill Buffington and Duncan Robertson.

Western Canadian Greyhound was now a corporate entity and owned all the stock of Central Canadian, but it did not yet own the company's physical assets. To address this, the Calgary meeting on October 18th was followed by an extraordinary general meeting held in Greyhound Corporation headquarters in Chicago on November 13, 1940 at which only Caesar, Maxwell and Moore were present, the rest of the shares being voted by proxy. The meeting ratified the actions of the previous meeting, completed legal requirements of registration and incorporation, and set in motion the transfer of the physical assets of Central Canadian to Western Canadian Greyhound. The meeting also gave approval for the new company to negotiate the acquisition of all the outstanding shares and physical assets of Trans Continental Coach Lines from Central Canadian.

A complicated but essential series of dividend declarations by Central Canadian in favour of Western Canadian, whose directors and officers were now one and the same, and a transfer of assets by payment from Western Canadian to Central Canadian followed. Central Canadian then applied to the Highway Traffic Boards of Alberta and Saskatchewan and the Public Utilities Boards of Manitoba and British Columbia for a transfer of licenses to the new company.

George Fay (center) and Barney Olson (second from right)
with officials at the Manitoba Transit Board, ca. 1940

On November 30, 1940 the transfer of the assets officially took place and Central Canadian Greyhound ceased to exist. An agreement to acquire the shares and assets of Trans Continental Coach Lines from Central Canadian was also ratified and Trans Continental also ceased to exist.

The operating transition went smoothly. Employees with Greyhound at the time recall no great changes in operation except in Duncan Robertson's financial area where some Greyhound Corporation accounting practices had to be adopted. Day to day, the business carried on much as it had, without the Olsons.

Early War Years

Travel was not restricted in the early war years. In fact, the number of Canadian service persons in training and the establishment of new military bases in the west created substantial leave travel as enlisted men visited or received visits from their families. Where Greyhound served military bases in the west, it had to put on extra schedules to handle the passenger loads.

Former driver Jack Rajala, who operated the Kingsgate run during the early war years, remembers the number of military wives he carried who were going to visit their husbands based on the west coast. Trying to save money, they travelled by bus rather than train, only to find that Canadian money was worth less than American during the U.S. portion of the trip.

The situation changed in November 1941 when the wartime transit controller announced the imposition of gas rationing. The number of routes and/or service on each route was seriously examined and, in some instances, eliminated. A further order from the controller the following spring prohibited the operation of buses for sightseeing purposes or the supplying of charter service of an unessential nature.

The greatest impact came when the transit controller issued an amendment effective November 15, 1942 restricting bus companies to operating passenger services only fifty miles in any direction, in order to save gasoline and rubber for the war effort. Although subject to special consideration in cases where no other form of public transportation existed, this restriction put a real crimp on Greyhound's operations.

The company was able to obtain special permission to run main routes such as Calgary-Lethbridge and Calgary-Edmonton, but the trip had to be made in two parts on two different days with passengers overnighting in Red Deer. In other instances the regulations could be stretched by having one driver take the bus to the fifty-mile limit and then turning it over to a new driver. Eventually the less important routes were affected and there was soon a surplus of equipment and drivers.

Just when operations seriously began to suffer, relief came in a directive from the Greyhound Corporation headquarters. This opportunity would give Greyhound an enviable reputation in wartime service and remain an inexhaustible source of pride.

The North West Service Command
In agreement with the Canadian government, in 1942 the United States embarked on building the Alcan Highway to shore up the continent's northern defences against the threat of Japanese attack. The United States Army Corps of Engineers, North West Service Command, intended to build a basic but passable road, 1,574 miles long, between Dawson Creek, British Columbia, and Fairbanks, Alaska, in eight months.

The Engineers immediately had trouble transporting military and civilian personnel, because the drivers assigned to troop truck transport were unfamiliar with the hilly, muddy and icy road conditions on the graded-out road northward from Dawson Creek.

As luck would have it, Ralph Bogan, one of the participants in the Mesaba Company from which developed the Greyhound Corporation and now one of the Corporation's chief executive officers, had been commissioned as a Colonel with the Engineers and had been appointed as an aide to the commanding officer of the project. Bogan contacted Fay in the fall of 1942 and asked him to provide the transportation, since Greyhound's American equipment wasn't designed for the rugged terrain, nor were its drivers familiar with the driving and weather conditions.

At the time, Fay was beginning to worry that some of Greyhound's under-utilized buses might be appropriated for wartime use, as there was a shortage of good transportation equipment in Canada. He was very interested in the opportunity the North West Service Command presented, as it was suggested that the U.S. Army would enter into a contract if a system using Greyhound men and equipment could be worked out.

Greyhound immediately took steps to become legally registered in both the Yukon Territory and

Alaska, and on December 23, 1942 agreed to a temporary contract with the United States government to operate on the Alcan Highway on a trial basis.

The Contract
The contract specified that Western Canadian Greyhound would make available at Dawson Creek, British Columbia, twelve of its "37-passenger standard Greyhound motor buses" and enough drivers, mechanics and dispatchers to ensure the operation of these buses in scheduled service. The buses, assigned special North West Service Command numbers, were subject to inspection by the contracting officer, the military official charged with administering the agreement.

Those to be transported in the area covered by the contract, Dawson Creek to Fairbanks, included "personnel of the military forces of the United States of America, civilian employees of the United States of America, and workmen and others employed by the United States of America and/or its contractors and agencies."

In return, the company would receive fifty cents per mile per bus per day, with a minimum payment of $80 per day for each bus guaranteed. As well, the government would provide suitable housing and mess facilities for the company's employees, office space for administrative and clerical employees, gasoline, oil, tires, the parts necessary to keep the buses operating, and shop facilities for storage and maintenance.

Greyhound men and equipment were on the scene before the contract was even concluded. On November 20, 1942, four of the company's best drivers, all unmarried men, were informed as they returned from their runs to prepare to go to Alaska immediately. These were Bill Brown, driving the MacLeod-Kingsgate run, Walt Hyssop, on the Lethbridge-Calgary service, Jack Tait and Don Luck. They were told to bring one suitcase and a sleeping bag and take the next bus to Calgary.

In Calgary the drivers watched as two 37-passenger buses were loaded on C. & E. flatcars. Chief mechanic Joe Kirk had specially provided these with fender skirts, a particularly strong heater and other necessities. Then, joined by mechanic Bill Broderick and superintendent of maintenance and transportation Lorne Frizzell, the four drivers boarded the train for the long trip to Dawson Creek, the jumping off point for the Alcan Highway.

Clear Necessity

The Northern Alberta Railway north of Edmonton was jammed with military and construction personnel, but the crew and buses arrived in Dawson Creek without incident. On unloading the buses, the crew found a crowd of people waiting to go up the highway, which had been closed to troop trucks because of problems they were experiencing with three bad hills between Dawson Creek and Fort Nelson. At the same time the aircraft usually flying up the highway were grounded because of bad weather.

Laden down with tool boxes, sleeping bags and other paraphernalia, a telephone crew piled into every available space on the buses, and the drivers drove off over what was basically a bulldozed track through the bush towards Whitehorse, almost a thousand miles away. In the hilly section between Dawson Creek and Fort Nelson the evidence for their need was clear to see. The sides of the road at the bottom of the hills were littered with trucks where the drivers had bailed out when they lost control. At one point they passed a yard with 700 wrecked vehicles in it!

Their own situation was not particularly rosy. On several occasions the crew and passengers had to get out and push the buses up a slippery hill or chop grooves in the ice at river crossings so the vehicles could get traction. Spelling each other off, the drivers pushed onward and arrived at Whitehorse in 65 below zero temperatures after a fifty-five hour non-stop trip.

At Whitehorse, the military authorities did not know what to make of the buses, as they had not been informed that Greyhound was coming. However, they were quite willing to take advantage of the opportunity, and after the buses were repaired and gassed up the drivers were immediately ordered to make the return trip.

The return trip was equally difficult and Frizzell decided that the buses were not geared low enough to handle the rough road. While the drivers and mechanic bunked in at the Dawson Creek Hotel, he returned to Calgary to go to work on the problem. A couple of weeks later a new lower-geared rear end arrived for one of the buses with instructions from Frizzell to install it and try it out on another run.

Because the Greyhound operation still lacked official status, the second trip was as problematic as the first. Fuel was not supplied and several times the drivers were forced to stop and suck gas out of nearly empty abandoned gas barrels. At one camp where nothing else was available, they used a half-barrel of diesel fuel that made the engine smoke, although the bus kept going. Nevertheless, the new rear end worked and the project now seemed feasible.

The original crew was soon joined by a few others, and they spent much of early 1943 bunked in at the hotel while they waited for further orders from Fay in Calgary. He was now trying to get the United States government to sign the contract that had been negotiated in December so that the service could officially begin.

Greyhound personnel assigned to the Alcan Highway at Whitehorse, November 1942.
Back Row: Frizzell, Mountie, Mountie, Brown. Front Row: Luck, Hyssop, Tait, Broderick

Initially, Greyhound personnel had to find fuel in abandoned gas barrels

Dawson Creek Explosion

While the crew was waiting for orders, a dynamite shed across the street from the hotel caught fire and exploded, killing twenty-two people. The drivers were lucky not to be badly hurt, even though Jack Tait was blown right out of the room in which he was staying into one across the hall. He emerged unscathed, carrying two children whom he had had the presence of mind to scoop up on his way out.

Standing on the railway station platform 200 feet away, driver Bert Wilson was hit by a flying timber that broke his leg. He was evacuated to Edmonton by air that night with the other injured. After receiving $2,000 compensation he decided not to go back. Bud Armstrong was walking past the temporary Greyhound office set up under Norman Lord's direction and was hit in the head with Lord's typewriter when it came flying through the window.

After the explosion Greyhound personnel slept on the buses with other Dawson Creek residents for several days until alternate accommodation could be arranged.

Operation Underway

Despite the length of time it took to sign the contract (the Secretary of War ratified it on April 16, 1943), the Greyhound operation was fully underway in February. Fay in Calgary was soon receiving glowing reports. On February 19th he received a letter from Tom Kirkham, a former Greyhound ticket agent who had gone to work at Trans-Canada Air Lines as supervisor of passenger agents:

I took the CNR out of Edmonton Wednesday night to Winnipeg. There must have been 200 US Army and US contractors employees on board.

I asked quite a few of them who had been working on the Alaska Highway if they had seen anything of the Greyhound Lines up there and they all answered yes. The answers varied but the consensus of opinion was that there were no finer buses or drivers anywhere and that it was one outfit that "sure knew what it was doing" or "they could teach a lot of our guys how to run things efficiently."

Buoyed by such reports, Fay decided to inspect the operation personally. He arrived in Dawson Creek in early March, accompanied by Lorne Frizzell, Bob Borden and Joe Kirk. Using a Greyhound Packard sedan, and carrying a letter of introduction from the commanding officer, the party took a tour of inspection along the highway.

By the time he returned from the trip, the Army Engineers were already requesting Greyhound to make more buses available. Unfortunately, there were no more to spare and the United States government began to buy its own to supplement the company's fleet. Greyhound agreed to provide drivers for these in a new contract that Fay had been negotiating for some time.

Dated June 15, 1943, the new contract had a major improvement over the first one, as it guaranteed Western Canadian a small profit. The contract

North West Service Command drivers with American military authorities at Whitehorse, 1943

estimated total monthly operating expenses at $59,130 and agreed that the government would pay a "Contractor's fee" of $1,304 per month over and above these costs. As well, it would pay a rental fee of $40 per vehicle per day and would, as in the past, reimburse the company on all direct expenses for fuel, supplies, equipment and services.

By the summer of 1943 the Alcan service was in full swing with the buses being driven 24 hours a day in the continuous summer light. Because the drivers worked in pairs, usually two drivers at a time were notified that they were to go on the highway detail. A bus would be picked up in Calgary, driven to Edmonton and then loaded on the railway for shipment to Dawson Creek, just like the first two. The twelve buses used were all built by Fort Garry Motor Body in 1941 and were equipped with Hall Scott horizontal, opposed-cylinder "pancake" engines.

Once the bus was unloaded at Dawson Creek the drivers worked a relay up the highway. They would pick up a load of passengers in Dawson Creek and share the driving up the first leg of the highway to Fort Nelson, where they would hand the bus over to another pair of drivers who would take it up the next leg to Whitehorse. All the driver teams worked on the first-in, first-out basis, the crew that brought the bus in handing it over to the crew in first who drove it up the next leg.

As the number of buses and crews working the highway increased, the Dawson Creek – Whitehorse section was broken into three legs, each about three hundred miles long, with relay points at Fort Nelson and Watson Lake. Drivers worked their way up the highway through the three legs and then drew the assignment of running a transit service that operated between Whitehorse and the various military and civilian construction camps that stretched some ten miles out from the city. This might have seemed a respite after the gruelling drive up the highway, but it was not, as each driver worked it for eighteen hours from 6 a.m. to midnight.

After this fourth leg, the men received a lay-over and then were assigned to start back down the highway or to go on the two northern relays, Whitehorse to Tok Junction and Tok to Fairbanks. Very few of the drivers ever got to Fairbanks as there was only about one trip a day north of Whitehorse compared with three or more a day coming into the city.

Road and Weather Conditions
Coping with the weather and the almost unbelievable road conditions left a strong impression on the men who drove the Alaska Highway. While there were inevitable mishaps as buses slid off the road, there were no serious accidents or injuries in over a million miles of operations over muskeg, icy roads and dangerous river crossings.

One driver remembered an occasion when he stopped his bus at the Robison River because of uncertain ice and the bus had to be pulled across by cable. His apprehension was not greatly relieved when he looked down through the crystal clear ice and twenty feet of water to see a brand new bulldozer sitting on the bottom.

At times the roads were so bad they were closed to all vehicles except the buses, which had to carry on. Along the route the bush was littered with the remains of planes caught in bad weather that had tried to use the road as a landing strip.

Despite the environment, most drivers took the job in stride, as they had been chosen for their winter driving experience. The road was constantly improved throughout 1943 and ploughed as frequently as possible in winter conditions. Even when the road was icy, drivers could stay between the snowbanks by keeping at least one wheel in a rut. Oddly enough, the worst conditions came when the temperature warmed up a bit in February and March, sometimes resulting in rain. Every driver dreaded the wet ice it created, as despite his skill, there was almost nothing he could do in such conditions.

Although the men on the North West Service Command put in long hours in harsh conditions, they were certainly well taken care of. Each man swore an official U.S. government oath of secrecy when beginning the job. He was then issued a military-style uniform with khaki pants and a sheepskin overcoat for cold weather duty. At the end of a leg the crews were put up in military dormitories or, if they were full, in a hotel. At Fort Nelson they even had their own barracks built.

In camp drivers received all the privileges of an officer, and many recalled the great meals they received in the mess hall or the 25 cent cigars they could purchase for 2 cents. While they were seconded to the project they were paid their normal salary by Greyhound and retained all their seniority in the company. Every six weeks they were allowed passage to Edmonton to take a two-week "furlough." They

The need for Greyhound drivers was evident all along the Alcan Highway

Military personnel pushing a bus up a slippery hill

could take the train, or if they were lucky they might catch a lift on the armed forces aircraft. Drivers remembered the numerous bottles of whiskey they had to produce on their return from Edmonton to obtain an empty seat on a "full" airplane.

"Arctic Bus Ride"
The fact that the Greyhound service had become a critical element in the construction of the Alcan Highway was attested to in an article written by Richard L. Neuberger, a former *New York Times* correspondent, who was serving as an aide to Brigadier-General James O'Connor, the officer in charge of highway construction. Originally appearing in *Argus* magazine, Neuberger's article, "Arctic Bus Ride," was read into the record of the 78th Congress of the United States on January 10, 1944 by Homer D. Angell, a member of the House of Representatives from Oregon, who himself had recently returned from Whitehorse:

"Night has blacked out the land by now. I fold an Army blanket over me and settle across my seat on the bus. Sleep comes quickly. We all awaken as the lights in the bus flash on, hours later. We are at Fort Nelson, where the road turns sharply westward toward Alaska. I look at my wrist watch. It is 4 in the morning.

"Two men have been driving our bus, each alternately sleeping or taking a turn at the wheel. Now two other drivers take over. E.R. Bavin, of Edmonton, and Grant Thompson, of Cranbrook, British Columbia, are replaced by Ray and Fraser Maxwell, brothers from Saskatoon, Saskatchewan.

"As the bus leaves Fort Nelson, its fuel truck replenished, the soldiers settle back to sleep once more. But I am wide awake; the sleep had been coaxed from me. I sit up in front and talk to Fraser Maxwell. I learn that all these drivers are men from the western Canadian division of the Greyhound Lines. They have come north voluntarily, signing up for stretches of 6 months each . . . Most of them come from Edmonton, Calgary, Lethbridge, Vancouver and Saskatoon . . .

"At the Watson Lake relay station, the Maxwell brothers gave up their driving posts and wearily sought out the barracks reserved for the bus drivers. Their places were taken by Bill Cherlenko, of Lethbridge, and Fred Enns, of Calgary. It was Fred's first week on the highway, and he was still goggle-eyed at the experience of driving for a thousand miles and not coming to a single town or village. 'Some wilderness,' expressed his primary reaction.

"On we rolled, toward our second sunset on the road. I thought of Fred's comment. We had been travelling nearly 35 hours and averaging 25 miles an hour, yet we had not come to any settlement. Here on the North American continent was an immense forest and mountain fastness, dotted only by isolated Indian villages, Hudson's Bay stores and mounted police posts, and now by relay stations and airports of the RCAF and the American Army . . .

"Our bus jounced on. We cross the headwaters of the Yukon River, and looked down at the greenish torrent which would end its individuality in the Bering Sea, 2,100 bleak miles away at St. Michael. I wandered what Jack London, who had taken boatloads of Klondikers through these uplands, would have written about our bus with its load of soldiers. I am sure he would have gone back through the skein of all our lives and woven a tale to match those of the men who travelled here by dog sled and hand-hewn raft."

Completion of the Highway

Once the building of the highway was completed in the fall of 1943, Greyhound's services were still required to carry personnel up and down the road. By this time the highway had also become a staging route for getting Russian pilots trained in the United States into Russia. Walter Hyssop had been paired with a driver who had worked for Red Bus Lines and could speak Russian. When the Army command discovered this, the pair was assigned to carry pilots back and forth from the camps at Fairbanks to the airstrip, where they were flown into Russia. Hyssop recalled one occasion, after Fairbanks had been fogged in for several days, watching 102 planes come down the runway making the flight across the Bering Strait.

While Greyhound was involved in the North West Service Command project, its other operations had personnel shortages. Many company men had volunteered for military service and most of the drivers and mechanics working on the Alcan Highway were those who had been turned down when they volunteered. Bob Borden had volunteered but the National Selective Service Commission placed such a high priority on the North West Service Command that it assigned him to serve on the project rather than in the armed forces. Company personnel shortages were most severe in the head office operation itself, with Fay, Frizzell, Pat Williams and Robertson left almost alone to keep the company on course through the war.

The Greyhound contract with the United States government was finally terminated in September 1944 when the government began to take over the responsibility for transporting the remaining personnel. During the year the number of buses and drivers had been slowly cut back so that there were only five vehicles left by the end. Bill Brown and Walter Hyssop, two of the original four drivers, were among the last to leave that fall, helping to drive the remaining cars and buses, carrying twenty-eight Greyhound people, out as far as the Peace River. Greyhound had helped accomplish a very important task.

Management Changes

As the Second World War drew to a close and Greyhound's involvement in the North West Service Command ended, Fay could look back on a period that had seen his company genuinely contribute to the war effort, and start to think about the future.

One matter that needed addressing was the company's management structure. The small, effective staff of the war years was Fay's style; he preferred to keep management in his own hands as much as possible. But as the company expanded through the acquisitions described in *Our Network, 1929-1940*, the need to delegate became obvious, and during the war the president had slowly begun to loosen the reins.

Duncan Robertson, the financial manager of the company almost from its inception, continued to be a key member of Fay's team. When Western Canadian was created, the company's slate of officers had understandably been dominated by executives of the Greyhound Corporation. With the exception of Fay as president, Robertson was the only Western Canadian employee to be appointed as an officer. Although he did not attend board meetings, as assistant comptroller and assistant secretary he was responsible for preparing financial reports for Greyhound Corporation headquarters. In 1944 he was provided with a very capable assistant, John Frew.

After Robertson, Lorne Frizzell was the most important member of the Western Canadian team. After the purchase of his company, Midland Bus Lines, in 1938, Frizzell was given the job of district superintendent in Edmonton, an area he knew like the back of his hand. But Fay recognized his capabilities and when the new company was created he decided Frizzell's expertise was needed at the Calgary head office.

Frizzell recalls that Fay came to Edmonton on his way back from Vancouver in the fall of 1940 and asked Lorne to drive him to Calgary. When they arrived, Fay announced to Frizzell in typical fashion, "Well, of course you're going to stay here," leaving his driver aghast. Since Fay's decisions were irreversible, Frizzell was soon ensconced in Calgary as general superintendent in charge of all drivers and transportation. It was only a temporary appointment, since Fay intended to create a new department to keep the growing fleet on the road and in good working order.

Accordingly, on March 1, 1941, Frizzell was appointed superintendent of maintenance and transportation, heading a department he would run under various titles for more than twenty-five years. And in December 1942, long-time company mechanic Joe Kirk was appointed mechanical superintendent responsible for all garages.

With the financial and mechanical areas of Greyhound's operations firmly placed in the hands of Robertson and Frizzell, Fay turned his attention to traffic. Speed Olson had looked after this concern as general superintendent during the company's first decade, but Western Canadian needed someone capable of handling an increasingly complex array of routes, schedules, ticketing and public relations.

Fay initially turned to Jerry Brown who had worked in the traffic field under Olson for several years. He performed well, but Fay had to find a replacement in 1941 when Brown volunteered for army service. His gaze fell on Bob Borden who had made his mark looking after Greyhound's Trans Continental interests in Winnipeg, and who was currently serving as district superintendent for Manitoba.

Borden was brought back to Calgary on a temporary basis as traffic manager, a position that he held throughout the war in addition to his responsibilities with the North West Service Command. When Brown returned from overseas, Fay was able to offer him either his old position as traffic manager, or the position of district superintendent in Vancouver, as Fred McLeod had decided to retire. Brown chose the West Coast, leaving the field open to Borden.

On April 1, 1945 Borden was appointed to the new position of general traffic manager at a salary of $550 per month. On the same date Robertson and Frizzell received raises to $575 and $600 per month respectively, in recognition of senior management's hard work and service through the war years. Pat Williams as director of safety and Joe Kirk as general superintendent of equipment each received $375 per month, and Grant Smith as a regional superintendent received $350 per month.

Changes in Compensation

In addition, at the end of 1946, a new bonus plan was instigated for management personnel. The board resolved "that this Company pay to such supervisory and semi-supervisory employees as may be designated by the President a bonus or additional compensation equal to one-twelfth of the salary of each such employee for the month of December, 1946, times the number of months and fractional parts thereof he has been in the employ of this Company during the year 1946."

These initial changes were followed by a rapid rise in management salary rates through the latter half of the decade. In April 1947 Borden was promoted to the new position of assistant to the president at a salary of $625 per month and was replaced as traffic manager by W.H. Morgan. Later that year Borden's salary was increased to $700 per month while Frizzell went to $675 and Robertson to $650. With increases virtually every year, by 1950 many managers were earning virtually twice the amount of annual income they had at the end of the war.

As for Fay, his salary also increased during this period, rising from $1,500 per month at war's end to almost $2,200 per month by the end of the decade.

Not only did management salaries continue to grow, but the headcount increased, particularly in middle management where several men would rise through the ranks to senior management positions. Among them were J.S. Frew, assistant comptroller, F.L. Mogen, general traffic manager, G.A. Savage, assistant manager, safety and claims, and D.R. Boyce, general purchasing agent.

John Frew had joined the company in 1937 as a trained accountant hired to assist Duncan Robertson. Floyd Mogen had begun his career as a Prairie Coach Lines ticket agent and then had replaced Borden in the Edmonton depot, eventually becoming depot manager. When his duties with the Alcan Highway ceased in 1944, he came to Calgary as chief clerk in the traffic department and then succeeded W.H. Morgan as traffic manager when he left the company in 1951. George Savage joined the company in 1941 and first served in the transportation department before becoming Pat Williams' assistant in safety and claims.

Outside the head office, Greyhound operations were handled by the regional superintendents, including long time employees Jerry Brown, Grant Smith and Bill deWynter, and a more recent addition, L.C. Chambers.

Board Activities

In the years after the war, the company decided to change the board's method of operation. To expedite its business the company needed a mechanism to approve major corporate expenditures between the annual board of directors meetings. The device originally used was called a "directors authority for expenditure" whereby a minimum of three directors could approve expenditures on the company's behalf, such expenditures to be later ratified by the entire board.

This procedure was modified in January 1943 when the board decided to act on a clause in the Articles of Association allowing for the creation of an executive committee, which had most of the powers of the full board when the board was not sitting. Forming the first three man executive committee were Fay, Wickman and Caesar. Thereafter, major expenditures were approved by "executive committee authority for expenditure."

The board also moved in 1948 to increase the capitalization of the company. On August 24, 1948, an extraordinary meeting of the shareholders altered the share capital to provide for an authorized capital of 200,000 shares without nominal or par value. On November 8 the board of directors authorized a five for one share split, cancelling the original 15,000 issued shares and issuing 75,000 new shares in their place. Finally, on November 30, 1948 a further resolution of the board declared a stock dividend of $1.25 million, "being part of the undivided profits of the company," with which the outstanding 125,000 shares were purchased.

Fay Begins to Retreat

The years of hard work and long hours in making Western Canadian the west's major interurban transportation company had taken their toll on Fay's health. He hated the cold Alberta weather and talked of moving to the West Coast.

In June 1943, Fay sold six hundred of his shares to the Greyhound Corporation, leaving him with 2,375. The board had continued to pay off the outstanding debentures from the sale, and in 1945 the board moved to pay $50,000 off the principal, leaving the principal at $100,000. When the war ended and the flood of acquisitions slowed to a trickle, the company began actively reducing its indebtedness.

Then, in June 1946, an important moment in the company's history was reached when Fay's remaining shares were purchased by the Corporation, making it the sole owner of Western Canadian. Although the price paid to redeem the shares is unknown, their book value alone was $50 each. Combined with the money he was still receiving from the redemption of the debentures on the sale of Central Canadian, the sale made Fay a wealthy man.

This undoubtedly had some influence on Fay's decision to move to the coast. In August 1948, he and his wife moved to Vancouver, eventually purchasing a home in the southwest Marine Drive area.

Although Fay had no intention of relinquishing the presidency of Greyhound, his decision inevitably influenced the company's operation. Despite his frequent visits to Calgary and constant telephone communication, the day-to-day operations fell to his three lieutenants, Robertson, Frizzell and Borden. Pat Williams also began to take on an increasingly important role, receiving the title of director of safety and claims, responsible for safety training, investigation of accidents and the settlement of all claims against the company.

Company Position

Greyhound's business had grown massively in ten years. In 1950, company equipment operated over 12 million miles, carried over 2.5 million passengers and generated total passenger revenues of $5.2 million, compared to just over six million miles, 1.25 million passengers and $1.7 million in revenues in 1940. Total company assets in 1950 stood at $6.5 million, over four times greater than they had been in 1940 at $1.5 million.

The Canadian intercity bus industry had come of age and the company was prospering with it. The pioneer years of Greyhound Canada Transportation Corp. were over.

The Borden Presidency
1956 – 1979

As Greyhound took steps to consolidate the gains made in the forties, Fay was beginning to tire. His successor, Bob Borden, would carry out the integration of the disparate Greyhound Corporation subsidiaries in Canada into one company – Greyhound Lines of Canada – and navigate the diversification boom with Boothe Leasing.

The tremendous development that Greyhound underwent in the decade after the war's end pleased Fay immensely. What had begun as a terrible gamble had made him a wealthy man. As the fifties progressed and his absences in Vancouver became more prolonged, it became clear that he was slowly preparing to ease himself out of the company.

One sign of this was the fact that the great flood of Western Canadian acquisitions of the war years ground to a halt. Fay seemed content to have the company remain the west's largest carrier.

Fay might have bowed out sooner but for the events to the south in the parent Greyhound Corporation. There Carl Wickman had retired in May 1946, aged fifty-nine, and was succeeded by Orville Caesar as president, with the other major power in the company, Ralph Bogan, becoming executive vice president.

This management change caused a lengthy power struggle, as the Caesar and Bogan camps fought for control of the company. At the same time, Corporation revenues began to decrease and the parent company began to take substantial dividends out of Western Canadian.

During the forties Greyhound Corporation had allowed Western Canadian to develop at its own pace, capitalizing acquisitions and making virtually no financial demands. However, this trend changed once the company began to make profits.

On August 29, 1952 the board of directors passed a resolution declaring a dividend of $2.50 per share, amounting to $500,000 on the 200,000 common shares outstanding. Similar dividend declarations were made in November 1953 and December 1954 and thereafter they began to increase, reaching $600,000 in November 1955, $800,000 in December 1956, and $1 million in September 1957.

Aware of this, Fay was determined to leave Western Canadian in a secure position when he stepped down. When he had moved to Vancouver he left management in the Calgary head office equally in the hands of Robertson, Frizzell and Borden. Fay was a fair man who allowed his executives to make a mistake once, but if they did not learn from their mistake they soon lost his confidence.

All three men performed well but the president's gaze increasingly fell on Bob Borden as the one with the skills necessary to succeed him. His first outward move in recognition of this came in April 1947 when he promoted Borden to assistant to the president.

Borden's Rise

Over the following years Borden's assignments gave him well-rounded training in all aspects of the company's business, building on his earlier experience as ticket agent, travelling passenger agent, district superintendent and traffic manager.

Borden's apprenticeship was long. Fay didn't make his move until ten years had passed. In 1956 at the age of fifty-nine, he informed the Greyhound Corporation of his intention to step down. The letter of resignation, dated February 21, 1956, was brief and to the point: "I hereby tender my resignation as President and General Manager of Western Canadian Greyhound

George Fay and Duncan Robertson, 1955

Lines, Ltd. to take effect as of March 1, 1956."

On the same day, February 21st, Robert L. Borden resigned as vice president and assistant general manager of the company, and the board passed a resolution that "R.L. Borden be, and he hereby is, elected President and General Manager of the Company, effective March 1, 1956 to serve as such until his successor is duly elected, at a salary of $17,500 per year."

Fay was coaxed to stay on as a consultant, and remained a director of the company. He was present at the next meeting on April 26, 1956, when the board unanimously passed a motion "expressing the Board of Directors' appreciation of the many services rendered to the Company over a great period of years by Mr. G.B. Fay, the former President, whose resignation was regretfully accepted, effective as of March 1st, 1956."

Although he remained a director until the company was dissolved in the reorganization of 1958, the April 26th meeting was the last that Fay attended in person for the company he had founded twenty-seven years before.

Thereafter Fay enjoyed his retirement on the coast, playing quantities of golf and becoming engrossed in rebuilding a seventy-foot rescue boat that he had acquired after the war.

During his first few years as president, Borden frequently called on Fay for advice and always found him happy in his retirement and willing to help in any way he could. Fay passed away in Vancouver in 1973, a giant in Canadian transportation history virtually unknown to the Canadian public.

Arthur Genet

After Wickman's death in 1954 while still chairman of the board for the Greyhound Corporation, the company chose Arthur Genet as the new chief executive. Genet was new to the bus industry, with a background in banking, railroads and finance. Within three years of his appointment he would lead the corporation into a morass of debt.

In 1956 Genet began his infamous "personnel development" programme, an attempt to match the right individuals in the Greyhound Corporation to the right jobs. Every Greyhound employee in both the United States and Canada underwent a battery of psychological, educational, physical fitness and other tests to assess his capability and suitability for the job, creating immense bad feeling throughout the organization.

The following year Genet began a nearly ruinous scheme of Greyhound-Rent-A-Car Services. Although

Greyhound's management team with a new Courier 95 in the early fifties.
Left to Right: John Frew, Lorne Frizzell, Bob Borden, George Savage and Joe Kirk

it did not include Canada, the line of business required large infusions of cash from subsidiaries to support the losses incurred.

Despite this poor track record, Genet made one extremely positive decision – to create Greyhound Lines of Canada.

Uniting the Country

The idea to unite the eastern and western Canadian interests of the Greyhound Corporation was not new in 1956, but it took Genet's impetus to achieve it. He had already simplified the complex American situation, integrating Greyhound operations into six geographic groups. The Greyhound Corporation's Ontario interests, now known as Eastern Canadian Greyhound Lines, were now ready to be taken over by new and aggressive management. However, the execution of the Canadian integration was left up to Borden and his associates.

In the past Borden had tried to convince George Fay to lay plans for such a move and had been surprised when Fay indicated that he was happy with what Western Canadian already had. Borden now had his chance to make Western Canadian Greyhound a truly national carrier.

The Ontario Subsidiaries

The Greyhound Corporation's first presence in Canada as Canadian Greyhound Lines, Ltd., had, as mentioned, coincided with the beginning of Canadian Greyhound Coaches in 1930, operating first between Buffalo and Detroit and shortly thereafter between Detroit and Toronto.

Canadian Greyhound Coaches and Gray Coach Lines, a Toronto Transit Commission subsidiary established in 1927, cooperated in offering through service over each other's routes. These included Gray Coach's Toronto-Hamilton-London service, begun in 1937, which connected south of London at Talbotville with Greyhound for service through to Detroit.

The arrangement on this route proved so successful that it developed into a joint service, with both companies providing buses, and it was eventually formalized as a new company, Toronto Greyhound Lines, Ltd.

Meanwhile, when the New York Central Railroad invested in the Greyhound Corporation in 1935, it had received a 35% interest in a new Greyhound operating affiliate known as Central Greyhound Lines. Canadian Greyhound Lines was integrated into Central Greyhound Lines as a subsidiary, and the new Toronto Greyhound Lines, in turn, became a subsidiary of Canadian Greyhound Lines.

An important but confusing array of changes took place in the relationship between Canadian Greyhound Coaches, Toronto Greyhound Lines, Central Greyhound Lines and Gray Coach Lines beginning in late 1939.

First, Toronto Greyhound purchased another large Ontario operator, Canadian-American Trailways Ltd., which offered service between Detroit and Buffalo via London, Brantford and Hamilton and through a subsidiary service between Windsor, Chatham and London. It also acquired a Port Huron-Sarnia-London route from Canadian Greyhound Lines.

Immediately afterwards, the Greyhound Corporation purchased Toronto Greyhound from Canadian Greyhound Coaches for $100,000. Service between Buffalo and Hamilton remained with Gray Coach, and it pulled out of Toronto Greyhound altogether.

These changes made Canadian Greyhound Coaches a long-haul carrier, providing an alternative service to that offered by Central Greyhound, while Toronto Greyhound Lines handled the shorter routes. During the war, buses in Ontario were placed under the same restrictions as they were in the west. At first these related to mileage, but in late 1942 the Department of Munitions' transit controller ordered Canadian Greyhound Coaches to suspend service over most of its routes owing to some duplication by Toronto Greyhound.

When this service was allowed to resume in April 1944, Toronto Greyhound's name was changed to Eastern Canadian Greyhound Lines. In 1945 it acquired the Nickel Belt Transportation Company, which operated North Bay-Sault Ste. Marie and Cochrane-Hearst-Geraldton.

Then, in 1948 the Greyhound Corporation made a concerted effort to buy out the railroad interests that held much of its stock. At this time Central Greyhound Lines was disbanded and its interests across the border in Michigan were put under the control of Great Lakes Greyhound Lines, while in Canada the situation was rationalized by merging Canadian Greyhound Coaches into Eastern Canadian Greyhound.

Eastern Canadian Greyhound

Eastern Canadian and Western Canadian Greyhound had similar operating structures. As Greyhound Corporation subsidiaries similar policies were enacted, and management and supervisory positions were duplicated in the two organizations. Like Western

Canadian's Fay and his trio of Robertson, Frizzell and Borden, Eastern Canadian was led by R. W. Budd, vice-president and general manager, who was assisted by auditor George Issell, operations manager L.J. Stewart and general traffic manager J.V. Murphy.

However, the two companies were not alike in size or income. In 1955 Eastern Canadian had $1.7 million worth of assets and generated about $1.9 million in revenues, while its western counterpart had $6.4 million worth of assets and generated $5.4 million in revenues. More importantly, Eastern Canadian managed to net only $24,000 in income while Western Canadian reported an impressive $620,000.

Genet's solution was to create a holding company, Greyhound Lines of Canada, responsible for both Western Canadian and Eastern Canadian Greyhound. The new company would be incorporated federally, as well as in Alberta, to overcome problems with provincial governments, such as the situation with the C.C.F. in Saskatchewan, and to allow it to offer shares to the public.

Going public with the company was a result of extreme political pressure exerted by the Diefenbaker government's strong policy position favouring Canadian ownership of Canadian industry. Sensitive to the anti-American feelings in the air, the Greyhound Corporation decided that offering Canadians a chance to invest in one of their most important public utilities would be a wise move.

Greyhound Lines of Canada

On September 11, 1957, Letters Patent were issued under the authority of the Secretary of State of Canada creating Greyhound Lines of Canada. Capital stock would consist of 200,000 cumulative preferred shares with a par value of $50 each and 1.5 million common shares without nominal or par value.

The first meeting of the directors of the new company was held on September 16th and a by-law passed specifying the number of directors (eight originally but quickly changed to ten), and outlining the titles and duties of officers. The positions designated included president and vice president, who had to be chosen from the board, and a comptroller, secretary and treasurer, who did not need to be members of the board.

An executive committee structure was also set in place, consisting of three members of the board elected annually who could exercise all its powers between meetings, subject to ratification at the next full board meeting. Appointments to the board fol-

Arthur Genet (second from left) with Bob Borden (third from left), 1957

lowed, including Borden, Genet and six other Greyhound Corporation executives.

A subsequent meeting on September 18th appointed Borden as president, Duncan Robertson as comptroller and Harry Zoltok as vice president, manufacturing, of the new holding company.

On the same day the Greyhound Corporation officially subscribed for 450,000 common shares of Greyhound Lines of Canada in return for conveying to it all the outstanding capital stock of Western Canadian Greyhound and Eastern Canadian Greyhound plus promissory notes amounting to $3.35 million. Special meetings of the boards of directors of those two companies agreed to transfer their shares to Greyhound Lines of Canada.

In addition, the Eastern Canadian Greyhound meeting had received and accepted the resignation of R.W. Budd as a director, vice president and general manager, and had elected Borden to fill these positions as well as appointing Duncan Robertson as comptroller and Lorne Frizzell as general manager of maintenance and operations. It further resolved to pay to Western Canadian Greyhound an annual amount equal to about one-quarter of Borden's increased salary, in proportion with Eastern Canadian's size.

With the legal and organizational framework for Greyhound Lines of Canada in place, the next step was to issue public shares. Here the company ran into some problems. Shares were to be listed on the Toronto and Montreal Stock Exchanges and were originally to consist of 60,000 5? % cumulative convertible preferred shares at $50 each and 150,000 common stocks fixed at $13.80 per share.

The issue was underwritten by three securities agents, Dominion Securities, Royal Securities and J.R. Timmins & Co., and a prospectus was approved on October 17th. Unfortunately, as their letter of October 31st withdrawing from this agreement pointed out, the agents found that "adverse changes" in the security market generally, and in the market for the Greyhound shares specifically, made it "impracticable and unwise" for them to try to market such securities.

The new board had to retract all the resolutions that had set the security sale in motion, and had to come up with a new scheme to make the shares more attractive. Seeking financial advice, the board implemented a solution on February 18, 1958.

By amending its Letters Patent, the company sub-

divided and changed its capital: the 450,000 common shares subscribed by the Greyhound Corporation were subdivided into 720,000 issued common shares; the unissued 1.05 million common shares remained as they were; and the 200,000 unissued preferred shares were changed into 630,000 unissued common shares, making a total of 2.4 million common shares. Divested of the preferred shares, the source of the problem, the directors approved an underwriting letter from Gairdner, Son & Co. that agreed to underwrite $3.5 million 5?% secured convertible sinking fund debentures and 180,000 common shares at a cost to it of $9.20 per share but to be marketed at $10 per share.

The convertible debentures, to be dated March 15, 1958, allowed the holder to convert the debentures at the rate of one common share for each $11.50 of debentures up to March 15, 1963 and $13.50 up until March 15, 1968. These steps were followed by the declaration of an initial quarterly dividend of 18.75 cents a common share payable on June 30, 1958.

The prospectus advertising the sale of the debentures and stock pointed out that Greyhound Lines of Canada had been created "for the primary purpose of affording Canadian investors an opportunity to share directly in the development of Greyhound operations in Canada." To that end, the common stock being offered represented 20% of the 900,000 shares the company intended to sell publicly.

Together with the convertible debentures, assuming they were all converted immediately, this meant "approximately 40% of the outstanding voting shares of the company would become available to Canadian investors."

In both cases the issues sold out quickly. By March 19, 1958 the company had permission to list the stocks on the Toronto Stock Exchange. The listing information showed that the 900,000 shares were held by 551 individual stockholders, 454 who held lots of between one and 100 shares and sixteen who held lots of over 1,000 shares. Numerous Greyhound employees who had taken advantage of the opportunity to invest in their own company were among the stockholders.

The stock prospectus told an impressive story: During 1957 the two subsidiaries had operated 7,308 route miles and had logged almost 317 million passenger miles.

Basic bus fare rates were generally 3 cents per

mile on short routes and 2.8 cents per mile on longer routes.

The companies owned 146 intercity buses and had an additional twenty-three on order for 1958. The majority of the buses were less than four years old, 137 of them having been manufactured by Motor Coach Industries.

Twelve depots were owned and operated outright. Many other company-owned depots were operated by a lessee.

The new company and its subsidiaries employed approximately 1,000 people, mostly unionized, and its labour record was considered excellent.

This bright picture was justified by the results of the new company's first year of operation. At its annual shareholders' meeting in Calgary on March 10, 1959 the annual report (the first ever produced by a Canadian Greyhound company) showed gross revenue of approximately $11.2 million and net income of approximately $1.1 million, or $1.215 per common share.

In his first report as president, Borden told shareholders that the company's two operating subsidiaries had added route mileage during the year, that its manufacturing subsidiary had sales in excess of $2.5 million, and that "measures are being taken to reduce operating costs, to improve revenues, and to modernize and up-grade our buses, terminals and buildings." He closed by predicting that "Greyhound should be able to retain or increase its share of the transportation market."

With the public launch a success, management tried to catch its breath, only to find that running three companies instead of one required much more effort than expected. There was a crying need to reduce operating costs and eliminate wasteful duplication.

Western Canadian Disappears

While Greyhound Lines of Canada was being created, the man whose idea it was left. Arthur Genet, under intense pressure due to the losses of his Rent-A-Car scheme, resigned as president and chief executive officer of the Greyhound Corporation and from the Canadian companies in July 1958.

His successor, Frederick Ackerman, a trained accountant, received his appointment with the expectation that he would restore sound management to the Greyhound Corporation and pull it out of debt. This critical eye applied to the subsidiaries as well.

Consequently, on May 27, 1959 the directors approved a draft agreement whereby Greyhound Lines of Canada would absorb Western Canadian Greyhound Lines, Ltd. effective July 1, 1959. Eastern Canadian Greyhound would remain a subsidiary, but its fiscal management, handled by Western Canadian, was to be transferred to Greyhound Lines of Canada. Western Canadian Greyhound Lines, Ltd., a name which millions of western Canadians had identified as the west's bus company for almost twenty years, disappeared.

Duncan Robertson

Sadly, along with Western Canadian disappeared one of the company's longest serving and most respected employees, Duncan Robertson. He died at fifty in March 1959, leaving a void in the Greyhound office and the hearts of his friends and fellow employees.

Because Greyhound's financial operations were becoming increasingly complex, the company moved quickly upon Robertson's death and the ongoing reorganization to strengthen this area.

When the directors appointed the company's new officers on May 27, 1959, the position of comptroller and assistant secretary was assigned to John Frew, Robertson's protégé for many years. Also among the officers appointed were Lorne Frizzell, assistant secretary and general manager of maintenance and transportation; Floyd Mogen, general sales and traffic manager; Pat Williams, general manager of safety, claims and personnel; and Norman Lord, assistant treasurer.

At the same time, the company launched a nationwide recruiting campaign for the new position of office manager. One applicant was a twenty-six-year-old chartered accountant newly arrived in Calgary from Regina. Jim Knight would become one of Borden's most trusted advisors and, eventually, his successor as president of Greyhound Lines of Canada.

Sixties Diversification

Greyhound Lines of Canada's annual report for 1962 was extremely upbeat. Borden called 1962 a "banner year" for the company and the Canadian travelling public, noting that "bus transportation is really coming into its own in Canada" and that "the trend is towards the highways – and this is where Greyhound excels."

Consolidated income for 1962 increased 19.2% over 1961 to $1.5 million, earnings per share jumped from $1.22 to $1.34 and dividends increased to $1.00 from 86.25 cents. Borden's debut as president had indeed been auspicious.

At this time, the Greyhound Corporation was engaged in a strong diversification movement under Frederick Ackerman and Gerald Trautman.

To this point Greyhound Lines of Canada had remained focussed on its core business of running a bus line, with one successful exception, Motor Coach Industries. It had briefly considered some of Greyhound Corporation's initiatives, such as the Greyhound Post Houses, but had rejected them as beyond the capabilities of a company its size.

But in the early sixties the Greyhound Corporation's whole philosophy was strongly directed to diversification. In 1963 the current favourite in the drive to diversification was Boothe Leasing and before long it appeared in Canada.

Boothe Leasing

In 1962, the Greyhound Corporation acquired Boothe Leasing Corporation for $14 million. Boothe Leasing was a San Francisco-based company that specialized in buying and leasing office equipment.

After its acquisition Boothe rapidly expanded into other areas of leasing, including purchasing five Boeing 707 jet aircraft airframes (all but the engines) for $50 million, which it leased to Trans World Airlines. Boothe also leased some of the first commercially available computer equipment in the United States.

On June 18, 1963, the Greyhound Lines of Canada board meeting set the wheels in motion to extend the business to Canada by creating a new wholly-owned subsidiary that would enter into a management contract with the Boothe Leasing Corporation in the United States.

The subsidiary was incorporated as Boothe Leasing of Canada Limited with authorized capital stock of $1 million ($500,000 of which was issued). H. Noel Crawford from the American company was elected as vice president, to be based in the Toronto head office.

The new company quickly launched into a series of purchases and lease agreements that made it a major factor in Greyhound's operations. In November 1963 it purchased twenty-four Carrett Tree Farmers, a type of automatic logging machine, from Capital Construction Equipment of Toronto for approximately $300,000 and leased them to Spruce Falls Power & Paper Company in Ontario.

In May 1964 Boothe purchased seven tugboats and eleven barges from the Yellowknife Transportation Company of Edmonton for $600,000 and agreed to lease them back to the company over a period of six years for use on the Mackenzie River at a minimum rental of $810,000.

Other types of transportation and specialty equipment were soon added, with three major acquisitions in 1965. In February 1965 the company purchased a used 204-B Bell helicopter in the United States for $231,000 and leased it to Bullock Wings & Rotors Ltd., a pioneer helicopter company working on northern geological surveys with major oil companies.

In April 1965 it purchased $350,000 worth of aerial survey equipment and leased it to Lockwood Survey Corporation, and in August the same year it acquired elevator and escalator equipment from the Otis Elevator Company for lease to Niagara International Centre Ltd.

Boothe required substantial capital investment for these and other diverse acquisitions, but these paled in comparison with what would become its major initiative.

The Wardair Deal

At this time the Canadian airline industry was beginning a period of tremendous expansion. Max Ward, a former bush pilot, saw the opportunity to establish charter services for an increasingly mobile Canadian public. His company, Wardair Canada Ltd., had already begun such service using DC-6 prop planes but to get into big league charter service he needed jet aircraft.

A mutual acquaintance, Cy Becker, introduced Bob Borden and Ward, who soon began discussing a deal. Ward wanted a Boeing 727 for charters to the United Kingdom, and because the Boeing company did not yet have one operating in Canada, it seemed possible that Boeing would be willing to grant some concessions.

The total cost of one Boeing 727 was approximately $5 million U.S., making it the largest single Greyhound undertaking in Canada to date. Understandably, D.P. Boothe, Jr., head of the Boothe Leasing Corporation, was brought in to explain the arrangement to the board of directors. The deal called for a ten-year lease term at $61,000 per month with a purchase option at 20% of its cost at the end of the term.

Boeing also agreed to a 20% "deficiency guarantee" in the event Wardair had trouble meeting its obligations. The board agreed.

While Boothe engaged in contract after contract, Greyhound's bus operations were growing quickly.

MCI's capital requirements and the Brewster acquisition *(see Our Network, 1956 – 1970)* were also putting pressure on Greyhound's capital. Boothe's Wardair contract forced Greyhound Lines of Canada to face its priorities.

Management was having difficulty getting a grip on the leasing business. It was an area Greyhound was unfamiliar with, and the Boothe leasing arrangements had little in common. As a result, Jim Knight was forced to spend much of his time analyzing the business case for each decision.

While the tax implications of leasing were very clear and favourable in the United States, the situation in Canada was less straightforward. Unfortunately, less generous depreciation and other tax factors in Canada generally meant the return was not as high as in the U.S.

Considering the immense capital requirements, Greyhound had serious doubts as to whether it could retain its expanding market position as one of Canada's foremost public carriers while pursuing other corporate goals.

Sale of Boothe Leasing

Borden set out his position at the board meeting on February 17, 1966. Because it would be necessary to raise $5 million by May 1st for the Wardair contract, he proposed to sell the stock of Boothe Leasing to its American counterpart, now known as Greyhound Leasing & Financial Corporation.

Borden argued in favour of this course of action "because the bus business in Canada is booming at the present time in much the same way it boomed in the United States seven or eight years ago and there exists a great opportunity for Greyhound Lines of Canada to expand its bus business."

Borden went on to say "it would not be practical to expand in both the bus business and the leasing business at the same time because of the amount of capital that would be needed."

Gerald Trautman, the new president of the Greyhound Corporation, suggested setting up a committee of Canadian directors to consider the proposal and report its findings to the board.

Despite some reluctance on the part of the Greyhound Corporation, it purchased Boothe Leasing of Canada (now called Greyhound Leasing & Financial of Canada Ltd.) and this was accepted by the board of directors at their meeting of April 14, 1966.

Greyhound Leasing & Financial Corporation acquired all the Canadian shares for their book value of $500,000 plus $13,000 in profits as shown on the balance sheet, as well as the $600,000 advance that it had provided Boothe Leasing of Canada when it was created.

The sale removed the thorny problem of raising $5 million to purchase the Boeing 727, although Greyhound Lines of Canada had to sign a note guaranteeing the money until the legalities of the sale of its Canadian leasing interests were completed and approved by the shareholders.

The initial decision to emulate the parent company had important consequences for the development of Greyhound Lines of Canada, but the decision to break away and chart its own course yielded solid benefits.

Advertising and Tour Programs

Beginning in the sixties, for the first time Greyhound put an emphasis on its advertising programs. For many years the company had relied on newspaper advertising to promote its services, frequently on a contra basis, and there was no separate advertising budget.

This began to change after the creation of Greyhound Lines of Canada, as the company met increasing competition from well-crafted railway and airline campaigns. By the early sixties it had its own Greyhound Travel Bureaus stocked with information brochures and schedules, and starting about 1965 Greyhound began aggressively promoting its special fares and services, particularly tour offerings, in other media.

Greyhound Travel Bureaus became a feature of new terminals in the sixties

A prime example of this was the new slogan, "Go all-Canadian Greyhound to Expo 67", used in newspapers, car cards and promotional literature and on radio and television. More publicity campaigns would follow. In the late sixties, Greyhound began cooperating with Air Canada in what were originally termed "familiarization tours" of the Canadian Rockies and the Pacific coast. Greyhound and Air Canada jointly promoted the tours. These campaigns, usually featuring the Royal Glacier and Royal Yellowhead Tours, were so successful that by the early seventies they had been extended to CP Air, Western Airlines and Japan Airlines.

Greyhound also promoted other tours and packages, such as long-weekend Toronto-Nashville "Grand Ole Opry" Tours and Northern Ontario "Fall Foliage" Tours, using the "Ameripass" programme where travellers received sixty days free travel in Canada and the United States for the low fare of $149.50, as well as "Skifari" Tours, which combined air transportation with week-long bus tours of the western ski slopes.

Go Greyhound . . . and Leave the Driving to Us

The special promotions carried their own slogans, such as "Bargains in Every Direction," "Swing Away with Playbound Greyhound," "Look at it our way," and "Ski away with Greyhound." But overriding all of these special slogans was the one originally generated by the Greyhound Corporation's advertising firm in the fifties, used in Canada with tremendous results.

This slogan soon achieved unique brand recognition: "Go Greyhound . . . and leave the driving to us."

Centennial Performance

1967, Canada's centennial year, proved to be an exceptional year for Greyhound. Thanks to Expo 67 in Montreal and many other celebrations, the whole country was on the move. Passenger miles increased 8% over 1966 to 590 million, double 1960 volumes. Package express increased by 12% and charter bus revenue, spurred by the many groups travelling to Montreal, increased 37% over 1966.

These performance figures translated into impressive financial gains. Consolidated gross revenue increased 13% to $29.7 million and consolidated net income increased 29% to $4.2 million. Earnings per share were 91 cents compared with 71 cents in 1966, and dividends 48.75 cents per share compared with 42.5 cents per share in 1966.

Promotion for Expo 67 initiated a whole new Greyhound advertising programme

Corporate Continuity

The seventies saw the retirement of many long-time Greyhound employees. The growing complexity of the business, the importance of new departments such as marketing and labour relations, and the demands of new acquisitions made it necessary for Borden to institute a formal "corporate continuity" plan to smooth out the succession process.

In a previous restructuring, Greyhound had increased the number of vice presidents and reallocated their responsibilities. As a result, prior to his retirement Lorne Frizzell had moved from vice president, maintenance and operations to a vice president whose role was assistant to the president. Joining him and the other existing senior manager, Harry Zoltok, vice president, manufacturing, were Floyd Mogen, vice president, marketing and traffic, and Bill deWynter, vice president, transportation and labour relations.

Two Greyhound pioneers, Bob Borden and Speed Olson, 1968

John Frew

Shortly after the restructuring, John Frew announced his retirement, and effective August 1, 1970, Jim Knight took over his responsibilities as comptroller and secretary. Knight was now an officer of the company and increasingly involved in decision-making.

Pat Williams

In March 1973 Pat Williams retired as assistant to the president, having moved to the position from director of safety, claims and personnel a short time before. He had enjoyed a long, fruitful career with Greyhound spanning almost forty years.

With Williams' retirement in 1973 and the earlier retirement of Grant Smith in 1966 as district superintendent in Vancouver, the most senior company employee left working in a management position was Bill deWynter, whose record went back to 1931.

Bill deWynter

As vice president, transportation and labour relations, deWynter's responsibilities included bus operations and the formulation and administration of transportation policies, programmes and procedures. He also conducted contract negotiations and grievance resolution.

Fellow employees recalled Bill as a master in deflecting labour complaints to the union office, making the union a buffer between employees and management. In 1976 he reached mandatory retirement age, after forty-five years of service, and was succeeded by thirty-two-year-old Bruce Tyson.

Bruce Tyson

A native of Hamilton, Ontario, Tyson grew up in Saskatchewan and went to high school in Edmonton. The day after graduation he went to work for Greyhound as an express agent in the Edmonton depot. Transferred to Cache Creek, B.C. as operations supervisor in February 1965, he received a phone call on New Year's Day, 1967 from Lorne Frizzell. Frizzell told him to be in Calgary on February 1st to take on the new position of chief clerk of maintenance and transportation.

After learning the ropes, he became Bill deWynter's understudy in 1970 and was appointed director of transportation and labour relations in 1975. Having observed and assisted deWynter for several years in his labour negotiations, Tyson was his logical replacement as vice president, transportation and labour relations.

Floyd Mogen

Next to Bob Borden, Floyd Mogen was the last remaining employee from the early years. As vice president, sales and traffic, he was responsible for fares and schedules and Greyhound's entire market-ing portfolio. Upon his retirement in 1978 after forty-three years of service, Mogen was replaced by R.N. "Bob" Parke, aged forty-eight.

Bob Parke

Parke was a native of Brandon, Manitoba. In 1950 he went to work for Greyhound as a ticket agent. After four years, he succeeded Russell Molleken as travel-ling passenger agent in Winnipeg, responsible for 135 commission agents in Manitoba and Saskatchewan.

In addition to agency visits and working with Greyhound's connecting carriers in Winnipeg, Parke put on travel shows advertising Greyhound in small-er prairie centres and visited junior and senior high schools to show the Greyhound Corporation promo-tional film "Freedom Highway."

In November 1956, Parke was promoted to the new position of city sales manager for Vancouver, working with agencies and interlining companies on Vancouver Island. He continued in this role for eleven years until May 1967 when Borden asked him to come to Calgary to become Mogen's understudy in the new position of director of traffic.

Because he liked the coast, Parke hesitated at first and asked regional manager Grant Smith what to do. Smith's advice was "if you don't go, they won't ask you again". Parke accepted the position.

During twelve years as Mogen's assistant, Parke spent much of his time at regulatory hearings and at meetings of the National Bus Traffic Association. This experience would prepare him well for the role he would take in 1978.

Borden's Assessment

As Bob Borden passed his fortieth anniversary with Greyhound in 1975 and looked ahead to retirement, he could be proud of his accomplishments. Under his presidency the company had achieved stable, lucra-tive growth, vastly expanded its network and become a truly national carrier. Borden wanted to ensure that Greyhound would prosper after he had departed.

He decided to emulate Fay's example: handpick a successor and groom him for the job. In fact, he took the concept one step further, developing a "corporate continuity" program where each top-level manage-ment position would have the incumbent's successor identified and trained to take over the position.

Both Borden and Fay had been operating men, completely at ease with the nuts-and-bolts of the bus business, knowing everything from scheduling to bus building to ticket sales. Under the modern era, lead-

ing a maturing industry, Borden realized that he was becoming increasingly more dependent on expert financial advice to make the decisions that kept Greyhound successful.

Jim Knight Receives the Nod

Borden decided to prepare Greyhound's top financial person, Jim Knight, for the presidency. In August 1975 Knight was promoted to vice president, comp-troller and secretary and in May 1977 to executive vice president.

To fill his shoes, in May 1976 Knight's former position of comptroller was assigned to Clive Cox, aged thirty-one, a Calgary native and Commerce graduate of the University of Calgary, who had joined Greyhound as chief accountant in 1972.

At the board meeting where Knight was promot-ed to executive vice president, Borden presented his corporate continuity plan as an organizational chart showing the incumbent executives and top-level man-agers with their proposed replacements. In its intro-duction, he provided the reasoning behind the plan:

This organizational chart depicts the current structure (officers, senior management and top level supervisory personnel) of Greyhound Lines of Canada Ltd.

It also shows those proposed for certain posi-tions upon the retirement of the present officers. The selection was made with the objective of ensuring that the transfer of each office will be achieved smoothly. It is imperative to maintain optimum efficiency in all aspects of the Company's operations during the transition.

All have served for many years in senior roles within the company. In each case the person proposed is the one whose duties have equipped him with the knowledge and experience to con-tinue and further accelerate the growth pattern of the Company.

Borden's plan was well received by the board, and with its adoption the period of transition that Borden referred to began in earnest.

Banner Years
1976

The last years of Borden's presidency were crowned with continued growth. In his 1976 annual report he stated that Greyhound's philosophy was "nothing is so good that it cannot be improved," and the results bore this out.

1977

Thanks in part to acquisitions such as Canadian

Coachways and through normal increase, in 1977 Greyhound operated nearly 850 million passenger miles a year.

Package express revenue had grown substantially, supported by the increased baggage and express space in the new MC-7 and MC-8 coaches, double that available in earlier MCI models. In 1977 express revenues reached $14.8 million compared with $2 million in 1967, an increase of almost 300%.

Consolidated gross revenues were $109.4 million and consolidated net income was $10.4 million, or $2.21 per share. Equally significant, Greyhound was now paying $2.5 million a year in licenses, registration, seat tax and property tax.

1978

By 1978 Greyhound was operating 367 buses over more than 14,000 miles of routes, carrying 6.5 million passengers annually and serving almost 900 small Canadian communities.

1979

In 1979, the last year of Borden's presidency and the company's golden anniversary, consolidated gross revenues reached $151.2 million, a one-third increase over the previous year, and net income $15.8 million, for earnings of $3.36 per share (stock had been split in 1967 and would split again in 1980). Dividends paid to shareholders totalled $1.25 per share.

Greyhound's 1979 annual report was titled "A golden tradition of service" in honour of its fiftieth anniversary and was prefaced with a summary of its achievements: "In half a century of service to the Canadian public, your Company has become the country's largest bus line in terms of route mileage, geographic coverage and revenues."

Borden's Leave-taking

Borden retired with a personal service record of forty-five years. As he took his leave, he expressed to the company's shareholders what those years meant to him:

On a personal note, I would like to say that in April 1980 I will have completed 45 very rewarding years with Greyhound Lines of Canada, which began as a young man when I joined Central Canadian Greyhound Lines as a ticket agent.

Over the years, I have seen the Company change and prosper, grow and endure, to become the premier carrier of Canada. I am proud to have witnessed so much of the Company's history in the making.

As it had for Fay, the board wished to have Borden's counsel available for the transition. Consequently, he was elected chairman of the board. He served until the board meeting of November 20, 1980, when he resigned as a director and officer of the company effective December 31,1980.

In appreciation for his long and faithful service the board adopted the following preamble and resolution:

WHEREAS, Robert L. Borden has served this Company and its predecessors for over 45 years, and as a Director, and President or Chairman of this Company from its inception on September 11, 1957 to the present time; and

WHEREAS, during his service as a Director, Bob contributed greatly to the growth and development of this Company through his knowledge, experience and expertise; and

WHEREAS, Bob's gracious concern for the needs of others and his sound judgment in human and business affairs have been an inspiration to his associates; now, therefore, be it

RESOLVED, that we, the Directors of Greyhound Lines of Canada Ltd., do gratefully and sincerely thank Robert L. Borden for his service to this Company and for his friendship and the pleasure of having been associated with him, and we bid him our best wishes for health and happiness in his retirement.

Sea Changes
1980-2003

The difficult economic conditions of the eighties and the emergence of cheaper air travel brought the realization that the bus industry was mature. Despite new president Jim Knight's efforts, Greyhound struggled until 1989, when Dick Huisman and the Fly Boys were brought on board to revitalize the company and its approach to customer service.

Jim Knight

James A. Knight was born at Invermay, Saskatchewan on February 11, 1934. After high school, Knight took a job with the Royal Bank. He fully intended to make banking his career, until paycheque envy drove him to article for a chartered accountant designation with Rooke, Thomas & Co. in Regina. After five hard years, Knight received his certification and began working for Deloitte, Plender, Haskins & Sells in Regina before moving to Calgary with his wife Roberta.

Knight was hired by John Frew for the Greyhound office manager's position and began his new career on September 1, 1960. For ten years, Knight shepherded the company's general accounting, financial statements, income tax, and general administration. The role kept him constantly under Bob Borden's eye, and Knight frequently proved his financial abilities and his value to the organization.

When John Frew retired in 1970, Knight was chosen as the new comptroller and secretary. Eventually, Borden decided Knight would be his successor, and in August 1975 he was promoted to vice president, comptroller and secretary, and again in May 1977 to executive vice president.

The Presidency

On January 1, 1980, Jim Knight took over the reins of Greyhound Lines of Canada and became president and chief executive officer.

Knight brought a different outlook to the Greyhound presidency. Founder George Fay had managed virtually every aspect of the company personally. Bob Borden had implemented some decentralization, but his forceful personality and operating style ensured that he still called all the important shots.

In contrast, Knight favoured a less autocratic management style. He believed in consensus-building and careful strategic planning to achieve the company's objectives. His first step was to strengthen the regional management concept that Greyhound had been paying lip service to for a number of years. Real control was given to the regional managers for four divisions located in Calgary, Vancouver, Winnipeg and Toronto, with head office retaining authority for policy decisions. At the same time, Knight gave his supporting management team of Bob Parke, vice president, transportation and labour relations; director of traffic Bruce Tyson; and comptroller Clive Cox more autonomy over their responsibilities.

Jim Knight

Greyhound's management team for the eighties.
Left to Right: Bruce Tyson, Jim Knight, Clive Cox and Bob Parke

1980

As Knight implemented his new approach, Greyhound enjoyed another exceptional year. In December 1980, Knight's first annual report cited a 14% increase in consolidated gross revenues to $173.2 million, with net income increasing over 37% to $21.7 million. Passenger volumes were up almost 5% over the previous year, new terminals had opened in Thunder Bay and Edmonton, Brewster Transport had increased revenues by 11%, and MCI had produced 1,300 bus shells and contributed gross revenues of $76 million, a 12% increase.

As well, Greyhound purchased $3.7 million of its own preferred stock and split its common stock two for one, making a total of 4.7 million outstanding shares. With the completion of this excellent year, the company looked forward to a repeat in 1981.

First Greyhound Strike

Unfortunately, the labour contract expired on December 31, 1980, and Greyhound began the new year faced with some expensive bargaining. The union's key monetary demands were for a 36% wage increase over three years, 14% for 1981 and 11% for the two following years, plus continuing the cost-of-living allowance (COLA).

Reflecting the reality of Canada's inflationary spiral, management countered with an offer of 27% over three years while insisting on dropping the cost-of-living clause that had been part of the contract from the early sixties. The union maintained that

Greyhound's recent record profits allowed it to pay more while management stated that the company's offer amounted to $20.1 million over three years compared to the union's demand of $34 million.

On April 22nd, 1981, last-minute efforts failed and 1,400 Greyhound employees went to the picket line for the first time. Public transportation was disrupted across the country and both sides were under pressure to settle.

Ten days later, a tentative settlement was reached and two days later employees were back at work. The settlement represented a compromise between the two positions: wages would increase 10% a year over three years, or 30% over the life of the contract, and the cost-of-living allowance was retained, with the proviso that it would not come into effect until the Consumer Price Index reached 33% above the December 1980 level.

Under the new contract, top drivers would receive 39.88 cents per mile in 1981, representing a salary of $28,000, based on average annual miles of 70,000, plus a 4% meal allowance. First class mechanics would receive $12.20 per hour, ticket clerks $10.20 per hour, and coach cleaners $9.47 per hour. The only other significant gain was a driver's guarantee of twenty-four hours off duty at home in any week.

Although the strike was settled relatively quickly, it was still costly for Greyhound, partly because of the media reports following the negotiations that produced public uncertainty and reduced ridership before and after the strike. To fix the declines, management advertised a national "Thank You Special" – a 50% discount on ticket prices between May 8-14, expressing "sincere thanks for your patience during the recent strike". The strategy worked and ticket sales quickly returned to pre-strike levels.

1981 Results

Despite the strike, 1981 proved to be another banner year. Gross revenue increased to $204.3 million, a new record, and net revenue to $24.7 million, and Greyhound announced dividends of $1.00 per share.

However, 1981's revenue punch was mostly due to MCI's sales and strong courier express revenues, boosted by a forty day Canada Post strike which helped increase package express revenues by 16%. As well, Greyhound was starting to realize gains from the new Sudbury-Toronto route authorities won in the fight with Gray Coach.

Unfortunately, Canada was now entering its most severe business recession since Greyhound's early days in the thirties. The decades of sustained economic growth and development the company had come to take for granted were rapidly ending. Continued limitless expansion was out of the question.

Recession

By the beginning of the new year, the first cracks in the boom Greyhound had ridden to unprecedented heights were beginning to show. The economy began to flatten out and the trend-setting Calgary real estate market started to turn around. The 1982 annual report was telling: despite increases in package express and charter revenues, gross revenues remained constant and net income fell back to 1980 levels.

As the recession deepened and unemployment statistics skyrocketed, fewer people could afford to travel. In 1983 Greyhound recorded a 3.8% decrease in passengers carried, the first decrease in many years, and 700,000 fewer operational miles. The decrease in miles reflected reduced frequency on low-ridership routes, as well as a softening charter market. Consolidated gross revenues dropped to $201.7 million, and MCI's revenue declined by $20 million from 1981.

Greyhound revenues did not return to 1981 levels again until 1984, when the company recorded $204.8 million in sales. Unfortunately, costs had risen significantly and net income was only $21.1 million compared to $24.7 million in 1981.

Jim Knight at the opening of the new Calgary depot on May 7, 1986

In 1985, as Greyhound prepared to open its new head office terminal in Calgary, Jim Knight hoped the worst of the recession was over, with revenue figures showing strong signs of recovery to pre-recession levels. At the same time, airline competition was increasing following deregulation. Airfares were as low as $199 Vancouver-Toronto return and industry ridership was plummeting. Under these pressures, Greyhound was becoming operationally driven rather than market driven.

U.S. Concerns

Over the decades Greyhound's American parent, the Greyhound Corporation based in Phoenix, Arizona, had progressively diversified the Corporation away from bus operations. The American bus lines had suffered ridership drops beginning in the 1960s as air travel became more popular, and diversification helped spread the revenue risk. In 1970, the Corporation purchased Armour and Company, which produced food and consumer products such as the famous Dial soap, and in 1976 it acquired the Greyhound Computer Corporation.

During this period the American bus line experienced serious labour troubles. Facing increasing competition and rising costs, it demanded significant concessions of up to 25%. The package was rejected almost unanimously, and in autumn 1983 the workers went on a seven-week long strike marked by violence and property damage. Eventually the workers approved a 3-year contract representing 17% wage and benefit concessions, but terrible damage had been done to the employer relationship and there was little faith on either side.

In 1986, when the contract expired, the U.S. employees rejected more demands for wage and benefit concessions, raising fears of a second strike. The Greyhound Corporation decided to shed the risk, and in 1987 the American bus business was sold to a private investment group led by Fred Currey in Dallas, Texas.

The sale ended a fifty-year partnership between the two Greyhound bus lines. Later that July, the new U.S. Greyhound began acquiring pieces of Trailways, Inc.

Weak Results

Although Greyhound Canada recorded strong overall revenues of $211 million, including passenger revenues of $80.3 million and charter sales of $9.1 million (thanks in part to Expo '86 in Vancouver), net income faltered.

As a performance measure, Greyhound Corporation's chairman John Teets, who replaced Gerald

Trautman in 1983, required an annual 15% return on equity from its subsidiaries. Greyhound Canada was able to sustain the necessary performance during the recession, but failed in 1986, due to poor operating results from subsidiary MCI and passenger volume declines.

More Strikes

Greyhound was concerned that it might be sold along with its American counterpart, and president Jim Knight asked the two Amalgamated Transit Union locals for concessions of up to 20%.

The contract for ATU, Local 1374, representing the Western Canadian workers, expired on December 31, 1986, while the contract for ATU, Local 1415 based out of Windsor expired October 1986. Both unions rejected the concession packages, and talks were scheduled with a federal conciliator.

Subsidiary Brewster Transport had already endured a one-year strike about a year previously, with the Canadian Labour Relations Board finding that the Phoenix head office of the Greyhound Corporation had influenced the negotiations to try and break the union by prolonging the strike.

Brewster Gray Line buses, May 1986

In 1987, overall sales improved to $240.8 million. The post-Expo slump brought passenger revenues down to $77.2 million from $80.3 million in 1986. MCI and courier express sales improved, and Greyhound announced a modest shareholder dividend of $1.20 per share. Unfortunately, the ongoing labour negotiations were unsuccessful and Greyhound Canada sustained its second strike, further harming its reputation for service.

1988

The year began well with the 1988 Calgary Winter Olympics, held in February. The company committed

1988 Calgary Winter Olympics.
One of the four Greyhound driver groups involved.
From Left to Right: John Pabst (Sudbury),
Dan Peterson Jr. (Penticton), Murray McGinn (Penticton),
Michael Boucher (Vancouver), Jacques Gosselin (Sudbury),
Bill Pankiw (Kamloops), Roy Bourgeois (Winnipeg),
Bill Anderson (Kamloops), George Cameron (Vancouver),
Dan Mudge (Kamloops), Warren Minnie (Winnipeg),
Gerry Kovaks (Regina), Rocci "Rocky" Amatto (Calgary).
In front: Mike Bailey (Penticton).
Missing: Al Erwin (Regina).

25% of its fleet and brought in drivers across Canada to complete the largest charter contract in Greyhound's history, helping the company achieve almost $12 million in charter sales that year.

As well, that summer Greyhound brought in a non-smoking rule that prohibited smoking on all but certain charter trips. The rule cut the company's repair and maintenance bills and received a customer approval rating of 85%.

However, although gross operating revenues increased 10% over 1987 to $263 million, passenger

On June 29, 1988 Greyhound launched a "Butt Out"
campaign banning smoking onboard its coaches

sales declined again to $76.2 million and dividends held firm at $1.20 for the third year. The annual report stated, "Greyhound's prices simply could not compete with airline prices, especially when travel time was factored into the relationship." Knight could see the writing on the wall.

Teets Makes a Decision

Back in Phoenix, chairman John Teets was very concerned about Greyhound's ridership declines over the past few years. Greyhound had lost touch with customers, management was repeating the same tactics year after year, and Teets wanted to shake up the organization. If the service could be improved, then hopefully the ridership would improve.

Departing from Greyhound's past policy of promoting from within, he decided to draw in some outside talent. Late in 1988 Teets hired hospitality and airline industry executive Dick Huisman, former executive vice-president of Canadian Pacific Hotels and senior executive with Canadian Pacific Airlines.

The Fly Boys

Dick Huisman's first act as the new president was to divide the company operations into three separate divisions by lines of business – Passenger, courier express and charters. He then performed a major reorganization, making several outside hires from the airline industry to staff the new divisions.

In May 1989, Huisman tagged John Munro as senior vice-president of marketing and operations. John Munro had headed up CP Air's marketing in the early 1980s and afterwards started two successful companies. He brought in Arthur Jackman, former

Dick Huisman, ca. 1990

head of Wardair's in-flight service, as Vice President, Marketing Services.

Huisman also selected Roger Pike as vice-president of market planning. A former CP Air marketing executive and consultant, Roger initially began consulting for Greyhound in March 1989 but was hired full-time that May.

Jack Sheneman, who had left Wardair two years earlier to work in marketing at Greyhound, became vice president, charters. Other airline hires included Walter Tytula and Kevin Lawless.

As well, Ron Parker, former head of Loomis, Canada's second largest national courier, became senior vice president and general manager of Greyhound's courier express division.

Identifying the Problem

In review, a number of things seemed to have gone wrong at Greyhound. As bus ridership steadily declined in favour of the private car and the air industry, the company failed to reinvest in itself. The infra-

Walter Tytula, ca. 1990

structure – buildings, agency network, fleet age – was deteriorating. People were losing pride in their company. They were coming to believe that bus was the transportation mode of last resort.

In this frame of mind, staff felt they could make decisions or treat people how they pleased. Front line service was deteriorating, and mistreated customers responded negatively, creating a self-fulfilling cycle. In autumn 1989 John Munro went to Dick Huisman and explained his belief that Greyhound had systemic cultural issues and that the industry was in a death spiral. As long as operations continued to follow in the same rut, there was nothing to market. Munro wanted to resign.

Instead of accepting Munro's resignation, Huisman retaliated by putting Munro in charge of operations to fix the problems.

Pan Pacific Survey

John Munro went to the Pan Pacific Hotel in Vancouver, then one of the premier hotels in North America and known for their exceptional standards. He asked their training personnel to travel the Greyhound network for a couple of months, to find out what the customer experienced.

> I wanted people who would not normally be bus passengers to ride on our coaches. So they put on their jeans and their sweatshirts and they rode Greyhound buses for about three months. I didn't want to know who was to blame, I didn't want locations, I didn't want names. What I wanted was to know what Greyhound looked like from the outside.

At the same time Munro commissioned research to find out how Greyhound staff felt about the company and what the riders thought about the product.

Munro expected Pan Pacific to come back with a training program. Instead, they came back and said, "Hire a janitor". They gave him pictures of depots across the country. They were filthy, coated with years of grime. The washrooms were not being cleaned and the managers and agents weren't being held accountable.

Dinner in the Washroom

Munro called the managers across the country and held a major meeting to share the results:

> I told them I could understand that we might have older buildings but that I could not understand the lack of cleanliness. If we can't clean it up and make it attractive, we shouldn't be in business. When the message didn't get through, I told them, Look, it has to be so clean that I want to be able to have a sit-down white table-cloth meal in a Greyhound washroom without telling you which one in advance.

The idea took off. In a matter of weeks Munro was eating dinners in Greyhound bathrooms from Thunder Bay to Vancouver. Signs were placed in the washrooms giving customers Munro's direct office number to call and complain. This went on for sever-

al months, until the media picked up the story while Munro was making a speech on a riverboat to the Kelowna Chamber of commerce.

The story went across the country. Munro did dozens of interviews. It was picked up by *MacLean's*, the *Globe and Mail*, *The New York Times*, international newspapers, and major TV stations. It even made Hollywood's "To Tell the Truth" program with Kitty Carlisle. Restaurants started to call asking, "Can we cater your next meal in the bathroom?" Munro's moment of exasperation had paid off.

Other Improvements

The research Munro had commissioned identified the following problems:

- Poor terminal customer service/lack of security.
- Difficulty obtaining accurate schedule and fare information. Customers called until they got the same answer twice.
- Aging fleet lacking in amenities.
- Lack of express inter-city service.

To address the problems Greyhound committed significant amounts of capital investment, beginning with the major terminals. The company hired a new group of terminal staff, dressed them in red blazers and gave them full authority to resolve customer problems, and increased facility security personnel. Greyhound also experimented with seat selection.

Roger Pike, ca. 1990

At the same time, Greyhound centralized passenger information by establishing a fully automated fare and scheduling information system. The system could be accessed through the local Greyhound terminal or 1-800-661-TRIP, and was extended to the agency network the same year. Arthur Jackman brought the system in on time and on budget. It launched March 1990 under the management of Mary Graviglio, and delivered much-needed consistency to the system.

Finally, to fix the fleet problems, Greyhound bought 52 "jet-like" new coaches with wider, plusher seats and installed onboard movie and stereo systems with personal headphones. The company also briefly experimented with 2 x 1 seating and implemented a complimentary snack bar.

Building a Better Seat

Customers had specifically complained about how uncomfortable the bus seats could be during long trips. To improve seat comfort, Munro approached the five seat manufacturers Greyhound dealt with on a worldwide basis and asked them to participate in a study to find the most comfortable seats.

The idea was to take the best seats from each company, put them on the bus, run them for four months and let the customer decide. All five said no thanks. They changed their minds when Greyhound wrote to each promising never to buy another seat from them, and the research project went ahead.

In essence, Huisman and Munro's approach was to introduce elements of airline management and upgrade Greyhound's image by making it an "airline on wheels" with a whole new focus on customer service. And sales grew.

In 1989 Greyhound experienced a strong revenue rebound, increasing 10% from 1988. An expected 6.5% post-Olympic slump in passenger ridership became an 8% increase. Courier express sales increased 25% and charter revenues grew by 10% to almost $11 million, operating 4.5 million charter miles. 1990 saw similar success and courier express increased again by 17.2%.

Inter-City Express Service (ICE)

In October 1989 the federal government announced significant cutbacks in VIA Rail services. As roughly 36% of Greyhound's network paralleled VIA's routes, this was an excellent opportunity to implement a new express service. In the public relations furor surrounding VIA Rail, Greyhound announced it would fill the void. Three months later, in January 1990 the

Developed to fill the gap left by VIA Rail cutbacks, the Inter-City Express service included on-board movies. March 1990

company introduced a new Greyhound Inter-City Express Service between key city-pairs, filing the gaps left by VIA. With fewer stops, service along such runs as Calgary-Vancouver was only 12 hours, compared to VIA's 18-24 hour trip.

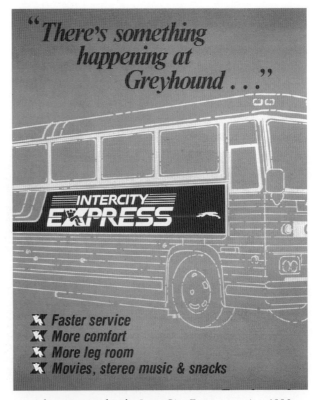

Advertisement for the Inter-City Express service, 1990

When the service was announced, Dick Huisman noted, "This is how we will not only fill the gaps left by VIA Rail cutbacks, but also grow the bus line." Greyhound was able to operate these routes at a profit where VIA Rail could not, because of Greyhound's innate flexibility to add and remove buses based on demand. The new inter-city express added 10,000 miles per day in scheduled runs and helped introduce the new fleet and improved amenities to a wide market. The consumer response was tremendously positive.

Greyhound also looked into negotiating interline travel packages with major Canadian airlines to allow Greyhound passengers to fly and ride the bus on one ticket. A few years later Huisman would twist this new intermodal concept and develop Greyhound Air.

Another Recession

In 1991 Canada was again seized by a recession and the bottom dropped out of the passenger market. Over the past two years Greyhound had invested almost $36 million of its capital to upgrade the terminal infrastructure and renew the fleet. To help pay for this the company was forced to increase prices, hoping the market would be inelastic to the increases.

This was only true to a point, and passengers began to turn away when the recession came. Greyhound had imposed an airline business model on the industry without realizing that its customer base still had significant differences from the airline market. That year Greyhound Canada's net income fell to $16.4 million.

Back in 1989 Greyhound had adopted a Loomis-style approach to its courier express services and created a separate division with cross-docks, trucks and tractor-trailers operated by third parties to handle its growing freight business. In 1991 it was clear that the separate infrastructure was far too costly, without the synergies present in the old system, and Greyhound began to disband it.

To try to preserve the increased freight volumes, following the lead of Greyhound Australia, the company launched an innovative pilot program to study using pup trailers attached to the buses. Achieving acceptance from the provinces took years, but the pup trailer concept had potential that would not be denied.

Route Rationalization

Following the 1987 sale of the American bus line, in 1990 the parent Greyhound Corporation had changed its name to Greyhound Dial Corporation and again in 1991 to the Dial Corp., adopting its name from Dial Soap, one of its best-known subsidiary products. John Teets was still in charge, holding Greyhound Canada on a tight rein. As 1991's poor results rolled in Teets demanded the company perform a comprehensive route rationalization.

Huisman and his team began classifying routes as profitable, making a contribution, or unprofitable. Most of the unprofitable routes were let go, but the regulatory process took time. At about the same time, the company revised its Eastern and Western operating divisions, assigning Winnipeg, Manitoba to the Eastern division to help make the regions more comparable in size, although virtually all of Winnipeg's business came from the west. This process went on for two years, eliminating almost 3 million annual route miles from the system.

Despite the whittling down process, in 1992

Bob Parke, ca. 1990.
He retired in 1992 after 42 years of service

Don Clarkson (in "Team East" shirt) and Dick Huisman
celebrating the purchase of Gray Coach, 1992

Greyhound reported revenues of $185.5 million and net income of only $10.6 million. Annual passenger volumes were 5.5 million. Earnings per share were $0.96, while capital expenditures had fallen to $10.7 million. However, the Gray Coach purchase that year brought invaluable Ontario route authorities that would make Ontario a large revenue producer for the first time in Greyhound's history.

Wheelchair Accessibility Begins

In addition to the route upheavals, the ongoing dismantling of the courier express division and the general state of worry, in 1992 Greyhound began a federally funded pilot project testing wheelchair accessible service in Alberta. The service used a prototype developed by Motor Coach Industries (MCI), a 45-foot intercity accessible bus equipped with both an accessible washroom and an on-board wheelchair lift. This groundbreaking work would set the stage for announcing national accessible service in 1995.

1993

On February 4, 1993, on the recommendation of the Minister of Transport and the National Transportation Agency, Greyhound successfully applied for an exemption order stating "minority public shareholders of Greyhound Lines of Canada Ltd. may increase the percentage of their voting shares in Greyhound Lines of Canada Ltd. from 31 per cent to 46 per cent". This probably had the effect of mitigating risk to the parent Dial Corp. while encouraging greater Canadian ownership.

That month the Board of Directors declared a special dividend of $5.00 per share, aggregating approximately $42 million. Greyhound had now consistently paid an annual dividend to shareholders during the past thirty years.

New Fare Products

To help encourage the faltering ridership, Greyhound launched marketing initiatives including the "Domestic Canada" pass aimed at the Canadian tourist market, "Companion 50% off" and "Family" fares, as well as city pair excursion fares.

According to the annual report, the campaigns were introduced to "respond to the impact of perpetual airline discount fares offered by the major carriers and airline charter operators. Sales . . . helped to significantly stem declines in ridership by diverting passengers to our services away from their personal car and other intercity transportation modes." In fact, the Canada Pass and Companion fare programs were so successful and appreciated by customers that

they have been offered in various forms ever since.

Recognizing the huge contribution they made to overall revenues, Greyhound took steps to recognize and develop "city pair" origin-destination trips, such as Toronto–Ottawa, Calgary–Edmonton and Vancouver–Kamloops. This initiative, led by John Munro, Kevin Lawless and Garry Clermont, was an extremely important step. Rather than treating a large corridor with several cities as a single unit, responding and marketing to a specific city pair with its own demographic characteristics definitely refined the company's advertising approach long into the future.

The company also developed a strategic alliance with McDonald's Restaurants and Sun-Rype Products Ltd. through 1993, which allowed Greyhound to advertise on tray liners in restaurants in Alberta and British Columbia in exchange for joint participation in a community program. Administered by McDonald's, the program provided transportation to non-profit organizations, for which Greyhound provided the coach and drivers.

Meanwhile, Dick Huisman's "Project Eagle" team began secretly investigating the potential for Greyhound to develop a discount airline and fight the airlines directly. The plan was ready to take to market in early 1994. Unfortunately, Canada was still feeling the effects of the recession, the travel industry was depressed and there was no money. The concept would sit on the shelf until 1995 when discussion was renewed.

Holding Our Ground

Despite high unemployment and low consumer confidence, 1993 revenues rose to $205.7 million and earnings per share reached $1.26. Annual ridership at approximately 6.5 million passengers was only marginally down, thanks to the new Gray Coach acquisition and the new Canada Pass and Companion fare offerings, and passenger miles totalled 707 million. Capital expenditures were now $9.3 million. Most importantly, net income was now up 31% over the previous year.

However, Greyhound's performance in 1994 was hampered by the Canadian economic situation. The recession had given way to a jobless recovery, and the intercity bus industry was not yet experiencing a turnaround. From an internal document, "It is now apparent that the changes in the Canadian market place that have resulted from the economic recession of 1990-91 are fundamental in nature and that the future of the company will be intrinsically different from its past".

To help boost revenues and complete the route Ontario network, in February 1994 Greyhound purchased significant route authorities from Ottawa-based Voyageur Colonial. As a company newsletter related, " . . . as much as 30% of 1994 revenues are anticipated to be generated in Ontario. These acquisitions have allowed the Company to grow volumes with relatively little incremental cost increases as advantage is taken of the existing Greyhound infrastructure." Serving the new routes with coaches diverted from charter service helped reduce costs for the new service. At the same time, in June 1994 Greyhound conducted more route rationalization exercises to manage the lanes and city pairs more effectively.

The company was also taking steps to cost-effectively improve its information technology. On February 28, 1994, Greyhound announced it was outsourcing its information system operations to SHL Systemhouse Inc. in a five-year deal worth $27 million, a move which vice-president of information systems Mark Richardson said would "help it deploy new technologies faster and branch into new areas of business. We are going to be saving money."

Share Volatility

In response to the poor business conditions and precipitous declines in traffic, beginning in April 1994 Greyhound's stock price fell from a high of just over $11 a share to less than $2 that October. The price continued to be depressed until late March 1995, when the price crept up above its top float line.

A float analysis by Steve Woods and Jan Arps for Stocks & Commodities Magazine in December 1996 described that a "complete turnover of Greyhound's float" of 14.1 million shares was achieved at that time, "giving a buy signal in the last week of March 1995". Whatever the reason, and despite Huisman's public protestations in April, the stock price slowly continued to rise, reaching almost $5 that June.

Special Projects

That spring, Greyhound entered the next phase of its accessibility program, rolling out accessible service using ten retrofitted coaches on major routes in four provinces. In a March press release, John Munro, now executive vice-president, stated, "Greyhound believes that access is a right, not a privilege, and that everyone, including the elderly and people with disabilities should have the right to travel in comfort."

Greyhound's stand on accessibility contributed to the company's established reputation for quality service, resulting in ongoing requests for Greyhound executives to give keynote addresses and a feature role in a customer service training package, "The Advantage: Service Quality". This video suite told the customer service stories of leading Canadian organizations from a behind-the-scenes perspective, and continues to be used today as a resource tool for management innovation.

Greyhound continued to investigate the feasibility of the pup trailer project, working with Dr. Moustafa El-Gindy, senior research officer for the National Research Council. In 1995, the experimental study by M. El-Gindy and X. Tong, "Analysis of a Bus/Pony-Trailer combination" was completed.

As per the abstract, "the results obtained indicated that a bus could tow a pony-trailer without degradation of the general safety performance standards of the bus. This may lead to increase of bus productivity by transporting more payloads." With this ammunition, the company renewed efforts to obtain permission from the provinces to run the combination on the highway.

Air Ramp-up

At the same time, Dick Huisman's airline dream began to take flight. The idea was put on the shelf in 1994, but 1995's recovery and the need to address the competition from the airlines and protect market share was a powerful motivator. Through the year the members of Project Eagle had been reworking the business case and investigating partners with which to offer the service.

With domestic business and pleasure travel forecasted to grow by 3.3% and 4.4% in 1996, in fall 1995 the vote was taken to go ahead with the air product, with the company creating the following vision:

Our goal is to introduce an air product and develop an integrated inter-modal "bus-plane-bus" product in combination with Greyhound's existing inter-city bus passenger service. Greyhound will introduce an air business product for the price sensitive business traveller linking Vancouver, Kelowna, Calgary and Edmonton with Toronto, Ottawa and Hamilton via a hub in Winnipeg (serving 19 city-pair markets).

In December 1995 Greyhound publicly announced it would provide "air service to Vancouver, Calgary, Ottawa, Toronto, Hamilton, Edmonton and Winnipeg, with Winnipeg as the hub. Striving to be the lowest cost provider of scheduled air service, Greyhound is negotiating with a third party provider of air service", with Greyhound retaining responsibility for all marketing, scheduling and ticket sales.

1995 Financial Results

Greyhound's financial results for 1995 continued to show revenue shortfalls to plan. By continuing cost reduction efforts, the company expected to realize $15.2 million in operating income on $182 million in revenues, compared to $11.4 million in operating income on $181 million in revenues in 1994.

1996

On February 6, 1996, Greyhound signed an Air Charter Agreement with Kelowna Flightcraft Air Charter Ltd. of Kelowna, B.C. The press release on February 11th announced the agreement "will provide the opportunity to link Greyhound's existing bus service with Kelowna Flightcraft's air network."

Unfortunately, serious regulatory approval issues concerning Greyhound's foreign ownership, as described in the April 12, 1996 ruling by the National Transportation Agency, forced Greyhound to delay the launch from its original date of May 12, 1996 to mid-July.

Greyhound Canada Transportation Corp.

To satisfy the foreign ownership rules, on May 31, 1996, Greyhound Lines of Canada Ltd. was restructured from a bus transportation, courier and tourism entity with a U.S. parent company, Dial Corp. (originally named The Greyhound Corporation), to become a bus transportation and courier company with no single, major shareholder or significant U.S. ownership.

The company was split into two companies, Brewster and Greyhound Canada Transportation Corp. (GCTC). As of June 1, 1996, Greyhound Canada Transportation Corp. became 76% Canadian-owned. The directors of the new company included Dick Huisman, president and CEO; Bruce Elmore, senior vice president, finance, CFO and corporate secretary; Garry Clermont, vice president and general manager, B.C. and Alberta; Dan Sguigna, vice president and general manager, Ontario; Roger Pike, vice president, government and industry relations; and Mark Richardson, vice president, management information systems.

On June 7, 1996, federal transport minister David Anderson acknowledged that Greyhound's restructuring satisfied domestic ownership requirements, and cleared the way for Greyhound Air to finally launch. The successes and frustrations of

Launch of Greyhound Air, July 1996.
From left to right: Tim Rothwell, Guy St-Denis, Greyhound Air pilot, Kevin Lawless

Greyhound's air service initiative are more fully described in the *Greyhound Air* Chapter.

The delays and expense associated with not one but two launch campaigns ate up capital, and on July 11 Greyhound Canada announced it had closed its previously announced financing of 2,750,000 Special Warrants, at a price of $5.50 per Special Warrant, for aggregate proceeds of $15,125,000.

In the first five months, the air operation recorded a $9.8 million pre-tax loss on revenues of $26.7 million. Meanwhile, the ground transportation business reported revenues of $175.3 million and net income of $5.5 million, including $105.4 million for the passenger business.

Executive vice-president John Munro was growing deeply concerned with the airline venture, and he resigned December 31, 1996, staying on as a consultant for the transition.

Looking for a White Knight

In 1997 it became increasingly apparent that Greyhound could not continue to sustain the losses caused by Greyhound Air. Although the airline received high marks from its passengers for excellent customer service, the high costs made it impossible to make a profit. Greyhound began looking for a strategic partner who could provide much-needed equity infusions.

During the spring and summer negotiations were held with several interested parties. Some were interested in purchasing Greyhound Air, some were interested in the bus operation, and some were interested in buying the entire Greyhound unit as a whole. Because of the amount of equity potentially involved, Greyhound sought advice from RBC Dominion Securities. Following review, RBC recommended that the Greyhound board accept the offer from Laidlaw Inc. as representing "the best opportunity to maximize value for the shareholders".

On September 2, 1997, Laidlaw Inc. and Greyhound Canada Transportation Corp. announced they had signed a definitive agreement under which Laidlaw would make a cash tender offer for all the outstanding shares of Greyhound. The friendly takeover was estimated at $100 million. Laidlaw held 650,000 shares previously purchased at $3 each and was offering a 53% premium on all outstanding stock.

Greyhound has publicly stated since last spring it has been seeking a strategic partner. Although the current peak summer travel season has produced satisfactory results for Greyhound Air, operating

losses are likely during the slower winter season ahead. As a result of its review of financial alternatives available to Greyhound, its board of directors has determined that recommending this transaction with Laidlaw to Greyhound shareholders is in the best interests of Greyhound shareholders. Laidlaw's offer is premised on Greyhound returning to its traditional role of providing quality inter-city bus passenger service and, as a result, Greyhound Air will terminate service effective September 21, 1997.

In compliance with the sale condition to shut down Greyhound Air, notice was given to Kelowna Flightcraft Air Charter Ltd. to terminate the air charter agreement, Brent Statton's role as senior vice-president, Air Services, was eliminated, and the air service formally ended September 21st.

Laidlaw's president and CEO James R. Bullock commented,

Greyhound represents an excellent opportunity for Laidlaw to consolidate its Canadian inter-city and tourism bus operations under a high quality, well recognized brand name. Our Winnipeg-based, Grey Goose intra-provincial scheduled service, and our Alberta and British Columbia tourism coach businesses will be integrated with Greyhound, augmenting its presence in those markets.

Laidlaw Acquisition of Greyhound Canada

On October 17, 1997, Greyhound Canada announced that its board of directors had resigned as Laidlaw Inc. had acquired more than 90% of its outstanding shares. A notice of compulsory acquisition was mailed to the remaining shareholders on October 20th. Upon the completion of the acquisition, Greyhound Canada was delisted from the Toronto Stock Exchange.

The new Greyhound board of directors was composed of officers of Laidlaw Inc. and its affiliates, including James R. Bullock, John R. Grainger, Ivan R. Cairns, Leslie W. Haworth, and Michael P. Forsayeth. John R. Grainger then succeeded Dick Huisman as president of the company.

Joining Laidlaw meant the opportunity to access and cross-promote Laidlaw's other companies, such as Grey Goose on the linehaul side, and Gray Line Victoria and Laidlaw Banff in charter and sightseeing operations.

During the airline period, the bus business had suffered from a lack of attention and conditions had deteriorated. The management team strove to refocus middle management and bring up the service while developing better operating data.

While continuing its focus on specific city-pair markets and passenger segments, such as students and seniors, in 1997 Greyhound launched the Travel Is Educational, Too! scholarship program for high school students entering university.

That year Greyhound achieved revenues of $178 million, before tax income of $12 million and net income of just over $10 million.

Intercity Bus Code of Practice

Through 1997 the company also continued its work through the Canadian Bus Association to develop with other industry partners a voluntary code of practice to provide accessible service to passengers with disabilities.

On July 9, 1998, federal transport minister David Collenette formally launched the Intercity Bus Code of Practice. The development process for the code had begun two years previously under the auspices of the Advisory Committee of Accessible Transportation (ACAT), with Greyhound participating through the Canadian Bus Association. As Minister Collenette related:

> What is unique about the Code is that it is not a government regulation or even a government document. It is a voluntary statement of commitment based on consensus between industry and consumers — a commitment to ensuring easier access to intercity bus travel for all citizens.

An industry first, the Code set out best practices for providing services in a safe and dignified manner to travellers with disabilities, including a three-step complaints procedure with ultimate recourse to Transport Canada.

1998 Financial Results

In 1998, following the Laidlaw purchase, Greyhound Canada expected total revenue of $232 million for all business lines and subsidiaries, with income before interest and taxes (IBIT) of roughly $20.5 million. Total passengers carried were 4.5 million. Scheduled passenger revenues grew 4% over prior year, especially in Ontario where the January ice storms paralysed the train system and kept cars off the road. However, El Nino's influence in the prairies resulted in a very mild winter and volumes were down. Greyhound's courier express division also did well, thanks to a postal strike that boosted volumes for most of the fall into December.

Regrouping

At the time of the Laidlaw purchase, Greyhound's bus operations were run by three regional vice-presidents: Roger Pike, vice president, Alberta and British Columbia; Gary Peppler, vice president and general manager, Manitoba and Saskatchewan; and Dan Sguigna, vice president and general manager, Ontario. With the air operation winding down, the division no longer made sense and Gary Peppler's role was eliminated. The operations were then re-divided, with Brian Gordon appointed vice president, western region; Roger Pike, vice-president, central region; and Dan Sguigna, vice president, eastern region.

Bruce Elmore resigned as chief financial officer and senior vice president, finance March 31, 1998, and was succeeded as director by Jack Tough, vice president, finance, Canadian Operations under Laidlaw Inc.

Another result of the sales was that on December 30, 1998, Greyhound adopted a new fiscal year terminating on August 31 rather than October 31.

Purchase of Greyhound Lines, Inc.

After the Phoenix-based Greyhound Corporation's sale in 1987 of the American bus line, Greyhound Lines, Inc. had struggled through more ruinous strikes and bankruptcy. In 1994 Craig Lentzsch became president and chief executive, and in 1998 Laidlaw Inc. decided to purchase the greatly improved organization.

Greyhound Lines, Inc. was then described as "the only nationwide inter-city bus operator in the United States", with "2,500 coaches serving 2,600 destinations with 18,000 daily departures", while Laidlaw Inc., based in Burlington, Ontario was known as North America's biggest ambulance and school-bus contractor.

On October 19, 1998, Laidlaw announced it had entered into an agreement and plan of merger with Greyhound Lines, Inc. of Dallas, Texas, to be adopted at a Special Meeting in January 1999. The transaction was valued at approximately $650 million, representing $470 million plus $180 million in debt assumption.

Describing the advantages of the transaction, Laidlaw CEO, James R. Bullock, noted:

> A united Greyhound operation serving travellers across Canada and the U.S. and Mexico has distinct advantages. Laidlaw becomes the largest inter-city passenger carrier and gains an otherwise unattainable platform and brand recogni-

tion for the expansion of the tourism and coach business in North America. Operating synergies are available in vehicle purchase, insurance, financing, head office and public company costs. We will be especially fortunate to have Mr. Craig Lentzsch, Greyhound's president and CEO, and his management team join Laidlaw. They have achieved a great deal, during the last four years, in restoring Greyhound's employee enthusiasm and service reputation, reflected in both increased passenger loads and satisfaction.

Successful Merger
On March 19, 1999, the Greyhound stockholders approved the merger with Laidlaw, making Greyhound Lines, Inc. a wholly owned subsidiary of Laidlaw Inc. James Bullock commented again:

> With Greyhound Lines, Inc. now part of Laidlaw, the company will be able to offer a truly North American bus service from Mexico to Alaska under one of the most recognizable brand names in the world. We look forward to the contribution which Greyhound's management team will make to Laidlaw's continued growth in its passenger transportation and package delivery businesses.

The long-term plan was to integrate Laidlaw's existing tour and coach operations with Greyhound Line's operations, and Bob Richards and Jack Tough were chosen to head up the integration team.

In July 1999, Michael Forsayeth of Laidlaw Inc. ceased to be president of Greyhound Canada, with Craig Lentzsch appointed president and chief executive officer and Jack Haugsland appointed executive vice-president and chief operating officer.

Over the following months Greyhound Canada then reorganized itself along the three lines of business: passenger services, courier express and travel services. Sguigna and Pike became vice presidents for the first two lines of business on a national basis, reporting to Jack Haugsland in Dallas, while a third department, charter and leisure services, split regionally, reported to Gordon Barr in Dallas.

Thus, after eleven years of separation, the networks of Greyhound Canada and Greyhound Lines, Inc. were reconnected, making it possible for passengers to travel all over North America using Greyhound.

Voyageur Colonial, Part Two
On November 19, 1998, Greyhound signed an agreement "to purchase the operating assets and assume certain liabilities" of Voyageur Colonial Ltd.

Canada Steamship Lines had been selling off portions of the Voyageur bus operations network beginning in 1990, and in 1994 Greyhound had picked up the valuable Toronto-Ottawa route plus some ancillary routes. Two years later, in 1996 another carrier, Trentway-Wagar/Coach Canada, bought the Toronto-Montreal operating rights.

Considering the high passenger volumes on the corridor, and backed with capital from new owner Laidlaw Inc., Greyhound Canada purchased the remaining routes, Ottawa-Montreal and Ottawa-Kingston, as well as the reasonably new 37-vehicle fleet. The Ottawa-Montreal route was especially lucrative, carrying up to 500,000 passengers a year, making it the second largest route in Canada. The purchase was finalized in February 1999 and a year later the driver group was integrated. That same year Greyhound Canada and Laidlaw began the process of transferring and integrating Laidlaw subsidiaries Grey Goose Bus Lines and Penetang-Midland Coach Lines.

Sudden Resignations
In March 2001, Dan Sguigna, vice president, passenger services, and Kevin Lawless, director, business development, resigned from the company to pursue other business interests. Kevin Lawless had joined with the other airline hires back in 1989, while Dan Sguigna, a former Greyhound Lines and Voyageur executive, originally came on board in February 1995.

The sudden resignations left a management vacuum. Craig Lentzsch appointed Roger Pike as interim vice president of passenger services in addition to his existing role as vice president, courier express. That June, Roger Pike was named Senior Vice President, Canadian Operations.

Roger Pike
Roger Pike had originally joined Greyhound in 1989 as a consultant before becoming vice-president of market planning under president Dick Huisman, whom he knew from CP Air. Over the next decade Pike held several different roles in operations, information systems in 1990, and government relations in 1992 when Bob Parke retired. He was the only sound internal choice to take control of Greyhound Canada.

Upon his promotion, Pike promoted Dave Leach to vice president, passenger services and Anthony Milonas to vice president, courier express, and the

Roger Pike

process to realign the company along lines of business continued.

National Express Group (China)

In Fall 2001, Greyhound Canada was approached by the National Express Group (China). From a press release:

> The New National Express Group, established April 20, 2001, is the only company approved by the Ministry of Communications for trans-provincial and trans-regional express transportation business. It is also a pilot company in China for the large-scale development of road transportation through intensive operations on the road network. The company has set up subsidiaries in coastal cities of east China. Currently, it has more than 300 luxury buses and 90 routes for passenger transportation.

After interviewing several large international passenger transportation companies, the National Express Group chose Greyhound to help modernize their bus transportation network in Shaanxi Province, seat of Beijing.

Although the idea sounded far-fetched, management realized the opportunity had genuine merit and pursued Greyhound's involvement. Following discussions and mutual visits to Canada and China, on October 21, 2002 during the 2002 China Road Transport Development Forum, Greyhound Canada signed an historic agreement in Beijing, China with Chairman Wang Yong-Li of the New National Express Group.

The consulting agreement was made to share Greyhound Canada's best practices in transportation management, courier express, tourism products, advanced technologies and safety management. Present for Greyhound in China were Roger Pike, senior vice president, operations; Lorne Anthony, director, business development; and Lorraine Card, director of safety.

During the signing, Wang Yong-Li told the forum that " . . . China still has a long way to go in technology innovation of road transportation. The cooperation with Greyhound is conducive to promote technological development of road transportation in China and absorb the advanced technology and management skills of developed countries."

Roger Pike responded, "With 73 years of experience and lessons, Greyhound is willing to begin an enduring cooperation between Canada and China in the field of road transportation." It was an historic moment.

Responses to September 11, 2001

Following the terrorist strikes in the United States and the grounding of air travel, Dave Leach, then vice president, passenger services, ordered the ramping up of the company's operations in Toronto, Ottawa, Montreal, St. Catharines, London, Windsor, Winnipeg and Vancouver to bring Americans safely home, handling huge volumes (+40%) on the international corridors from coast to coast in close coordination with Greyhound Lines, Inc.

In the aftermath the company transported free-of-charge two buses of volunteers in support of the New York clean-up, followed by a convoy of Bobcats and other construction vehicles. Greyhound met with the Canadian Security Intelligence Service (CSIS) and Transport Canada to develop its network safety plan from a Canadian risk perspective; initiated an internal safety review of its operations and facilities; and launched an education and awareness program to help empower front-line staff and reassure passengers. Greyhound then helped form the new Task Force on Bus Safety in conjunction with Transport Canada and Labour Canada and the Amalgamated Transit Union (ATU).

Canada Loves New York, November 30 – December 2, 2001

That November Greyhound participated in the Canada Loves New York Committee, which coordinated this feel-good sightseeing event with the City of New York and developed affordable transportation plans to bring as many people as possible to the city for the celebration of New York.

Led by Senator Jerry Grafstein, committee mem-

THE WHITE HOUSE
WASHINGTON

NOVEMBER 27, 2001

I am pleased to send warm greetings to all those taking part in the "Canada Loves New York" celebration. And a special welcome to our Canadian friends traveling to New York City for the weekend of November 30.

The United States and Canada are strongly linked by ties of family, friendship, trade, and shared values. Our countries have stood shoulder to shoulder in war, peace, trial, and triumph, and we again stand together today to defeat terrorism. I applaud the "Canada Loves New York" Committee and the Canadian people for making this event possible in celebration of our solidarity. By responding to Mayor Giuliani's invitation to come to New York, you demonstrate your share as lands of freedom and opportunity.

Best wishes for a wonderful weekend in New York City.

*President George Bush and Mayor of New York
Rudy Giuliani sent letters congratulating the organizers of
Canada Loves New York, November 30-December 2, 2001*

bers included George Cohon (founder of McDonald's Canada), Michael Budman (co-founder of Roots Canada), Earle O'Born (president and CEO, The Printing House Limited), and several others. Greyhound representatives included Stuart Kendrick, Warren Delany and Rob Wade. This event was a major success and enjoyed high attendance, attracting over 20,000 Canadians.

Roger Pike Retires

On February 28, 2003, Roger Pike, the last remaining "Fly Boy" from the Huisman days, retired from Greyhound Canada and was succeeded by Dave Leach as Senior Vice President, Canada, who assumed control of the company from the Toronto regional office.

Dave Leach

Dave Leach began his career with Greyhound in 1986 as a baggage handler in Edmonton. Leach held several operations positions over the next four years before becoming operations manager, Edmonton in 1990. He left the company briefly in July 1994 to work for the Saskatchewan Transportation Corporation (STC), but returned in April 1996 as

general manager for the B.C. region when George Carscadden retired.

Over the next three and a half years he reorganized the B.C. management team and developed a new relationship with the union. Labour relations had become non-existent with a backlog of over seventy outstanding grievances. Leach conducted a meeting with all union representatives in B.C., since called the "Coquitlam Summit", resulting in the resolution of all but 3 grievances and forming the basis for driver operating procedures within B.C. Leach also successfully defended Greyhound's relationship with its owner-operators when challenged by the union in arbitration.

In November 1999, under Greyhound's reorganization by lines of business, Dave Leach was appointed general manager, national GCX operations and moved from Vancouver to the head office in Calgary. There he successfully negotiated and implemented new compensation for the agency network and P&D operators. This new compensation-based focus of the agents and P&D operators contributed significantly to growth. He also successfully communicated the pricing strate-

Dave Leach, speaking at the November 2001 driver recognition ceremonies. Photo courtesy Bill McCarthy

gy developed by Ivan Wannamaker, and provided support to the sales and marketing department to communicate and implement nationally. The new pricing structure resulted in a yield increase of nearly 8%.

Leach also assessed and reorganized the national operations team and developed a strategy to standardize national GCX operations, including new standard operating procedures and measurement criteria.

Following the management shake-up occasioned by several staff departures, in June 2001 Leach was named vice president, passenger services, and relocated to Toronto. Responsible for managing driver operations, fleet planning and overseeing labour and government relations, he was also responsible for the successful integration of Grey Goose Bus Lines into the company, bringing 139 new members into the Amalgamated Transit Union from the Union of Canadian Auto Workers.

Leach also developed commuter service and infrastructure initiatives for Southern Ontario and instituted "intelligent fleet allocation", allowing the company to save hundreds of thousands of bus miles.

With this strong operational experience, Dave Leach was a natural for the role vacated by Roger Pike. Appointed senior vice president, Canada of Greyhound Canada Transportation Corp. on March 1, 2003, Dave Leach brings a vigorous, grounded perspective to Greyhound management. A recent nominee for "Canada's Top 40 CEOs under 40" program, sponsored by Caldwell Partners and the Globe & Mail, Dave Leach has a truly open door policy and is known for taking the "high road" during disputes.

Today, Leach's senior management team includes Ron Love, vice president, finance; Karim Lalani, controller; Stuart Kendrick, vice president, passenger services; Brad Shephard, vice president, revenue development and analysis; Bill Betton, director of operations, Greyhound Courier Express; Scott Narowski, director of revenue development; Ivan Wannamaker, director, national sales, Greyhound Courier Express; Lorraine Card, director of safety; Lisa Trueman, director of human resources; Chris Batty, director, labour and management relations; Howie Boyda, regional manager, maintenance; Dave Welbourne, director of audit services and Jim Wingerter, director, claims and loss control.

With this team in place, Dave Leach looks forward to positioning Greyhound Canada as a customer-focused operation that is technologically up-to-date, fully accessible, and environmentally sound, so that in the years to come Canadians will realize, "You're going places. Go Greyhound."

CHAPTER THREE

OUR NETWORK

1929 – 1940

reyhound Canada is one of the very few companies in Canada that started in the west and built east. From the beginning, Greyhound has grown its network through strategic acquisitions and interline partnerships. Today, Greyhound Canada carries more than 6.5 million passengers a year across our national network running from Vancouver, B.C. to Montreal, Quebec, with interline connections throughout North America.

1929–1930: FIRST STEPS

On November 30, 1929, when Greyhound was first formed, its operations consisted of the 45-mile Nelson-Trail route, Nelson-Kaslo and Nelson-Nakusp as a result of the Kootenay Valley Transportation Company purchase.

Founders Fay and Olson immediately added Calgary-Nanton, Calgary-Fort MacLeod, Fort MacLeod-Lethbridge and Fort MacLeod-Cardston from their purchase of the Foothills Transportation Company, Ltd. Service through Calgary-Macleod-Lethbridge service began in March, while the Calgary-Edmonton service was inaugurated in May 1930 using the Canadian Yelloway name, but operated by Greyhound.

First Calgary-Edmonton run

Greyhound operator Grant Smith was the first to make the Calgary-Edmonton, on May 23, 1930. He had a rough schedule and instructions to stop and try to sign up agents along the way. When he left Calgary he didn't have a single passenger, but duly stopped at each centre on the schedule, noting the time taken to travel between stops and talking to potential agents in drugstores and hotels.

Smith's coach remained empty until he reached Leduc where a railway crew was waiting to go to Edmonton. They took one look at the bus and decided to give it a try, allowing Smith to sell the first eleven tickets on the run to those working for the competition – the C & E Railway. When he reached Edmonton he pulled his bus into the old recreation hall on 100th Avenue and 101st Street used as a depot by a few operators in Edmonton and stayed overnight. The next day he headed back to Calgary with one passenger.

The first Calgary-Edmonton run had been far from lucrative, but that did not disturb Fay and Olson. They knew it would take time to build a clientele.

That June, Fay and Olson were ready to open Greyhound's first depot in Calgary. The opening was followed by Greyhound's first newspaper advertising campaign. The company's first advertisement appeared in the Wednesday, June 25th, 1930 edition of the *Calgary Herald*:

> *Travel by Motor Coach at*
> *Lower Fares between*
> *Calgary and Edmonton*
> *$5.15 one way*
> *$9.25 round trip*
> *two trips daily*
> *7:45 a.m. and 1:30 p.m.*
> *Calgary and Lethbridge*
> *$3.85 one way*
> *$7.00 round trip two trips daily*
> *8 a.m. and 2 p.m.*
> *Motor Coach Depot*
> *Herald Building*
> *M9699*
> *Yelloway-Greyhound lines*

Central Canadian Greyhound route map showing interline connections, 1932

The same month, the Department of Public Works agreed to extend the company's Lethbridge-Cardston run to Waterton Lakes for the summer and the first schedule became effective June 25th. Later that summer, Greyhound applied to operate between High River and Lethbridge via Vulcan, and this was granted in early September.

Alberta–B.C. link

Fay's next step was to obtain running rights between the company's Alberta and British Columbia operations, since this route held the key to making interline connections with carriers in the United States.

The Alberta-B.C. link was difficult to get since it required Greyhound to obtain licences from two different provinces' regulatory agencies, neither of which was familiar with setting up interprovincial services. Greyhound intended to use the route from Fort Macleod to Pincher Creek and then west through the Crowsnest Pass, linking up with its existing B.C. operations at Cranbrook.

In July 1930, under the merger with Canadian Yelloway Lines, Greyhound acquired operating rights between Calgary and Edmonton. Then, in August, Greyhound applied to the Alberta government to begin one round trip daily service effective September 15th from Fort Macleod to Crowsnest at the British Columbia boundary via Pincher Creek, a distance of seventy-two miles.

On September 5, 1930, Greyhound made a similar application to the British Columbia government for service between Cranbrook and Crowsnest, a distance of ninety-five miles.

However, both provinces pointed out that the company could not transfer their respective licences from one vehicle to another. This meant that the coaches would have to meet and exchange passengers at the border. Barney Olson then went to Victoria to try to lobby for an exception to the ruling.

Unfortunately, he was unsuccessful. In a letter to Fay on September 9th, he reported, "Now in regards to substituting an Alta. coach in B.C. territory, this is strictly a Provincial Police matter and I took it up this morning with Inspector Hood here in Victoria, and he informed me that there was no such thing as substituting in the by-law."

Despite the extra expense, Greyhound decided to go ahead and began the service on September 15th. The next day, Greyhound launched a second advertising campaign in the *Calgary Herald* under the slogan "Ride the Greyhounds."

The advertisement listed the cost of round-trip fares to Edmonton, Lethbridge, Cranbrook, Spokane and Seattle, and highlighted connections at Spokane for Portland, San Francisco, and Vancouver, B.C.

Interline Agreements

Because the transportation network in the thirties was a very decentralized collection of small bus lines, a passenger might have to travel on several different bus companies to get to his destination.

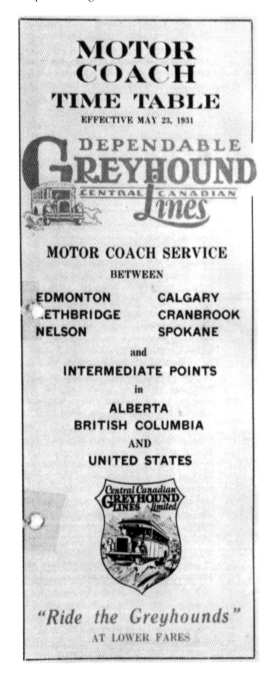

Greyhound timetable from May 1931

Interline agreements make it possible for a passenger to buy just one ticket at his point of origin and be sure that all lines would honour the ticket. Interline agreements of the time could be formal or informal agreements where the seller of the ticket agreed to reimburse the other carriers for their portion of the passenger's travel.

In 1931 Greyhound Coaches worked out interline agreements with several small Alberta bus lines, including Midland Bus Lines and Sunburst Motor Coaches in Edmonton, White Bus Lines in Red Deer, Red Bus Lines in Calgary and Johnson Bus Lines in Lethbridge.

Except for an abortive attempt to run a service between Red Deer and Sylvan Lake in 1931, Greyhound seemed content to let these smaller companies provide a feeder service for its main lines between Edmonton, Calgary and Lethbridge.

Canada–U.S. Through Service

The successful linking of the B.C. and Alberta operations immediately allowed Greyhound to begin offering through service to the Pacific Northwest of the United States, thanks to several interline agreements with American carriers.

Through Kootenay Valley Greyhound had inherited an interline agreement with Auto-Interurban Lines of Spokane, Washington for service between Spokane and Trail, B.C. Greyhound then negotiated another in 1930 with North Idaho Stages of Sandpoint, Idaho between Spokane and Cranbrook (later Creston).

Through the B.C. company Greyhound also had two other agreements with American companies. In order to offer service all the way to California it would need to extend its interline agreements beyond Spokane, first with Union Pacific Stages and Washington Motor Coaches to Portland and then with Pacific Greyhound Lines from there to San Francisco.

Road Conditions in the '30s

At this time few roads were paved or even gravelled. The Alberta government was spending a pittance on road construction and virtually nothing on maintenance. Twenty years later, after the Depression and World War II, even in 1959 there were fewer than 560 paved miles in the entire province of Alberta.

Although during winter the coaches were inadequately heated, the roads posed the greatest problem, as they were frequently covered with ice or blocked by drifting snow. After frequent delays and several trip cancellations, Fay took action. Greyhound bought an International truck and mounted a snowplough on the front of it to clear drifted roads. Two drivers operated the creation, one driving and one swamping, first clearing the Calgary-Edmonton road and then turning their attention to other routes. Early Greyhound driver Norm Chalmers was particularly adept, getting the big side wing plow to throw the snow off in both directions, closely followed by the bus.

Greyhound was not the only one benefiting from this service, as witnessed by the convoy of trucks and

Greyhound's plough breaks the way on the Calgary-Edmonton highway, 1930-1931

private vehicles following Greyhound's snowplow. In future years the government would be sufficiently shamed by the fact that a private company was being called upon to perform a public service to purchase more of its own snowplows, but in the meantime Greyhound's public image benefited greatly.

As well, huge potholes filled with water often made the roads impassable, forcing the government to impose road bans. Sometimes Greyhound had to dispatch a bus from the destination end of a run to meet the bus from the originating end and transfer the passengers at that point. Greyhound employees would even go out in a truck to pump out such holes before the government decided to issue a ban.

The Lethbridge Prison Racket

Lethbridge generated some of the most interesting problems and solutions of Greyhound's early operations. One of these included the nearby provincial jail. Since Calgary didn't have a jail, Greyhound did a brisk business transporting prisoners between Calgary and Lethbridge. Most days there was at least one prisoner and often there were five or six.

Convicted prisoners were brought down to the 8 o'clock bus in Calgary by paddy wagon and placed in the back seat. The Mounted Police escort was supposed to sit with them but often sat up front where he could chat with the driver. After dropping the regular passengers at the Lethbridge depot the bus ran out to the jail, where the escort delivered the prisoners.

The Mountie's comfortable chats with the driver ended when one prisoner figured out how to pen the safety bar on the back of the bus. The prisoners all vamoosed while the police escort was up front with the driver.

Discharged prisoners were also a benefit to Greyhound. On discharge each prisoner was brought into town by prison truck and given $5 and a Greyhound ticket back to the place where he had been sentenced.

The depot workers in Lethbridge recalled that scarcely a day would go by that a discharged prisoner didn't come in and try to get a refund on the ticket. The tickets were a special issue, white in colour, and the agent would patiently explain that the ticket was non-refundable without authorization from the provincial government. However, the ticket would usually show up later that day in the hands of some unsuspecting traveller who had bought it in the beer parlour next door.

Cent-a-Mile Excursions

During the early thirties Fay was able to convince the Department of Public Works to allow Greyhound to offer round-trip excursion rates (usually 125% of a one way fare) just as the railways were doing for special seasons, such as Easter or Christmas, or for special events, such as the Calgary Stampede.

Greyhound always tried to keep its tariffs about 10-20% below those of the railway competing over the same route, although the various regulatory bodies didn't always allow Greyhound to maintain the spread.

As an extension of this, Greyhound soon began marketing "Cent-a-mile" excursions. These became extremely popular – sometimes the Lethbridge ticket office sold twenty to thirty a day.

1933–1934: RACE TO THE SASKATCHEWAN BORDER

In 1933, Greyhound began to move towards the Saskatchewan boundary, the start of an inexorable push east that would be key to Greyhound's future expansion strategy.

Robert J. Duncan

Robert J. Duncan was a small Calgary operator who began a service between the city and the town of Hussar in 1927 as "Calgary and Eastern Bus Lines". In the next few years he added several other routes: Calgary to Arrowwood and Gleichen in 1928, Calgary to Olds in 1929 and Calgary to Medicine Hat in 1932.

On November 21, 1933, Fay reported to the Alberta board that he and Duncan had reached a "satisfactory agreement" on the transfer of Duncan's Alberta lines to Greyhound, marking the beginning of Greyhound's practice of buying out the opposition.

Sometime that year Duncan moved to Saskatoon and began operating a licence between Medicine Hat and the Saskatchewan boundary under the name of Arrow Coach Lines. The following year, 1934, the same pattern emerged and Greyhound purchased the rights.

Dewitt T. Johnson

In 1932 another small operator, Dewitt T. Johnson of Lethbridge, who had begun running a service to Coutts in 1930, began servicing Medicine Hat from Lethbridge.

By 1933 Johnson turned his attention to his Coutts connection to the United States and a new line between Lethbridge and High River. Receiving notice in early November that Johnson intended to drop the

Lethbridge-Medicine Hat service, the chief clerk of Alberta's Department of Public Works wrote to Fay: "If you desire to take over this franchise, we will be pleased to consider your application."

Fay jumped at the chance, and on December 5, 1933 Greyhound began operating round trip daily service between Lethbridge and Medicine Hat using one of its new 16-passenger buses.

In 1934, Johnson, now operating under the name of Alberta-Montana Bus Lines, dropped his route between Lethbridge and High River via Vulcan and Greyhound took it over as well.

Other interline agreements with Saskatchewan carriers now provided Greyhound passengers with through connections to Saskatoon, Regina and Winnipeg.

1935–1937: CANADA-US CONNECTIONS

With the Saskatchewan doors fully open, Fay turned his attention to obtaining more convenient connections for travellers from Alberta to the United States and the west coast. The old interline agreements with Auto-Interurban Lines between Trail and Spokane and North Idaho Stages between Creston and Spokane worked well for passengers who began travel in the Kootenays, but were not as convenient for prairie travellers.

In order to offer service all the way to California, Greyhound wanted to extend its interline agreements beyond Spokane, first with Union Pacific Stages and Washington Motor Coaches to Portland and then with Pacific Greyhound Lines from Portland to San Francisco. This was initially delayed by a dispute with the Greyhound Corporation over the Greyhound trademark (see *The Depression Years* Chapter).

On May 21, 1935, the Greyhound Corporation in the U.S. ratified the trademark licence allowing Greyhound to use the name and trademark over a territory

> East of a line from Trail, British Columbia to Tête Jaune Cache, British Columbia, via Vernon, British Columbia, also the entire Province of Alberta: also territory in Saskatchewan west of a line drawn from Orkney, Saskatchewan to Canwood, Saskatchewan via Swift Current, Saskatchewan and Saskatoon, not to include the licensing of an operation to any company between Saskatoon and Prince Albert, Saskatchewan.

As a result of the agreement, Greyhound's routes in Canada were now identified in American advertising as Greyhound Corporation connecting lines.

The same day, Greyhound signed interline traffic agreements with Pacific Greyhound, Northland Greyhound and Washington Motor Coach, which allowed it to offer service from Canada to California.

To get around the high costs associated with a foreign company operating into Canada, Washington Motor Coach bought the part of the route extending from Spokane to Bonner's Ferry and then filed for the rights to run from Bonner's Ferry to the Canadian border at Eastport, Idaho. At the same time, Fay received authority to operate a new route between Fernie and Kingsgate, B.C. on the Canadian side of the border. Fernie, B.C. and Spokane, Washington thus became overnight stopover points for American and Canadian citizens travelling on Greyhound routes.

Jack Rajala, who drove the first bus on the service in May 1935, recalled he had only two passengers for his first connection, and when he met the American bus it only had one for him. However, business soon increased, thanks in part to the American advertising, and the route became one of Greyhound's most lucrative.

New Public Services Act, 1936

Until spring 1936, all of Greyhound's Alberta route licences were issued under the comparatively accommodating Public Vehicles Act of 1927. However, as the number of public service vehicles on the road mushroomed, the government realized that stricter procedures and regulations were needed to ensure orderly service and public safety. Consequently, on May 1, 1936 the new Public Service Vehicles Act was proclaimed and the first Highway Traffic Board appointed.

The Board's business was split between truck and bus operations: preparing classification and tables of freight rates, formulating regulations for the operation of trucks and buses, and revising the tariffs covering bus fares. The new Act also required all applications for Public Service Vehicle Certificates to be considered by the Board at a public hearing.

The Alberta act and similar ones in other provinces marked the end of the bus industry's pioneer period. From this point the relative freedom the early bus operators enjoyed in running their businesses disappeared as the industry came of age and became increasingly regulated.

George Fay attended the first public hearings in

Calgary of the new Highway Traffic Board on September 2-3, 1936. He vigorously defended Greyhound's service record and successfully renewed all its licences. With this appearance Fay began a task that would occupy much of his and his successors' time and a large portion of the company's legal budget in the decades ahead.

$99 Circle Tour

In 1937, Lethbridge native Tom Kirkham went to work in the ticket office, where he and fellow depot worker Bud Armstrong soon became famous for going into the beer parlour and shouting out the bus departures with service to a string of about fifty different towns and cities from Lethbridge to Los Angeles.

Kirkham was fascinated by bus schedules and in between arrivals in the winter he would research tariffs and ticketing methods. As Lethbridge was a major transfer point between north-south and east-west Greyhound traffic, Kirkham set himself a challenge. He decided to work out a trip around North America that would use connecting Greyhound lines and include Vancouver, Los Angeles and Montreal, for less than $100.

Using the many schedules and tariffs to hand, he succeeded in a month. The trip ran Lethbridge-Vancouver-Los Angeles-Atlanta-Boston-Montreal-Chicago-Winnipeg-Lethbridge, and cost $99. Passengers could board at Calgary or Edmonton for an extra $1 or $2 respectively.

Kirkham sent the idea to traffic manager Jerry Brown in Calgary, suggesting the company advertise it to every teacher in the province. Known as the "Circle Tour", the trip was indeed very popular with teachers, almost the only ones who had the time and money to take such a trip in the Depression.

Kirkham's Baggage Tag System

Because the British Columbia government charged high licence fees, the company tried to minimize the number of buses licensed for B.C., usually about three in Lethbridge and Macleod to handle the westbound traffic. Lethbridge was the bus transfer point. As the excursions grew in popularity, Lethbridge began having problems processing baggage. The buses westbound from Winnipeg arrived in Lethbridge in the middle of the night. The night staff would try to read the tags in the dark to see if the bags should be taken off, transferred to a northbound bus or be put on the bus continuing west, and errors were increasing.

Tom Kirkham's solution was to colour-code the tags by province of destination: Manitoba, Saskatchewan, Alberta and British Columbia. This simple yet ingenious solution earned Kirkham a $10 a month raise, and Greyhound still uses this baggage tag system today.

1938: CONSOLIDATING THE PRAIRIES

Greyhound's next move to the east was big, gaining control of two of the largest companies and much of the most important route mileage in Saskatchewan and Manitoba. The two companies were Trans Continental Coach Lines, owned by Barney Olson, and Prairie Coach Lines, owned by R. Peverley.

Trans Continental Coach Lines

Barney Olson's Trans Continental Coach Lines Limited operated several routes in Manitoba including Winnipeg-Virden. Barney had taken the company as far as he could with his resources, and bringing it into the Greyhound fold seemed the smart thing to do. Fay probably convinced him that an organization that spread itself across the four prairie provinces would be a very attractive and saleable asset.

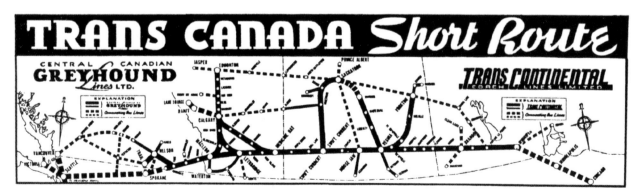

Trans Canada Short Route

Prairie Coach Lines

Prairie Coach Lines of Regina, Saskatchewan, which operated many of its routes under the name of Checker Greyhound, had been running a service between Calgary and Regina since 1933, and was also running between Regina and Virden, Manitoba, providing the link between Central Canadian and Trans Continental.

The company's owner, R. Peverley, was deeply into debt from expanding too quickly and Fay offered him a way out. If his creditors approved and the government agreed to transfer the licences, Fay would pay off the creditors and give Peverley a consideration over and above his debts. In a tight spot, Peverley agreed to consider an offer.

The Acquisition Agreement

The manoeuvre to accomplish the two acquisitions was complicated. Its implementation hinged on Fay acquiring an option on Prairie Coach and an agreement with the two Olsons defining the process.

On April 8, 1938 the three men signed a memorandum of agreement outlining the steps:

• Fay would negotiate an option on Prairie Coach Lines.

• Barney Olson would sell Central Canadian all the franchises and assets of Trans Continental Coach Lines including four depreciated coaches and two new coaches for an estimated cost of $50,000.

• Olson would pay Central Canadian Greyhound $10,000. As payment to Barney Olson for Trans Continental, Central Canadian would create $75,000 of preferred shares and allot them to him.

• Barney Olson would transfer $10,000 worth of preferred stock to Fay for which he would pay Olson $5,000 in cash.

• Speed Olson would subscribe for $5,000 worth of preferred stock for which he would pay Barney Olson $3,500.

A new company would be formed under the laws of Alberta having authorized capital of $50,000 divided into 500 shares and Central Canadian would purchase enough stock in the company to allow it to purchase Prairie Coach.

Barney Olson would be appointed president and managing director of the new company with full authority to carry out all actions pertaining to the ordinary business of the company, with the exception of policy and purchase of equipment which would be referred to the board of directors of Central Canadian and with the exception of all matters relating to traffic agreements and matters of finance which would be under the control of Fay.

Full control of the new company would be vested in the board of directors of Central Canadian Greyhound.

On completion of the organization of the new company, the salaries of each of the three would be equal. Barney Olson's salary would, as far as possible, be paid by the new company and not be a drain on Central Canadian.

On April 12, 1938, Fay acquired an option from Prairie Coach Lines, setting the wheels in motion.

On April 14th the new company, named after Olson's old Trans Continental Coach Lines Ltd., was registered in Alberta with head offices in Calgary. The subscribing shareholders, holding one share each, were Greyhound's lawyer, Percy L. Sanford, a secretary, Edith Nerland, and Speed Olson.

On April 22nd the shareholders agreed to take over George Fay's option to purchase Prairie Coach Lines Limited and to deposit a cheque for $4,950 in a Regina bank in the joint name of Trans Continental and Prairie Coach. On April 25th the directors of Central Canadian agreed to purchase 400 shares of Trans Continental's capital stock by transferring to it all the assets purchased from Barney Olson and paid it $40,000 in cash, allowing Trans Continental to make the deposit.

The same day, the directors of Trans Continental met and the two shares belonging to Sanford and Nerland were transferred to Fay and Barney Olson, who became secretary-treasurer and president of the company respectively. Then the new officers tidied up the books and authorised Fay and Barney Olson to arrange for an extension of time for payment of $25,000 owing to the National Trust Company.

Then, in late May 1938 Trans Continental's directors approved the acquisition of an option from Grey Goose Bus Lines Limited to purchase its operating franchise between Winnipeg and Oak Bluff on Highway No. 3 and between Oak Bluff and Reston, Manitoba on Highway No. 2. Later, in September they approved the purchase of two 37-passenger coaches at $15,000 apiece from the Fort Garry Motor Body and Paint Works Limited in Winnipeg.

Retrieving Prairie's agents

In 1938 future president Bob Borden's task as the new general passenger agent was to "resurrect" the many agents previously working for Peverley's Prairie Coach. These agents had lapsed over the winter in the absence of service on many of Prairie's routes. This was important work, for small town commission agents formed the very backbone of the Greyhound sales force and the drivers often relied on them for assistance in emergencies.

Borden travelled the back roads of Saskatchewan, visiting small town garages, hotels and stores to talk to former Prairie Coach agents and prospective new Greyhound ones. Borden then visited agents all over the system from Trail to Winnipeg, training them on ticketing procedures, addressing their needs and trying to collect receipts from agents whose reports were tardy. Some things never change.

Borden began his task with a brand new Ford. That October, the car had 110,000 miles on the odometer and was completely worn out.

Alberta Expansion

To date, Greyhound had mainly focussed on southern B.C., southern Alberta, Saskatchewan and Manitoba. However, although one of the company's most important routes ran north from Calgary to Edmonton, where it established a depot in May 1931, Greyhound lacked a strong identity in northern Alberta.

There were several small bus lines in Alberta, mostly dating from the late twenties, including Northland Rapid Transit run by J. Victor Horner between Edmonton and Barrhead, Collins Brothers (later Canadian Coachways) who served Athabasca from the capital, and R.F. Latimer who operated between the city and Thorhild. But the most important company in the area was run by a particularly astute and knowledgeable bus operator, Lorne Frizzell.

Lorne Frizzell

Born 1905 in Great Falls, Montana, Lorne Frizzell came to Alberta in 1911 when his father, a locomotive engineer, got a job running a steam donkey on the construction of Edmonton's High Level Bridge. He spent a few years in Barrhead, eighty miles north of Edmonton, and then moved to Edmonton about 1916 to complete his schooling.

After a frustrating year in university in 1922, Frizzell saw a need for trucking service between Edmonton and Barrhead, where he had numerous acquaintances in the business community. In 1923 he and partner Norman Lord began the truck line with one vehicle, using Frizzell's farm as a headquarters,

and soon added a second truck. But by 1926 Frizzell felt that there was not enough freight business to sustain the lines. While driving as a spare driver for Horner's Northland Rapid Transit he decided to go into the bus business, choosing the name Midland Bus Lines, Limited from a railway that his father had worked for once in Colorado.

Midland Bus Lines

While Lord carried on with the truck line, Frizzell converted a 7-passenger Buick into an 8-passenger bus by stretching the wheelbase, and began running a service to Vegreville, sixty-five miles east of Edmonton. By June 1929 he had extended his original route eastward to Innisfree using a 14-passenger Reo custom built for him in Edmonton.

In 1931 Frizzell made his first move west of Edmonton, taking a sixty-five mile route to Evansburg from another line that went broke. Then, moving east, in 1932 he began serving Vermillion and in 1933 he gained Lloydminster at the Saskatchewan border. From there Frizzell and Grey Goose Coach Lines started an alternate service (one year each) between Biggar and Unit to keep competitors from running Biggar-Edmonton.

Grey Goose was an important Saskatchewan carrier operating between Prince Albert, North Battleford, Lloydminster and Saskatoon. In February 1936 Midland Bus Lines, which now included Norman Lord as a 25% partner, purchased all of Grey Goose's Saskatchewan assets, including roughly ten buses, and its franchises. Frizzell's improved fleet now included Grey Goose's ten buses, a model V Yellow coach, a model 65-2, 29-passenger White and two 21-passenger Kenworths. Midland was now the second largest stage line in Alberta with a network of routes in northern Alberta and Saskatchewan.

Fay and Frizzell

Fay and Frizzell's good relationship dated to 1929 when Fay first visited Edmonton in an attempt to get the franchises for southern Alberta. Frizzell had connections in the Department of Public Works through his trucking business and his bus line, and introduced Fay to the people in the department who got him his interview with the minister.

In fact, after Brewster Transport had discontinued its Calgary-Edmonton service, Frizzell considered taking it over, but was deterred by his small fleet and the wretched quality of the Calgary-Edmonton gravel road. When Greyhound opened its Edmonton depot Frizzell became one of its major users, paying

Greyhound a commission based on the percentage of total tickets sold (i.e. if Midland sold 20% of the tickets then Midland paid 20% of the operating expenses).

Midland Bus Lines also had an interline agreement with Greyhound, a real benefit to Greyhound as Midland sold many more tickets over Greyhound lines than vice versa. The working relationship was further strengthened in 1937 when the two companies made a combined purchase of some Kenworth buses from Seattle to obtain a lower unit price. Thereafter Midland did all of Greyhound's Edmonton maintenance work in its garage as well.

Late in fall 1938 Fay invited Frizzell for dinner in Red Deer. Over the meal Fay said he could see that Midland was the key to transportation in the northern part of the prairies over Highway No. 16. Not only did it operate extensive services itself, but it also had agreements with Arrow Coach Lines between Saskatoon and Yorkton, Saskatchewan, and with Clark Transportation between Yorkton and Winnipeg, thereby controlling the northern route between Edmonton and Winnipeg. In contrast Greyhound passengers bound for Winnipeg had to go south to Calgary before heading east, adding four to five hours to the trip.

Fay also agreed that Edmonton would be an important hub for bus transportation and correspondingly Greyhound needed good representation there. As a result, he was prepared to make Frizzell a generous offer for Midland's business and equipment and was prepared to guarantee him a top management position, district supervisor in Edmonton.

Frizzell had about twenty-five employees working for him. After receiving Fay's promise that they would keep their jobs and seniority, the deal was sealed in early December 1938. In fact, some long-serving Greyhound employees were heard to gripe "who bought out who?" when they saw how well the Midland employees were treated.

OUR NETWORK
1940 – 1950

1940–1942: THE ALBERTA–B.C. LINK

75 Once the legal niceties of the sale between Greyhound and Trans Continental were complete, Fay devoted his attention to his long-standing goal, the running rights between Calgary and Banff. Having sewn up routes through four provinces, Greyhound was determined to finalize its Alberta-B.C. link and consolidate its network.

With the recent completion of the Big Bend Highway, this route was not just a potentially lucrative tourist run, but the key to developing Greyhound's service to the west coast through Canadian territory. Fay's tenacity in pursuing this goal against persistent and hostile opposition truly illustrates his business sense and ingenuity.

Big Bend Highway

In 1925, A.W. Campbell of the Department of Railways and Canals discussed the desirability of an all-Canada motor road at a meeting of the Canadian Good Roads Association in Edmonton. The first action seems to have been taken in the Depression by the Department of Labour when, to stimulate employment, it offered to pay provinces one-half of the construction costs of any highway that a province designated as its section of a national motor route. The Big Bend Highway was built on this basis.

The highway was intended to loop around the Columbia River's northern arc (the "big bend") to link existing roads at Golden and Revelstoke, providing a more direct link between the prairies and the Pacific coast than the route through the northwestern United States.

Construction initially proceeded rapidly, but was delayed by the effects of the Depression and the high cost of materials. By this time most provinces had begun to use gravel on roads, but good gravel was in short supply and relatively expensive on the prairies. Most roads were still built with clay and were not sufficiently raised to prevent snowdrifts and washouts.

However, by the end of the decade many roads were gravelled and a portion of Greyhound's old nemesis, the Calgary-Edmonton Highway, was paved. The Big Bend was finally finished in 1940, just before the demands of the war put a stop to new road construction.

Greyhound needed this route to complete its network, but unfortunately Alberta's largest, most successful and most influential bus company, Brewster Transport, held the rights.

Brewster Transport

George Brewster had obtained a licence from the B.C. government to operate from the eastern boundary of the province over the Big Bend to Revelstoke. Through an arrangement with B.C. Coach Lines from Revelstoke to Vancouver, beginning in July 1940 the Brewster Transport Company offered Banff to Vancouver service over what it advertised as the "Trans-Canada Evergreen Highway".

The service was actually provided by the Brewster Bus Service, operated by George Brewster. During the depths of the Depression, Brewster Transport president Jim Brewster was unable to keep many employees, including family members, on the payroll. He gave his brother George the option to run the Calgary-Banff service independently. George Brewster jumped at the chance and was offering daily return service from Banff to Calgary in a small Ford bus.

Bad Blood

Fay and Jim Brewster were not on the best of terms,

dating to Greyhound's establishment in Alberta on the Calgary-Edmonton line, stripped from Brewster by the government due to Brewster's spotty service. Outmanoeuvred in that battle, Jim Brewster vigorously resisted attempts by Greyhound and other non-resident operators to move into the lucrative mountain national parks tourist market, which his company largely controlled.

The Rocky Mountain Association

To protect his market, in 1939 Brewster spearheaded the creation of the Rocky Mountains Parks Motor Livery Operators' Association, an organization of park transportation companies headquartered in Banff and Jasper. This association's goal was to negotiate an exclusive franchise with the federal government for motor livery service within the parks, and the negotiations took some time. Fay submitted a brief opposing the franchise, but to no avail. On July 3, 1940 the association signed an agreement with the Parks Branch giving it the exclusive franchise, in return for 5% of each member's operating revenues.

Secondary Park Gate Rights

Fay had not put much hope in the brief, and unfazed, put another gambit in play. Approaching the Highway Traffic Board, he convinced it to give Greyhound "secondary" (summer only, no local service) running rights between Edson and the Jasper Park gates and between Calgary and the Banff Park gates "for the purpose of giving increased service to the large number of tourists who desire to travel by bus over these lines."

A model 150 "Silversides" delivered to Greyhound in 1940

With these provincial rights in hand, Fay then persuaded the Parks Branch to let him bring his buses into the Banff and Jasper townships. Here the restrictions on the size of the buses allowed on park roads, and the franchise agreement prevented Greyhound from seeking running rights past the towns.

Brewster was undoubtedly annoyed by Fay's success in gaining secondary rights into Banff, and soothed his wounds by concentrating on the new service his company was offering over the recently completed Big Bend Highway.

Subverting the Association

Unfortunately, Jim Brewster's joy was short-lived. Fay had found a way to compete with both Brewster's tourist livery business in the parks and the Pacific coast service.

Group of Greyhound passengers along the road to Jasper, 1940

As transportation beyond Banff township was restricted to those holding membership in the Motor Livery Operators' Association, Fay secretly approached one of the smaller members, R.F. Colebrook, and worked out an agreement with him. By its terms Greyhound brought passengers as far as Banff where they transferred to the Colebrook coaches, which met all the size and licensing criteria to conduct park tours or pass through them.

Grand Circle Tour

At the same time, Fay took advantage of the recently completed Banff–Jasper Highway, another Depression project, to offer a "Grand Circle Tour" that included Edmonton, Jasper, Banff and Calgary for the rock-bottom price of $16.80, about the same as the cost of a fare from Lake Louise to Jasper on a Brewster bus. Fay subsidized some of the regular sightseeing tour runs and advertised them at bargain prices, further undercutting the competition.

Using the Greyhound-Colebrook agreement, Colebrook buses picked up Greyhound's passengers in Banff and transported them via the Banff–

Greyhound Circle Tour advertising

Windermere Highway to link up with Greyhound's connections through the Crowsnest Pass and Kootenay Valley.

Secondary Big Bend Rights

Although Fay approached the B.C. Public Utilities Commission for secondary running rights over the Big Bend route, his request was denied for summer 1940. Undeterred, after the purchase by the U.S. Greyhound Corporation and subsequent renaming of the company to Western Canadian Greyhound, Fay applied again and was successful. Greyhound now had secondary running rights over the Big Bend.

Brewster Succumbs

Jim Brewster protested what he called Fay's "smart practices" and complained that an American-controlled company was taking money from the pocket of a Canadian one, but without result. Six months later, losing money on the run and knowing Greyhound would cut its fares if he tried to compete head on, in spring 1941 he discontinued Brewster Transport's service and instructed his comptroller, Lou Crosby, to sell Brewster's Big Bend rights to Greyhound. The final price was $1,000.

Driven 'Round the Bend

Notoriously full of curves and hills, running through desolate, unpopulated territory, the Big Bend highway gave Greyhound's drivers some of the trickiest driving they experienced anywhere. As an example, driver Ed Dunn was on a holiday trip to the coast and asked the regular driver, Harold Selke, if he would like him to take the wheel for a while. Selke agreed.

Used to the wide-open, straight roads of the prairies, Dunn had difficulty navigating the curves and hills at highway speed. After less than an hour, Selke came up front and said, "O.K. Ed, I'll take over now, you've got us about half-an-hour behind schedule."

More Shenanigans

Despite this success, Fay was not yet finished with the Brewster family. He still needed the primary rights on the Calgary-Banff route.

To get these, he secretly acquired stock in a second Banff member of the Motor Livery Operators' Association, R.K. Madsen. Negotiations to purchase an interest in Madsen's company began in earnest early in 1941. Bob Borden vividly recalled many trips at Fay's direction to meet with Madsen in Banff at prearranged locations, or driving Madsen back to Banff from Calgary in the middle of the night after a meeting. Secrecy was needed so Brewster would not find out and interfere.

On February 21, 1941, Greyhound purchased $20,000 of Madsen stock. Through this new subsidiary Greyhound became a member of the Motor Livery Operators' Association and could take part in its exclusive franchise.

Cadillac Fleet

Two months later, on April 18, 1941 Greyhound purchased five beautiful, convertible Cadillac sedans and four International 12-passenger bus chassis for Madsen at a cost of $32,000.

The new Madsen equipment was to be used in competition with Brewster Transport's somewhat older fleet, but that was only one reason why Fay purchased it. It was also bait for George Brewster, who was starting to run a little sightseeing business himself.

Greyhound Cadillacs at Banff, 1941

Once the Madsen equipment was operating, Fay approached Brewster and made an offer that was difficult to refuse. If Brewster would turn over the Banff-Calgary rights to Greyhound, the company would give him the Madsen Cadillacs and buses for his own sightseeing fleet. Greyhound also agreed to send him any passengers who came into the park for sightseeing purposes, and to give him the overload rights for the Greyhound Banff-Calgary local service.

Apparently the offer caused a debate between George and his brother Jim as to who actually owned the Banff-Calgary rights, but an agreement was reached by early 1942, perhaps because Fay indicated he was willing to put some cash into the deal.

Banff-Calgary Rights

On January 28, 1942, Greyhound acquired George Brewster's service between Banff and Calgary, including the licences and his two Ford buses, for a cash consideration of $20,000 and the aforementioned sightseeing equipment.

Fay could have been forgiven for pausing to gloat, but he didn't have the time. He was already deep into extending Greyhound's interests farther west. Fay clearly intended to establish company-owned routes, rather than connecting lines, right through to the Pacific coast. The way to do this was through the now tried and true method of acquisition.

Connecting the Coast

Before Greyhound began its service over the Big Bend Highway in 1941, Fay went looking for an agreement with a B.C. company licensed to carry passengers to the coast from Revelstoke, where his company's licence terminated.

At this time there were two main operators in the region, B.C. Coach Lines and B.C. Greyhound Lines.

Begun in 1929 by R.V. Wilkinson and C.M. Blackwell, B.C. Coach Lines' routes centered on Kamloops, initially offering service east to Salmon Arm, southeast to Vernon and Nakusp and from Princeton to Spence's Bridge. By 1941 it also held rights from Kamloops to Revelstoke and from Prince George to Quesnel, as well as from Quesnel to Vancouver through another company with which Wilkinson and Blackwell were associated, Cariboo Stages Ltd.

B.C. Greyhound Lines

B.C. Greyhound Lines was the creation of Fred B. McLeod, a native of Nanaimo who began a small local bus service out of Penticton in 1930. It gradually expanded in the Okanagan Valley until 1934, when it acquired another small company, Interior Greyhound Lines, providing it with routes extending through the valley north to Salmon Arm and then west to Kamloops.

At Kamloops, Interior Greyhound had connections with Cariboo Greyhound Lines, a company formed in 1931 that operated from Kamloops south to Oroville, Washington and from Vancouver to Prince George over the new Cariboo Highway. McLeod created B.C. Greyhound Lines in 1935 to consolidate his existing interests, and then purchased Cariboo Greyhound, operating it as a subsidiary of his new company.

B.C. Greyhound gradually extended its licences westwards towards the coast from Kamloops, finally achieving its goal in 1940 when McLeod bought out Blue Funnel Lines, his main competitor on the

Kamloops-Vancouver route. Blue Funnel then too became a subsidiary of B.C. Greyhound Lines.

Fay knew Fred McLeod well since the early thirties, and his second appearance before the B.C. Public Utilities Commission in the fall of 1940 was in concert with B.C. Greyhound. Fay was applying for through rights over the Big Bend to Revelstoke and McLeod was applying for a licence from Kamloops to Revelstoke.

Fay's case was strong and he argued it forcefully: The granting of the applications . . . will connect the now existing motor coach systems of British Columbia with those of Alberta, Saskatchewan, and Manitoba on a sound, economical basis, . . . ensure efficient and reliable operation and eliminate unnecessary transfers, delays, lack of comfort and make possible co-operation that will meet all the requirements of public convenience and necessity.

Citing "public convenience and necessity," the Commission granted the two licences, preparing the way for through service over the Big Bend beginning in summer 1941. Greyhound now had secondary running rights over the Big Bend.

Option on B.C. Coach Lines

The sale to Greyhound Corporation took place shortly afterwards, and with the resulting infusion of capital Fay tried to acquire B.C. Coach Lines' operation between Revelstoke and Vancouver and thereby obtain full running rights over the Big Bend.

Negotiations were initiated with Wilkinson and Blackwell, and in April 1941 Fay acquired an option on B.C. Coach Lines and Cariboo Stages, Ltd. (a different company than the similarly named Cariboo Greyhound), the total purchase price to be $55,000. At the same time Fay applied afresh to the Public Utilities Commission, asking for approval of the transfer of the two companies' licences to Western Canadian Greyhound.

To his amazement, the Commission refused, slapping his wrists with their contention that "the public interest will be best served by giving protection to existing license carriers who are giving or who are ready and willing to give good service to the public."

The Commission was referring to the fact that the licence granted to B.C. Greyhound had not even been tried out and that the company had assumed obligations of $40,000 to establish its Revelstoke-Vancouver service. It concluded that the request was "unfair" and that it "would result in direct injury to

the B.C. Greyhound, and might even prove fatal to that company."

The option to purchase B.C. Coach Lines and Cariboo Stages was not picked up and Greyhound lost its $5,000 option deposit. Instead, Fay operated the existing interline agreement with B.C. Greyhound successfully for three summers, until 1944 when the wartime transit controller froze the operation. After discontinuing Big Bend service for the winter of 1943-44, as it normally did, in 1944 Greyhound was not permitted to re-establish its summer routes between Golden and Revelstoke or between Banff and Cranbrook over the Banff-Windermere Highway.

B.C. Greyhound Buy-out

Rather than treat the situation as a drawback, Fay saw it as an opportunity to achieve the objective the Public Utilities Commission had denied him in 1941.

B.C. Greyhound wartime schedule

Shutting down the Big Bend service would hurt the B.C. companies more than Greyhound, so it was an ideal time to attempt a buy-out.

Negotiations with Fred McLeod and his minority partner, Ivor Neil, began in spring 1944. On May 2nd Fay took a proposed agreement to a special directors' meeting in Chicago with three top Greyhound Corporation executives, Wickman, Caesar and Ralph Bogan.

The group unanimously approved the acquisition of all the common shares of B.C. Greyhound Ltd., 552 shares of Cariboo Greyhound Lines, Ltd., and all the shares of Cariboo Garage Limited, the terminal operating arm of the company, for a total price of $316,000. This included the option payment of $90,000 and the balance of $226,000 in semi-annual installments of $18,000 each with an interest rate of 5% per annum on the unpaid balance.

As part of the agreement, Western Canadian also guaranteed to pay $17,000 of liabilities of Cariboo Greyhound Lines and Cariboo Garage Limited, and to sell back O.K. Valley Freight Lines, Ltd., a wholly-owned subsidiary of B.C. Greyhound Lines, to McLeod and Neil.

Fay now had direct access from the prairies to Vancouver and the Pacific coast through Canada on Greyhound-owned lines. Greyhound was now also linked with the Cariboo Waggon Road. Fay had finally realized his Pacific dream, though at a heavy price.

Greyhound bus at 100 Mile House on the historic Cariboo Highway, 1946

1941–1946: SASKATCHEWAN
Arrow Coach Lines
Back in 1933, Fay had attempted to create a northern link between Edmonton and Winnipeg through Saskatoon to complement Greyhound's existing southern route through Calgary and Regina. This had led to negotiations with R.J. Duncan, the majority owner of Arrow Coach Lines, Ltd., which held licences on routes from Saskatoon to Yorkton and from Saskatoon to Regina through Moose Jaw.

Duncan was already building up Arrow Coach when Greyhound bought out his Alberta routes in 1933 and 1934, but in the process he had to take in a number of smaller partners to provide capital. At the beginning of the war Arrow's debt began to drag it down and the minority owners wanted out. Arrow was ripe for a Greyhound bid.

On November 18, 1941, Greyhound and Arrow reached an agreement wherein Greyhound assumed all the assets and liabilities of Arrow by purchasing 45,000 shares of the company for roughly $56,000. Greyhound had accomplished the first step in connecting Saskatoon with Winnipeg.

Clark Transportation
Beyond Yorkton, the route was controlled by the Clark Transportation Company Ltd. Clark's owners, W.M. Hill and C.T. Clark, were not initially interested in selling, but Fay eventually made them an offer they couldn't refuse. At the same May 2nd meeting which approved the purchase of B.C. Greyhound, the directors also approved the purchase of Clark Transportation for $275,000.

Red Bus Lines
Finally, Fay had his eye on Red Bus Lines. Running between Calgary and the Saskatchewan border at Alsask, Red Bus Lines was one of Alberta's pioneer bus operators, first beginning service in 1929 between Calgary and Drumheller. The owner, W. Poxon, was ready to sell and in 1944 Fay received permission to make this purchase as well.

The C.C.F. Threat
Greyhound had always tried to maintain good relations with the provinces where it operated, seeking a low political profile. However, in June 1944 the C.C.F. swept to power under premier T.C. "Tommy" Douglas, western Canada's first socialist government. This government believed in state ownership of utilities and related industries, and soon publicly announced it intended to take over the province's bus lines.

Shortly after the election, Grant Smith, district superintendent for Saskatchewan, received a visit from a newly appointed government official. After introducing himself, the man came to the point. "We're going to take over your bus lines," he stated. A stunned Smith took in the story and told him he'd better talk to the boss.

With the official still in his office, Smith telephoned Fay in Calgary and gave him the news. At first there was silence on the line. Then Fay spoke up. "Are you drunk?" Smith attempted to get the official to talk directly with Fay, but he refused to do so, promising he would be in touch soon enough.

The matter quickly became a public issue, with Public Works Minister J.T. Douglas stating, "the people of Saskatchewan may reap the benefits of the highways which they have paid to build and maintain."

That fall a government negotiator contacted Fay, asking him to state a fair price for the equipment the company operated in the province. Fay refused to do so, pointing out that the company's business in the province consisted of more than just equipment, since the licences it held were valuable in themselves and Greyhound paid a hefty amount in taxes for the right to have them.

Greyhound's intra-provincial service consisted of twenty-six buses running on the routes Regina-Watrous-Manitou Beach, Saskatoon-Rosetown-Alsask, Saskatoon-Prince Albert, Carlyle-North Portal, Regina-Yorkton, and Moose Jaw-Assiniboia. At the time, all Saskatchewan licences were for service within the province's borders because wartime restrictions prevented inter-provincial service.

Fay then referred the problem to Greyhound Corporation headquarters in Chicago, which made strong representation to the Saskatchewan government, and discussions ground to a halt.

Inter-Provincial Rights
In December 1944, in the midst of the standoff, the federal government lifted restrictions on inter-provincial bus traffic. Greyhound immediately applied to renew its inter-provincial services. The Saskatchewan Highway Traffic Board granted the licence, but any jubilation Fay may have felt was tempered by the statements of Deputy Premier C.M. Fines, who publicly stated the Traffic Board could simply cancel the licences when the provincial government was ready to take over the bus lines.

These inter-provincial services consisted of eight daily runs through Saskatchewan to Alberta and Manitoba, operating on three different routes. The primary route was Highway No. 1 from Calgary through Medicine Hat, Swift Current, Regina, Fleming and Portage la Prairie to Winnipeg; a variation on this route ran south from Regina to Stoughton and then east to Winnipeg; and the northern route ran via Highway 16 from Edmonton through Lloydminster, Saskatoon and Yorkton to Winnipeg.

Nationalization Program
By spring 1945, the Douglas government's first priority for its nationalization program was the proposed bus line takeovers. The Minister of Highways stated as much in public speeches. When the Crown Corporations Act received first reading in late March, reliable government sources informed the press that the first crown corporation to be set up would be a government bus and truck company.

However, despite the passing of the Act, for several months the government took no immediate steps to make good on its threats. This was due to two things: first, Greyhound's unexpected resistance to the offer to purchase its equipment, requiring the government to purchase buses from other sources, and second, the time to prepare and pass the legislation that would allow the government to nationalize provincial businesses. In particular, it was not clear that the province legally had the power to nationalize Greyhound's inter-provincial operations.

Douglas Acts
After weeks of denial, despite intensive Greyhound lobbying behind the scenes, on December 5, 1945 Public Works Minister J.T. Douglas announced that Saskatchewan would move into the bus business on April 1, 1946, the date when the annual operating licences granted by the Highway Traffic Board expired, and that forthwith private bus lines could operate only in areas of the province not served by government lines.

The announcement also pointed out that the government would operate service over 3,300 route miles and that it had placed an order for "thirty new modern type buses."

This public announcement was followed in February 1946 by a letter from J.R. MacDonald, Chairman of the Highway Traffic Board. Sent to Greyhound and each of the ten smaller operators in Saskatchewan, it read:

The Government had decided to commence bus operations over certain routes in this province and on a point of policy has directed this Board to reserve these routes for such operations. Therefore, you are hereby notified that certificates of registration authorizing you to operate the routes hereunder mentioned will not be issued to you for the registration year 1946-47, which commences on April 1, 1946.

This notice put Greyhound in a bad position. In an attempt to cut his losses, Fay decided to forget about the local runs and fight for the key inter-provincial routes. J.T. Douglas quickly recognized that the government could not stop Greyhound from running through Saskatchewan but contended that it could prevent Greyhound from offering any service to provincial customers:

> We cannot prevent the Greyhound line operating an inter-provincial run across the province but we can stop private bus companies, operating inter-provincial runs through the province, from picking up passengers in the province.

In discussions with a government negotiator, a transportation expert imported from England, Fay argued that the Saskatchewan government did not have the right to cancel the pick-up rights on the inter-provincial licences, and referred him to Greyhound's lawyers. In return, the negotiator threatened to have Greyhound's equipment confiscated if it attempted to operate in the province, and the company took the threat seriously. However, Greyhound's remaining connections included the R.C.M.P., who indicated they would give Greyhound enough warning to get their equipment out if worst came to worst.

Greyhound Saskatchewan service just prior to government nationalization in 1946

Lawyers for the two sides wrangled for several months, with Greyhound's counsel threatening to appeal under the B.N.A. Act all the way to the Privy Council in Great Britain. When it became clear that neither party felt sure of its case in court, they turned to compromise.

Compromise

The government agreed to let Greyhound offer local service on its three inter-provincial lines. In return, the company agreed not to challenge the confiscation of the purely provincial routes, that the new crown company, the Saskatchewan Transportation Corporation (STC), would compete for local service on the three routes, and that Greyhound would assist the new company with getting on its feet.

Fay undoubtedly derived some pleasure from an editorial that appeared in a Saskatoon newspaper the day after the new Saskatchewan Transportation Corporation began, for he kept a copy in his file:

> This newspaper has previously had occasion to comment upon the light-hearted, casual way in which the CCF Government of Saskatchewan has entered upon some of its major industrial experiments. It has often seemed to this newspaper that the Government has gone into some of its businesses without any real knowledge of the problems involved and without any real consideration of the service it must render and with a minimum of organization to meet the demands it is presumed to cater to.
>
> Nothing could better illustrate this lack of intelligent planning than the incident that took place at the bus depot here on the morning of April 1. This was the day the Province took over a number of bus lines in Saskatchewan – among them the run from Saskatoon to Prince Albert formerly served by Greyhound Lines. The passengers gathered at the bus depot. The express was there. But there was no bus.
>
> Greyhound could not run the trip to the northern city because its franchise had expired at midnight, March 31. The new Government-operated line, apparently overlooking the fact that some persons might still be interested in a bus service from Saskatoon to Prince Albert had no bus there either. And so the travellers and the express were left on the sidewalk while the new Crown company held a caucus to ponder what might be done in this "emergency" situation.
>
> There can be no excuse at all for the

Government's failure to provide service on the route from Saskatoon to Prince Albert. The roads have been good enough for the Greyhound to operate the line continuously. And if, as Mr. Douglas said last week, the Province had been disappointed in receiving its new equipment from the factories, there was no reason why arrangements should not have been made to rent a bus for the route or to permit the Greyhound Lines to continue serving it.

Silver Lining

Fay certainly considered the confiscation of Greyhound's intra-provincial routes as a blow. Greyhound had paid good money for the rights and had received no compensation. At least Greyhound had won the critical battle for its inter-provincial rights.

In hindsight, however, the confiscation was the best thing that could have happened. Greyhound retained the lucrative main lines while the riskier local runs were no longer a concern or responsibility. These feeders were now the responsibility of the Saskatchewan government, which had to run them no matter what the economics, and it immediately began to lose money on them. In a province as sparsely populated as Saskatchewan, Douglas may have saved Greyhound from some tough future decisions.

Greyhound's service thereafter ran on four trans-Saskatchewan inter-provincial routes, including Edmonton-North Battleford-Saskatoon-Yorkton-Winnipeg, Calgary-Swift Current-Moose Jaw-Regina-Winnipeg, Regina-Redvers-Reston-Winnipeg, and Saskatoon-Alsask-Calgary. Today, Greyhound Canada operates service on all of these routes except

for the Regina-Redvers-Reston-Winnipeg route on which service was discontinued in the early 1990s.

Western Canadian Greyhound marketing brochure, 1945

Post-war Housekeeping

Having previously bought almost every company in sight, after the war Greyhound either made minor acquisitions or divested under-performing routes. In particular, Greyhound purchased routes from B.C. Coach Lines and from Vernon-Salmon Arm Coach Lines to solidify its position in British Columbia's Okanagan Valley.

A 1948 map illustrating the results of Saskatchewan's nationalization scheme

In July 1946, it purchased from B.C. Coach Lines, Ltd. certain routes and equipment to a value of $60,000. The routes included Kamloops to Revelstoke, Kamloops to Vernon and Revelstoke to Vernon, while the equipment consisted of two Hayes and one Reo 26-passenger coaches and an MCI 28-passenger coach. Then, in October 1947, Greyhound purchased a route from Vernon to Salmon Arm, one International coach, one Kenworth coach and an Oldsmobile sedan from Vernon-Salmon Arm Coach Lines Ltd. for $22,500.

On the divestiture side, a typical example was the decision in March 1945 to sell off a route between Cold Lake and Vegreville, Alberta that Greyhound had acquired with the purchase of Midland Bus Lines in 1938. Greyhound sold the franchise for $5,000 to Sunburst Motor Coaches Ltd. of Edmonton, an early Alberta bus company whose owners, A. Erickson and R.E. Brown of Westlock, had begun the company in 1930 with a service between Smoky Lake and Edmonton.

Alberta Roads

The pent-up demand for road improvements, unobtainable during the war, was further frustrated by the successful demands of northern residents, particularly in the Peace River district, to have monies designated to building roads for them.

For example, the Peace River Highway Conference held in Edmonton in 1948 endorsed a four-point programme whose major tenet was that the government "allocate in immediate and future years, a major portion of road maintenance and construction expenditures for a highway development program to embrace northern Alberta and particularly the Peace River area."

In 1949 there were fewer than 560 paved miles in the entire province. One of Greyhound's busiest routes, No. 3 through the Crowsnest Pass, did not receive its first coat of asphalt until 1952. However, during the fifties western Canada's main roads were gradually paved, funded by the profits from increased oil production.

Another important development would begin to take shape during this decade – the construction of the Trans-Canada Highway.

1956 – 1970

The creation of the combined Greyhound Lines of Canada in 1957 partially realized president Bob Borden's dream of extending the company beyond Western Canada, but the eastern and western operations still existed in isolation from one another. During the sixties Borden would realize three milestones for Greyhound: the completion of the Trans-Canada Highway, allowing Greyhound to run cross-Canada service from Ontario to B.C.; the acquisition of long-time competitor Brewster Transport; and the acquisition of Canadian Coachways, a sturdy northern operator.

1958–1965: VANCOUVER–TORONTO SERVICE/THE TRANS CANADA HIGHWAY

No one knows for sure who first conceived the idea to build a motor road connecting Canada coast-to-coast. However, a J.M. Wardle, an engineer in the Department of the Interior at the end of the First World War, is known to have submitted a report to his department suggesting construction of a cross-Canada highway as a post-war project.

The idea was definitely taken up in 1925, when A.W. Campbell of the Department of Railways and Canals mentioned the desirability of an all-Canada motor road at a meeting of the Canadian Good Roads Association in Edmonton. After the war, the project was formalized as the Trans-Canada Highway Act of 1949, and seven provinces recognized it through Dominion-Provincial agreements.

Statistics

The cost to complete the Trans-Canada was initially estimated at $300 million, and the government contributed $150 million in 1950. When the highway was finally completed in 1960, four years late, the

Greyhound advertising in the 1950s

actual cost was $825 million, nearly triple the original estimate, due in part to construction delays in the rugged area north of Lake Superior, and through the Rogers Pass section in the Selkirks.

The Act specified pavement widths of 6.7 metres and 7.3 metres, wide shoulder widths, low gradients and curvature, as few railway crossings as possible, and a maximum load-bearing capacity of 9.1 tons per axle.

Construction was not completed in western Canada until 1960 and the highway would not officially open until 1962, but as the different sections were completed Greyhound began running service.

Connecting the Dots

Bob Borden had inside information on the route the Trans-Canada Highway would take north of Lake Superior, thanks to a company lawyer who obtained a copy of the proposed alignment from a political friend in Ottawa. With this information he was able to identify the acquisition targets that would allow him to link Greyhound's western lines to the city of Toronto. Starting in May 1958, Greyhound began to acquire the final keys to its future Vancouver-Toronto through service, beginning with Moore's Trans-Canada Bus Lines.

Moore's Trans-Canada Bus Lines

Moore's was a small bus company operating between Winnipeg and Kenora in the Lake of the Woods district of western Ontario. Originally called Moore's Taxi Limited, the company began offering trucking and public transportation over the route in the early 1940s.

George Fay first began negotiations to purchase the bus operation from Moore in 1944, who wanted $300,000 for the combined operations. Greyhound was willing to pay $70,000 for the bus line, but the deal failed when no purchaser could be found for the taxi and truck business.

Knowing the path the Trans-Canada would take, Borden recognized that Moore's company was indispensable to the Manitoba-Ontario portion of the link. Happily, by 1958 Moore's was now purely a bus line, and Greyhound soon acquired it for the bargain price of $100,000 – just $30,000 more than the company had offered fourteen years earlier.

Eastern Canadian Greyhound

In order to bring all the lines for the proposed Vancouver-Toronto service under one company, on February 17, 1960, Greyhound purchased the licences held by fellow Greyhound Corporation subsidiary, Eastern Canadian Greyhound.

An Eastern Canadian Courier 200

The $2.25 million purchase included "all operating rights, motor coaches, other equipment, fixtures and stores relating thereto" of its northern division between Sault Ste. Marie, Sudbury and North Bay, fleshing out the northern Ontario network.

ECGL timetable illustrating northern division purchased by GLC in 1960

Sudbury-Toronto Operating Rights

In March 1961 Greyhound applied to the Transport Board for operating rights between Sudbury and Toronto, both to complete its Trans-Canada Highway network and to tie in with its own Toronto-U.S. services, recently purchased from Eastern Greyhound.

The problem was that Gray Coach, a Toronto Transit Commission (TTC) subsidiary, held the licence and wasn't interested in sharing it. Greyhound and Gray Coach did have interline agreements on some Ontario services, such as the Toronto-New York line, but the Sudbury relationship was acrimonious and connecting passengers were experiencing lengthy delays. Gray Coach vigorously opposed Greyhound's application.

Unfortunately, on October 31, 1961 the Board denied their application on the basis of "public necessity and convenience". As well, Greyhound and Gray Coach were taken to task for the delays passengers were experiencing changing buses at Sudbury:

> Further, we are of the opinion that, if joint operations in the past have been carried out successfully by the applicant company and its affiliates and the respondent company, the Board fails to see any good reason why this cooperation should not be applied to the present case. We, therefore, feel that both parties, Greyhound Lines of Canada Ltd. and Gray Coach Lines Limited, should take immediate steps in order that the present delays, causing great inconvenience to the travelling public at Sudbury, be eliminated as far as possible.

The Traffic Board then recommended that these delays be eliminated by a through service jointly operated by Greyhound and Gray Coach. Subsequently, in 1962 Greyhound made an agreement with Gray Coach to purchase miles so its buses could run into Toronto on the 270-mile Grey Coach route between Sudbury and Toronto, but the matter rankled. A few years later, in 1966 Greyhound offered $12 million to the TTC for Gray Coach, but was turned down.

Small purchases

Greyhound continued to piece together other small routes. For example, in May 1962 the company paid Canadian National Railways $52,800 for two MCI buses and the operating rights held by it between Port Arthur and Longlac in northwestern Ontario. Greyhound also applied to the Ontario Highway Transport Board for licences over the new section of highway being built between Port Arthur and Sault Ste. Marie.

Trans-Canada Opens

The long-awaited completion of the Trans-Canada Highway officially took place on September 3, 1962 when Prime Minister John Diefenbaker declared the highway open at a ceremony at the height of Rogers Pass, British Columbia.

Rogers Pass was an auspicious location for Greyhound, because the new road through the rugged Selkirks eliminated the hair-raising Big Bend route the company had operated since 1941, saving several hours of schedule time and allowing for year-round service.

Although the official opening took place in September, Greyhound began running schedules over its "All Canadian Route" starting June 1st:

> The first regularly scheduled passenger bus to travel over an all-Canadian route via the new section of the Trans-Canada Highway, which traverses Ontario's ruggedly scenic Upper Lake Superior Country, left Toronto Friday.

Greyhound Courier Challenger at Rogers Pass opening ceremonies, September 3, 1962

This will inaugurate an East-West bus link that has never before been possible. Buses travelling east and west will provide daily service via Canadian territory, eliminating the need for passengers to pass through the U.S.A. on their way between Canadian points . . .

In view of the present U.S. exchange rate, it is also believed that the new cross-Canada service will have the effect of keeping travel dollars in Canada. In addition, it means an extra 1,500 miles of highway over which Canadian businesses and individuals can ship packages and parcels via bus express.

The 3,000 mile run between Vancouver and Toronto will be completed in three-and-a-half days. Between Calgary and Toronto, through service will be provided without change of bus – although there will be frequent rest and meal stops, and passengers may enjoy stopover privileges if they wish.

The travelling time between Calgary and Toronto will be reduced by seven hours.

This one-bus service has been made possible by an agreement under which Greyhound buses will travel on the 270-mile Gray Coach Lines, Limited route between Sudbury and Toronto.

Through cooperation between Greyhound, Gray Coach Lines, Colonial Coach Lines Ltd. and provincial bus systems, inter-connecting service will enable bus passengers to travel across Canada from the Pacific Coast to the Maritimes.

Bob Borden watches Ontario Highways Minister William Goodfellow cut the ribbon to inaugurate Trans-Canada Highway service, June 1, 1962

Bob Borden attended the ceremonies at the Ontario Legislature that sent the inaugural bus, loaded with media, on its way. His remarks noted that the event was "a milestone in the history of our country's transportation." It was also the realization of his greatest dream.

Rapid Growth

In 1963, Greyhound initiated the first "through-express" schedules between Vancouver and Toronto. These became so popular that within a year the company had to double the service to satisfy the demand. In 1964 Greyhound finalized an agreement with Colonial Coach Lines Limited to allow through service between Montreal and Calgary. Similar agreements with other provincial bus systems soon made it possible for passengers to travel from the Pacific Coast all the way to the Maritimes, as predicted in the June 1, 1962 press release.

Bob Borden and Calgary mayor Grant MacEwan sending giant ticket to Mayor Jean Drapeau to inaugurate service to Montreal in 1964

By 1965 Greyhound was offering three trips a day between eastern Canada and Calgary and four trips a day between Winnipeg and the Pacific coast, contributing to a record 190 million passenger miles along the Trans-Canada Highway, a 15% increase over the previous year.

Greyhound created its Trans-Canada Highways Tour division in 1962

Trans-Canada Highway Tours

The new Trans-Canada Highway represented a tremendous opportunity to develop Canadian tourism, both domestically and overseas. To address the potential market, Greyhound created a new division, Trans-Canada Highway Tours.

The division offered a deluxe tour package, called "Royal Glacier Tours," between Calgary and the Pacific coast over the new Rogers Pass section of the highway, featuring daytime travel, hotels, sightseeing trips and most meals. Working closely with airlines and travel agents, including the company's own Greyhound Travel Bureaus, it extensively advertised the tours in the United States and throughout Europe. The division also created highly popular packages such as "Skifari" and "Grand Ole Opry" tours.

Business was so good that in its first annual report, covering the first 4-month June to September season, the division was able to boast its tours attracted visitors from 150 centres in Canada and the United States, the largest number coming from New York City, closely followed by Toronto.

$99 Grand Circle Tour

In 1964, Greyhound Lines of Canada and the Greyhound Corporation began promoting the "99 Days For 99 Dollars" Travel Plan. Under this plan, which later developed into the Discovery Pass/Canada Pass programs, passengers could travel anywhere in Canada and the continental United States for one low fare, with unlimited stopover privileges.

In Canada this was called the "$99 Grand Circle Tour" as Canadians were invited to travel along the Trans-Canada Highway and then go south to the United States to visit Los Angeles, New Orleans, Miami and New York. The plan was wildly popular: in 1965 Greyhound reported a 25% passenger increase in just one year.

BREWSTER TRANSPORT ACQUISITION 1965

While Greyhound was developing its Trans-Canada services, the owners of the Brewster Transport Company, the world's largest private sightseeing company and Greyhound's oldest and most bitter rival, suddenly offered to sell their business. Although the price was heavy, the opportunity could not be missed.

Origins

Brewster Transport's roots date back to 1892 when twelve-year-old Bill Brewster and his ten-year-old brother Jim, sons of Banff dairyman John Brewster, were requested by the manager of the Banff Springs Hotel to take a fishing party out on the trail. The trip became the basis for W. & J. Brewster, a profitable outfitting and guiding concern. After winning exclusive outfitting and livery concessions from the Canadian Pacific Railway in 1904-1905, the newly capitalized Brewster Brothers built up a fleet and extended their services to Lake Louise, Field and Glacier House. By 1915, the renamed Brewster Transport Company owned a large horse-drawn fleet and 146 head of driving horses.

Unfortunately, in June 1915 the federal government passed an Order-in-Council giving private and touring automobiles free use of park roads. Brewster quickly began adding motorized fleet, buying five Overland touring cars in 1916, and converting used Kissel trucks using framework and seats from the old horse-drawn "tally-hos" into three of Canada's first buses in 1917.

Brewster's "auto tally-ho", ca. 1917

Brewster soon moved on to manufactured vehicles from White Motor Company in Cleveland, Ohio. By the late twenties White Motor Company had sales offices in Montreal, Toronto, Calgary and Vancouver, and a major branch office in Winnipeg, which made it difficult for future Greyhound founder George Fay to sell Yellow coaches in Alberta and B.C. Fay didn't succeed in convincing Brewster to give Yellow a shot until 1929, shortly before he left to launch Greyhound, when he sold them two enclosed 17-passenger Yellow Model WAs costing $6,950 and $8,200 respectively.

In the mid-twenties Brewster began to expand from national parks sightseeing, establishing the first sightseeing business in Hawaii and working to develop stage lines in Alberta. By 1930 Brewster's fleet had reached 79 vehicles with a total carrying capacity of 880 passengers.

Brewster got into scheduled passenger service by accident, courtesy of the Banff-Windermere highway. Early in the twenties the federal and British Columbia and Alberta provincial governments cooperated to build the Banff-Windermere Highway, which opened in 1923. This event was a major step forward in western Canadian highway construction and provided an excellent highway link with the United States.

A few years later, Brewster cooperated in offering "Rawhide Trail Tours," a package created by an interline agreement between the CPR and the Great Northern Railway for excursion parties. The leisurely tour, which ran Waterton Lakes-Cranbrook-Radium-Golden-Field-Lake Louise-Banff, using the Banff-Windermere Highway, cost Brewster substantial deadheading, which the company decided to eliminate by carrying passengers between Calgary, Lethbridge and Waterton Lakes under the separate entity, Royal Blue Lines.

The Feud Begins

As a result, when the Public Vehicles Act came into force in 1927, Brewster Transport won the licences for the Calgary-Waterton Lakes and Calgary-Banff routes as well as the Calgary-Edmonton run. Brewster served the latter route for two years before it was taken away in 1929 for poor service and awarded to Greyhound, sparking the feud. The relationship had simmered ever since, though things began to improve after Jim Brewster's death in 1947. Brewster's management passed to Lou Crosby, reporting to a board of directors representing Brewster's family, and Crosby had his own fish to fry.

Crosby extricated Brewster from some unprofitable interests, such as the Sunshine Lodge, and acquired better ones, such as service stations at Banff, Field and Jasper, where it expanded in 1955. By this time the company was operating 95 pieces of equipment – 52 buses, 29 cars and 14 baggage trucks – with a total seating capacity of 1,500 and a net asset value of $1.3 million.

Brewster-Rocky Mountain Partnership

For many years Brewster Transport's major rival in the mountain national parks tourist livery business

Brewster-Rocky Mountain-Gray Line fleet, ca. 1960

Brewster's Mount Royal Hotel, one of its several hospitality interests, 1964

was Rocky Mountain Tours and Transport Ltd. By the mid-fifties the two companies realized their head-to-head competition was killing the return on many routes, and they decided on a partnership. In 1957, they pooled their transportation interests in a new business, Brewster-Rocky Mountain-Gray Line, two-thirds owned by Brewster and one-third by Rocky Mountain Tours, creating a virtual sightseeing monopoly.

Time to Sell

This happy state of affairs lasted until February 1964, when Lou Crosby died after fifty-seven years of service. The lawyer representing the Brewster family's interests on the board recommended the company be sold so that the family could rely on an annual guaranteed income rather than unpredictable dividend income.

Brewster first approached the CPR, which was only right considering it had given the company its big start in 1904 – Brewster had held its mountain hotel transportation concessions ever since – but after some delay the railway indicated it was not interested. Jack Hayes, the new Brewster president, then contacted Greyhound.

Borden was surprised by the approach, even though in recent years the two companies had been on better terms. In fact, in 1959 Brewster Transport

became responsible for operating Greyhound's bus depot in Banff.

Upon review, the proposition was attractive, not only because it meant an opportunity to settle an old score, but because Brewster Transport and Brewster-Rocky Mountain-Gray Line had solid financial statements as the near-monopoly player in the sightseeing market. Brewster was a bus line operator with a proven record and an excellent reputation in the tourism business, a niche that Greyhound wanted to pursue. Brewster's infrastructure interests, such as the hotels and service stations, suggested an attractive diversification opportunity.

The Offer

In July 1965 Borden made an offer to the Brewster Estate and the MacLeod Estate, owner of Rocky Mountain Tours, to acquire all the stock of Brewster Transport and Brewster-Rocky Mountain-Gray Line for a total of $2.5 million cash. The offer was accepted, but the deadline to close the transaction was scheduled before the next Greyhound board of directors meeting.

Keen to ensure the deal, Borden took the unusual step of writing the board members and seeking their approval for the transaction. All agreed, and the deal was ratified at the succeeding meeting in August 1965. Approval was also required from the CPR and the federal government. After some anxious moments and questions about an American-controlled company taking over one of Canada's oldest transportation interests, both approved.

Later that year Brewster Transport, now a wholly-owned subsidiary, acquired all the stock of Brewster-Rocky Mountain-Gray Line to simplify the corporate structure, and purchased seven used MCI model 96 Couriers from Greyhound to upgrade its sightseeing fleet.

After the purchase, Greyhound immediately began a massive advertising campaign to cash in on Brewster's image as a famous mountain tourist transportation company in conjunction with Greyhound's own highly valuable brand footprint. Greyhound's 1965 annual report devoted an entire page to explain to the shareholders the importance of this acquisition:

In its major 1965 expansion project, your Company acquired the largest tourist interests in the Western Canadian national parks of Banff, Yoho, Kootenay and Jasper. During August, the purchase was announced of all outstanding shares of Brewster Transport Company Limited, which will operate as a separate division of your Company.

Since 1909, the Brewster name has been associated with the development of tourist amenities in these mountain parklands. The operation has grown from horse-drawn transportation and pack trains to modern servicing facilities, accommodations and a large fleet of vista-domed sightseeing coaches, limousines and cars. The sightseeing fleet is being further modernized by the addition of 7 new vista-domed coaches.

As a result of the purchase, which made front-page news in the Western Canadian press, your Company has acquired a sightseeing organization operating throughout the national parks area, a chain of hotels and chalets and related services.

The very next year, Greyhound experienced a windfall when the CPR's "Dominion" transcontinental train was pulled off pending a Canadian Transport Board review. As a result, most Canadian and American tour groups were using Greyhound's Royal Glacier Tours. Tour bookings were up 42% over the previous year, and most of the inflow groups used Brewster Transport once they reached the Rockies. In August 1966 Borden reported that he felt the company was not going to be able to handle all the business coming its way that summer.

Greyhound had enormously increased passenger miles, added new tour services, increased its package express business, acquired Brewster Transport, and made major developments in bus building. In 1969, in the middle of all this expansion they identified yet another acquisition: the Canadian Coachways System.

CANADIAN COACHWAYS

The Canadian Coachways story has a lot in common with Greyhound's own. Initially a small Alberta bus line serving rural communities north of Edmonton, it began to grow as post-war oil exploration developed the Alberta and British Columbia northern economies. Eventually, it attracted the attention of a large American company, International Utilities, which wanted to diversify its holdings from gas utilities.

Founded in 1929 by the Collins brothers, Percy and Jack, the company began service over the 100 mile Edmonton-Athabasca "road" using a 7-passenger touring car. The brothers squabbled early and Percy started his own line, which took over what later became an important route between Edmonton and Mayerthorpe when Lorne Frizzell discontinued service on it in 1933.

In 1935 the brothers got back together, incorporating their separate interests into Canadian Coachways, Ltd. They soon expanded north of Edmonton, adding routes to Lac la Biche, Lac la Nonne and Breton. During the war they grew their fleet by several Western Flyers, MCI's major competitor, which they patronized for many years.

Expansion

After the war, Alberta's north began to open up when the highway to the Peace River country was completed. George Fay applied for the rights to the Edmonton-Dawson Creek route, but Coachways had the inside track because of its existing Athabasca service. Running via High Prairie and Lesser Slave Lake, the original route proved to be touch-and-go until 1955, when it was shortened by over 100 miles by using the company's old Mayerthorpe route to the new Whitecourt cut-off.

Another major addition occurred in 1950, when the Collins brothers bought out Gateway to Yellowknife Bus Lines. Gateway provided a connection from Edmonton through to Hay River in the Northwest Territories via the Mackenzie Highway.

By the early fifties Jack Collins sold his interest in the company and Percy Collins brought his son

A Coachways PD4104 crossing a trestle bridge at Taylor, B.C., 1957

Mickey into the business. Coachways expanded again in 1955 when it began service over the Alaska Highway from Dawson Creek to Fort Nelson. The following year these routes were extended to Whitehorse and in 1958 they reached all the way to Haines Junction.

These rudimentary northern roads were extremely difficult to travel and required strong, versatile equipment. Coachways experimented with several different vehicles, including an experiment to re-equip used Courier 100s with Cummins diesel engines, but this proved to be a failure. Coachways then turned to General Motors, purchasing three 4104s. Although they occasionally had to be pulled out of mud holes by Caterpillar tractors, these buses proved to be very tough.

Another experiment followed in 1956 when president Mickey Collins designed a combination bus-truck, the "Bruck", built by Western Flyer using old company Flyers. The Bruck had sixteen seats and 400 cubic feet of express space, reflecting the important role parcel express played in cross-subsidizing the thinly populated northern routes. It was so successful that Coachways eventually built a dozen, some with twenty seats and 600 cubic feet of cargo space.

During the company's final period of expansion under the Collins family, in the early sixties Canadian Coachways added several small bus lines. These included Alaskan Motor Coaches, Inc., extending the company's service all the way to Fairbanks and Anchorage, Alaska; Yellowhead Coach Lines, providing a route over the new Yellowhead Highway between Kamloops and Clearwater, B.C.; and Pembina Bus Lines, inaugurating the first company service south of Edmonton to Drayton Valley. The company also began to take on industrial bus contracts, such as providing service to U. S. and Canadian Air Force bases, and moved into the school bus field as well.

Sale to International Utilities

In 1965 Mickey Collins sold Canadian Coachways to International Utilities Corporation, an American company that already owned Northwestern Utilities and Canadian Western Natural Gas in Alberta and wanted to diversify into the transportation field. As I.U.C.'s Coachways System Division, the company immediately pursued another slate of acquisitions using the influx of new capital.

That year Coachways acquired Prince Coach Lines and its subsidiary Rupert Bus Lines along with their important 500-mile line between Prince George and Prince Rupert. The same year the company picked up Riverbend Trailways, serving the Mica Dam, and the bus division of the White Pass and Yukon Railway. A major addition in 1966 was one of Alberta's few remaining pioneer companies, Robert Horner's Sunburst Motor Coaches and Northland Arrow Lines, bringing in another 2,000 miles of mainly rural routes north and south of Edmonton. In a separate acquisition, International Utilities bought another major British Columbia operator, Vancouver Island Coach Lines.

Back on the Block

International Utilities had apparently hoped to bind these bus lines together and challenge Greyhound Lines of Canada as the west's foremost bus company. Unfortunately, many of the routes were just marginal. The low returns, International Utilities' inexperience in the bus industry, and the extremely high maintenance costs quickly created large deficits. After four years, the parent company decided to curtail the drain on its finances and in 1969 turned to Greyhound as the obvious buyer.

Greyhound had been watching its northern competitor for some time, and even had some cooperative arrangements, such as a combined service on the new Royal Yellowhead Tours Greyhound launched in 1968 following the opening of the Yellowhead Highway.

Many in the Greyhound organization thought the potential acquisition was a terrible idea, but Borden believed it merited consideration. As Edmonton natives, Borden and Lorne Frizzell understood the opportunities in the northern frontier.

Aware of Coachways' difficulties, Borden demanded their financial statements for analysis. The analysis found that Coachways had lost $260,000 on operations in 1968, $100,000 of which was a non-recurring loss from the sale of assets. Greyhound calculated that, if the Greyhound and Coachways oper-ations had been combined in 1968, the resulting synergies would have earned Coachways $312,000. The synergies were based on eliminating the Coachways garages in Edmonton and Calgary, employee reductions and insurance cost reductions.

On the day before the Greyhound board met to discuss the proposed acquisition, using the analysis, Borden successfully convinced Greyhound Corporation CEO Gerald Trautman to support him on the acquisition, which had a strong element of risk and could easily miscarry. Greyhound was only interested in acquiring three of the four parts of the Coachways System: two wholly-owned subsidiaries, Canadian Coachways (Alberta) Ltd. and Canadian Coachways (B.C.) Ltd., and a wholly-owned operating company, Alaskan Coachways Ltd.

In contrast, International Utilities wanted $3.6 million for the three plus a fourth subsidiary, Vancouver Island Transportation Company, Ltd., which was valued at about $2 million alone. Borden's research had convinced him that the Vancouver Island operation would be nothing but a liability, certain to lose money, but I.U.C. was not willing to make a deal without including it. The gamble involved agreeing to pay the $3.6 million purchase price, but only on the condition that I.U.C. keep the unwanted subsidiary.

The acquisition

Despite the high cost, Borden and his advisors felt sure they could soon make the Coachways System profitable and recoup the investment. The deal was approved at the August 21, 1969 board meeting, and

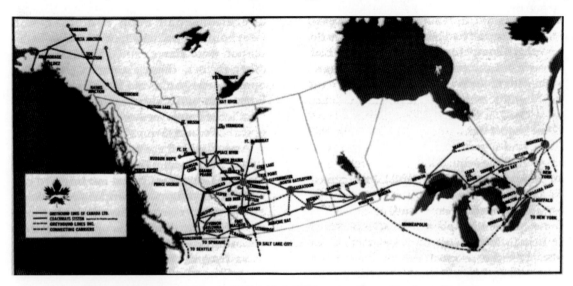

The Coachways acquisition in 1970 added 6,700 route miles to Greyhound's services

I.U.C. quickly accepted it. However, the official purchase did not become effective until January 29, 1970, after it received approval from the Canadian Transport Commission.

Greyhound gained a substantial list of assets and rights from the deal, including bus depots, garages, and seventy-five buses. Much of the fleet were MC-Is, but many others reflected the eclectic mix of vehicles Coachways had used, such as Western Flyer Canucks and General Motors PD4107s and 4903s.

Operating Rights

Coachways operated 6,700 route miles in Alberta. British Columbia, the Yukon and the Northwest Territories and more in Alaska. In fact, Greyhound had to receive the approval of the U.S. Interstate Commerce Commission before the acquisition of Alaskan Coachways Ltd. became official.

Under the acquisition, Greyhound's bus miles were set to climb by seven million a year, an increase of 25%, and its gross bus revenues were predicted to increase by 22% – a rosy future indeed, as Greyhound reported to its shareholders:

This acquisition has been effected at a favorable time for your Company. As the pace of industrial development quickens, the population of the Canadian North is increasing. Moreover, there is a growing interest in the travel opportunities afforded by the region. These factors point to a mounting demand upon the Coachways facilities now owned and operated by Greyhound.

Although Canadian Coachways' equipment and routes for the most part quickly integrated into the Greyhound network, unfortunately considerable staff reductions were required, including thirty people in the Edmonton headquarters and about seventy surplus drivers. Greyhound quickly eliminated the Edmonton garage, combining the maintenance operations with its own facilities there.

Although most of the senior Coachways management went their separate ways, one major personnel gain was Leif Laustsen, Coachways' superintendent of maintenance and former Sunburst Motor Coach mechanic. In 1970 he moved to Calgary as superintendent of equipment under E.H. O'Brien, director of maintenance.

MC-7 Supercruiser on the Yellowhead Highway in front of Mount Robson, early seventies.
Thanks to the Coachways acquisition in 1970, Greyhound now ran service to the edge of the Arctic Circle

1970 – 2003

1976–1978: BATTLE WITH GRAY COACH

Back in the early sixties when it was establishing its Trans-Canada Highway network, Greyhound was stymied by Gray Coach when it tried to get Ontario operating rights between Sudbury and Toronto.

Gray Coach, who owned the rights, hotly contested Greyhound's 1961 application, and the Highway Transport Board agreed, ordering the two parties to make some sort of arrangement so passengers would not be penalized when transferring between the two bus companies. Greyhound wound up having to purchase miles from Gray Coach in 1962 so it could run its service on the 270-mile Sudbury-Toronto Gray Coach route.

To try to get around the issue, in 1966 Greyhound offered $12 million to purchase Gray Coach from its parent company, the Toronto Transit Commission (TTC), but was turned down. There the matter sat, for a decade, until 1976, when Greyhound decided to try again.

The Application

That year Greyhound applied for licences to operate express routes between Sudbury and Toronto and Toronto and the New York border, which were controlled by Gray Coach Lines. At the same time, Stock Bros. Lines Ltd. of Orillia, a subsidiary of Travelways Ltd., applied for rights on another Gray Coach route between Toronto, Barrie and Orillia.

Expecting a fight, Greyhound management did their homework. Local management, including Norm Aitken, district supervisor, spent six weeks straight without a day off travelling on the bus between Sudbury and Sault Ste. Marie talking to passengers to identify potential witnesses. Willing witnesses were

then formally interviewed before being approved by the company lawyer in Thunder Bay.

Norm Aitken and Bob Parke, vice president, sales, then called on every reeve, mayor and councillor between Sudbury and Thunder Bay to ask for their support. The same exercise was repeated between Toronto and Buffalo. Aitken even went to Manitoulin Island and successfully persuaded the chiefs of five Aboriginal bands there to appear as witnesses. Aitken felt that Greyhound presented the "best calibre of witnesses of any hearing that I've ever attended".

The First Hearing

Hearings on the application began April 21, 1976 and lasted seven days. Greyhound's lawyer, E.A. "Fast Eddie" Goodman presented 70 witnesses who gave evidence supporting Greyhound's application. The evidence was a litany of complaints against Gray Coach about lost luggage, sluggish, rude drivers, problems transferring between Gray Coach and connecting bus lines, and terrible on-time performance. As well, president Borden testified that Greyhound was prepared to expend $5 million in garage and depot facilities in Toronto if they won the rights.

According to *Bus & Truck Transport* magazine, Gray Coach's legal defence "offered no substantiating evidence to support its claim that it will lose passengers and revenue to Greyhound. It refused or was unable to provide financial statements. It would not even come up with figures to show how many passengers had to change buses at Sudbury. When one witness had the temerity to complain about Gray Coach service, the company's counsel suggested that if she didn't like it she could fly instead".

Greyhound Successful

At the conclusion of the hearings the Board reserved

its decision. Seven months later, on November 22, 1976 the Board ruled in Greyhound's favour and a certificate was issued, launching a media storm. Borden ordered his Ontario troops to establish the express service the next day, knowing Gray Coach would appeal.

As a government-owned operation, Gray Coach pulled out all the political stops to try and have the Transport Board's decision overturned. True to the protectionist environment of the time, Greyhound was roundly criticized for being 61.5% American-owned. One stunt involved a group of Ontario members of provincial parliament being photographed taking a protest ride à la Rosa Parks, but on a Gray Coach bus.

Review ordered

After intensive lobbying, transport minister James Snow, acting for Ontario premier Bill Davis's minority Progressive Conservative government, ordered a review, and the Ontario Highway Transport Board undertook a second set of hearings on January 24, 1977. To prepare, on January 6 Greyhound distributed quantities of "Transportation Surveys", polling passengers at Winnipeg, Thunder Bay, Sudbury and Toronto on the new and expanded service.

The new hearings, the longest in the Transport Board's history, lasted for thirty-six days. Thirty-six witnesses appeared and 192 exhibits were submitted. Greyhound managers Jim Knight, Floyd Mogen and Bob Parke attended every session. Bob Borden was present for most of the hearings as well, occasionally tearing himself away to attend to other company matters in Calgary.

Gray Coach cried foul in the hearings, claiming that the Transport Board's November decision forcing them to share their three most profitable lanes with competitors would reverse a projected profit of $779,000 for 1977 into a loss of $756,000.

In response, Greyhound submitted an 84-page document describing four different operating plans Gray Coach could take to generate a profit of up to $1.25 million in a competitive environment, without cutting feeder route service, by better scheduling, reduced maintenance staff and changes to vehicle depreciation.

Public vs. Private

During the hearings Liberal leader Dr. Stuart Smith and New Democrat leader Stephen Lewis charged that the Transport Board had exceeded its legislative authority politically, if not technically, by approving the route sharing in the first place, since the province did not have a cohesive policy on inter-city bus transportation. In particular, Lewis's position was that the public corporation, Gray Coach, should be protected at the expense of the private, Greyhound.

At the conclusion of the hearings the Board again reserved its decision. On July 21, 1977 the Board upheld its original decision, permitting Greyhound to run on the Toronto-Sudbury and Toronto-Buffalo lanes, and criticized Gray Coach for being inefficient and only marginally profitable. In his report to Minister Snow, transport board chairman Edward Shoniker cited Gray Coach's poor management and soaring labour costs, recommending the company be reorganized with a board of directors separate from the TTC, instead of part-time appointed officials.

The next day, July 22, Greyhound district manager L.O. Forbes sent a memo to all drivers in the Sudbury division advising them to expect visits from the press in the Toronto terminal and to pay special attention to their appearance, "to present ourselves in the best possible light" during the post-judgement scrutiny period.

Gray Coach then took the appeal to Cabinet.

Six months later, on January 25, 1978, the Cabinet upheld the Transport Board's decision, although it did instruct Greyhound to implement certain pooling arrangements with Gray Coach on the routes. In Greyhound's annual report for 1978, Borden happily stated, "these decisions are beneficial to your Company and will enable it to continue to provide better service in Ontario and especially in Northern Ontario."

BRITISH COLUMBIA

At the same time, British Columbia was making its own moves in bus transportation. In 1973-1974, the mood was disturbingly evocative of the Saskatchewan government's 1944-1946 partially successful bid to annex the bus business. B.C.'s NDP government began readings of Bill 70, the Transit Services Act.

Section 2 of Bill 70 gave the government far-reaching powers to purchase or "otherwise acquire" lines of buses, and Greyhound was quite concerned that the government would attempt to expropriate its operations or refuse to renew its annual licences to operate in the province. If the province decided to take this avenue and put on its own buses, Greyhound could be forced to operate closed-door from the B.C.-Alberta boundary into Vancouver and back, without pick up or delivery privileges between the two points.

Over several tense days in late April and early May 1974, while Section 2 was undergoing final reading, Mr. A.V. Fraser, Member for Cariboo and Mr. McClelland, Member for Langley took turns questioning B.C.'s Minister of Municipal Affairs, as quoted in Hansard:

"Bill 70, Transit Services Act, is another typical takeover bill of the NDP where it takes over all the transportation facilities in the province the exception probably being the CNR and CPR if they so desire. As an example, what happens to Greyhound Bus Lines in this authority granted to the Minister?"

"Does the government intend to cancel the operating franchise that Greyhound Bus Lines has with this government now?"

"I would like to see the Minister of Municipal Affairs say that he is not going to cancel the licence of the private enterprise carriers of this province and that they will continue to operate."

The Minister repeatedly refused to answer the questions. On May 3, 1974, Mr. Fraser then went on record praising Greyhound, saying:

I have no shares in the Greyhound bus line, but I want to tell you that they have the expertise, the people, the experience, and they don't run just in the little lowland Fraser Valley. They run all over this province and have for years. The people of this province from Hope north all through the Kootenays and the Cariboo and the north appreciate their experience and they don't want to see them put out of business and then taken over by the civic stage lines who don't even know how to put a set of chains on. They'd even get stuck when there was a cloud in the sky! They have no idea how to operate under the conditions that Greyhound has to operate. I would like to hear the Minister say that clearly here they have no intention to put Greyhound or other private enterprise bus line out of business, because this bill certainly gives them the authority to do just that.

The Honourable Mr. Cocke spoke at some length, finally saying:

The Member for Langley (Mr. McClelland) asked about Greyhound. There are no plans to remove Greyhound (. . .) They seem to be providing a very good service at the moment.

The Minister then went on to suggest that perhaps a publicly operated service was needed to fill gaps where Greyhound did not or no longer chose to run, such as "the area between Prince Rupert and Prince George, which was subsequently picked up by a private operator."

Mr. McClelland then responded,

One brief comment before Section 2 passes and I'd like to thank the Minister for finally telling us and assuring us that he has no intention of canceling the opposition franchise of Greyhound and also admitting to us that he does intend to go into the intra-provincial bus line business and from the looks of the bill we also will be going into the manufacture of buses, probably a money-losing operation like Western Flyer and I guess, because of Section f(2), we can also expect to be going into the restaurant and hotel business as well and I'd just ask the Minister, Mr. Chairman, when and where we can expect the first Lorimer Hilton to be erected?

1992: GRAY COACH ACQUISITION

According to its history published in 1987, Gray Coach Lines, Limited (Gray Coach) was established by the Toronto Transit Commission (TTC) as a separate entity in 1927, "to ensure that the intercity business did not impose any financial burden on people who rode TTC's other conveyances".

Despite its gloomy forecasts during the battle with Greyhound in 1977-1978, Gray Coach had done reasonably well, with annual profits reportedly in the $2 million range.

In early 1986 Gray Coach brought William "Bill" Verrier on board as president, to refine the operation and further increase profitability. Bill Verrier came to Gray Coach from a senior management role at Eastern Provincial Airlines in Newfoundland, and retained his enthusiasm for the industry.

Service Cuts

Sometime in 1988, Bill Verrier began implementing service and line reductions on low-income routes to improve profitability, causing labour unrest. In December 1988, the drivers staged brief walkouts lasting half a day, stalling service across Gray Coach's territory. They also threatened a wildcat strike in mid-January 1989 following rumours that Gray Coach would abandon its London-Kitchener and Owen Sound-Barrie/Collingwood routes.

Gray Coach denied the rumours for some weeks and promised the communities that their service

Official opening of the Coquihalla Highway with B.C. Premier Bill Bennett, 1986

would continue. The Ontario Highway Transport Board indicated that no applications were pending from Gray Coach, and that in fact there hadn't been since 1986. However, behind the scenes Gray Coach negotiated with Penetang-Midland Coach Lines (PMCL) and Chatham Coach (Cha-Co) to take over the service so Gray Coach could discontinue its own on the low-income routes. PMCL and Cha-Co filed their applications in February 1989, and Gray Coach was set to withdraw on March 5, 1989.

This news was received with outrage from the union and concern from the affected communities. On February 21, 1989, MPP Ms. Bryden appeared before the House demanding the Minister of Transportation intervene:

I am gravely disturbed by the news that Gray Coach Lines is planning to abandon the Owen Sound to Barrie and the Kitchener to London bus routes on March 5, 1989. I would like to ask the Minister of Transportation (Mr. Fulton) if he has approved this plan.

Gray Coach, which is wholly owned by the Toronto Transit Commission, was given exclusive rights over profitable routes many years ago, with an obligation to provide quality service for less-profitable and even money-losing routes. Is the minister prepared to let them abandon this responsibility? Is it in the public interest to return to the chaotic situation of unco-ordinated private bus line operators which preceded the establishment of Gray Coach Lines

and produced a variety of standards of service? The March 5 closedown of the Gray Coach routes will leave a substantial number of residents in the areas served by these routes with no reliable alternative public transportation. It will also result in the loss of jobs for a large number of Gray Coach employees located in these communities.

I urge the minister to refuse approval of the line abandonment until he has listened to the residents and the employees affected and is prepared to guarantee that the ministry will see that quality service is provided to these areas. I also urge him to give us a policy statement on the privatization of the bus transportation service in this province.

The transfer was put on hold and hearings were set for May 1, 1989 at the Ontario Highway Transport Board. In the meantime, the union tried to lobby its cause. On April 28, 1989 Raymond L. Hutchinson, president of the Amalgamated Transit Union, Local 113, for Gray Coach, wrote to Metro Council and others protesting the planned eliminations and expected lost jobs. However, at the hearings the transfers were approved.

Sale to Stagecoach

Sometime in either June or October 1990 (various reports), following negotiations with Brian Souter, the TTC sold Gray Coach to Stagecoach (Holdings) Ltd. of Scotland. Stagecoach paid at least $16 million and acquired 100 buses in the transaction. Stagecoach had

successfully reorganized several public transit companies, and the increasingly indebted Gray Coach represented an opportunity to exercise their model in Canada.

As part of the reorganization, in November 1991 Stagecoach sold off Gray Coach's northern routes from Toronto to Sudbury and North Bay to Ontario Northland Transportation's bus operation for $7 million. The new company developed a new computerized onboard register system, and consequently eliminated Gray Coach's agency network, except for a handful of key agencies – Toronto, St. Catharines, Niagara Falls, Cambridge, Guelph/Kitchener and Owen Sound. This proved to be disastrous, as the agency network was Gray Coach's only direct contact with most of its customer base.

Gray Coach Lines Coach #2533 leaving the Metro Toronto Coach Terminal on Airport Express service, December 1991

Stagecoach also recognized that Gray Coach's massive labour costs needed to be brought under control if the operation was to be made profitable again. Unfortunately, Stagecoach's approach was seen as rather adversarial and they were largely unsuccessful in gaining concessions from the union. Within a year and a half Gray Coach was deep in the red and in bankruptcy protection.

Verge of bankruptcy

In 1992 Gray Coach and its subsidiaries Gray Coach Travel and Stagecoach Canada Leasing were on the verge of bankruptcy. Current liabilities were $8.7 million and long-term debt was $14.5 million.

Labour costs for drivers (paid hourly), platform and terminal represented 42% of revenues, while maintenance came to 30.6%, not to mention high coach depreciation, and coach rental costs that represented a third of charter revenues. Gray Coach also had an expensive lease for five coaches to serve the peak summer charter season. Greyhound's 1978 assessment of Gray Coach's cost issues was proven accurate.

Because of these crushing labour and fleet costs, Gray Coach's scheduled service operations contributed a total margin of less than 3%. In fact, the only things holding the company up were sightseeing, the Toronto airport shuttle contract, and bus parcel express.

Greyhound Makes an Offer

Like Brian Souter, John Munro of Greyhound's vice-president, operations, was originally from Scotland, and the two had a good relationship. As Gray Coach's troubles mounted, Munro called Souter to ask him how he liked Canada now. They met a couple of months later and mapped out the beginnings of a sale on a napkin in a restaurant across from Toronto's Royal York hotel.

Based on the negotiations, on July 9, 1992 Gray Coach was approved to receive relief under the Companies' Creditors Arrangement Act until October 13, 1992, when the sale agreement between Stagecoach and Greyhound was expected to be complete.

Gray Coach desperately needed to trim wages and was locked in union negotiations. In exchange for a portion of the company, the drivers took a 10% wage rollback effective August 16, 1992, helping slow the bleeding.

In order to cut costs, Gray Coach management were ordered to eliminate anything that didn't directly contribute to the bottom line. This went so far that Gray Coach was no longer maintaining operating statistics in its last few months. By the time of the purchase, Gray Coach " . . . had not only stopped counting passengers, it had stopped counting dollars".

Under the terms of the Share Purchase Agreement dated October 23, 1992, Greyhound paid $9.2 million for the shares of Gray Coach, acquiring the scheduled, charter and parcel express bus transportation operations, as well as the sightseeing and airport express. Bruce Elmore signed for Greyhound and Bill Verrier signed for Gray Coach, essentially his last act as president for the company. The purchase was completed sometime in December 1992 or January 1993.

Routes Acquired

Through the purchase Greyhound acquired assets of $9.8 million in coaches and $2.4 million in property, including the Lakeshore Garage. However, far more important were the valuable route authorities, which in essence created Greyhound's southern Ontario commuter service and short-haul business.

Before the acquisition, Greyhound's Ontario presence was essentially Toronto-Sudbury and Toronto to Buffalo/Detroit, plus a small route between St. Thomas and London via Highway 3. Through the purchase Greyhound gained the following:

- Toronto-Guelph-Kitchener
- Toronto-Guelph-Owen Sound
- Toronto-Grimsby-St. Catharines-Niagara Falls and Buffalo. Gray Coach's service to Buffalo began in 1928 after the Peace Bridge was completed at Niagara Falls.

As well, Greyhound now owned the Gray Line Toronto sightseeing franchise and Niagara Tours. Gray Coach previously obtained the Gray Line franchise on February 14, 1967, probably anticipating spillover sightseeing from Expo 67 in Montreal.

Gray Line Toronto operated two distinct sightseeing tour products, active from April 1 to the first week of November: the Toronto city tour, and the Niagara Falls tour, a 9.5 hour tour including a ride aboard the Maid of the Mist tour boat to the base of the world-famous Canadian Horseshoe Falls and a full buffet luncheon, with an afternoon/evening tour option available.

Gray Line Toronto sightseeing brochure, 2004

Double deckers on Gray Line Toronto sightseeing service. Gray Coach livery, 1992

Gray Coach #2545 at York Street and Queen's Quay West, Toronto, November 1991

Finally, Greyhound took over Gray Coach's Toronto airport shuttle contract, which is now operated by Pacific Western Transportation (PWT).

Labour Integration

Integrating the former Gray Coach drivers into the Greyhound system took some time. Compared to the hourly paid Gray Coach drivers, Greyhound driver pay is mile based, which meant it would be far cheaper for Greyhound to use its own drivers on the comparatively low mileage Gray Coach routes. Because they had received part ownership in Gray Coach in exchange for accepting the wage concessions, the Gray Coach drivers were in a position to derail Greyhound's acquisition, if they felt their work would be threatened.

Under a side agreement to the acquisition, Greyhound agreed with Amalgamated Transit Union, Locals 1630 and Local 1415 not to cross utilize manpower or equipment until the two unions had the opportunity to integrate their membership or state seniority.

There were also cultural integration issues. At Greyhound, drivers could be fired not just for safety violations, but also for poor customer service and theft. Greyhound expected some pretty serious changes and there was friction between the two groups of employees. Greyhound's union, Amalgamated Transit Union, Local 1415, led by president Bill Noddle, supported Greyhound's renewed commitment to customer service under president Dick Huisman, and helped lead the value transition.

On July 1, 1994, the employees covered under Gray Coach Lines Inc., ATU, Local 1630, Toronto, Ontario were rolled into the ATU, Local 1415 collective agreement. This followed the expiration of ATU, Local 1630's final agreement ratified August 6, 1992, effective July 1, 1992 to June 30, 1994.

VOYAGEUR COLONIAL LIMITED

Under its original name, Provincial Transport, Voyageur's presence in Quebec and eastern Ontario dates back to 1928. Provincial Transport grew quickly, acquiring 31 independent Montreal bus lines in June 1929. During the Great Depression, Provincial Transport bought Ottawa's Colonial Coach Lines for its coveted Ottawa-Kingston and Morrisburg-Renfrew routes, as well as 11 coaches. Provincial Transport soon bought three more companies, giving it the Toronto-Montreal and Ottawa-Montreal schedules and 30 more coaches.

Voyageur Name

In 1960 Provincial Transport Enterprises was purchased by Paul Desmarais of the Power Corporation.

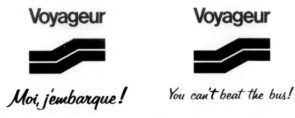

In 1969, the different subsidiaries, which had continued to operate under their original names and livery, were branded with the Voyageur name and the distinctive green and blue logo. Voyageur Colonial was based in Ottawa and operated the major Ontario-Quebec inter-provincial routes, while Voyageur Inc. was based in Montreal and handled the Quebec intraprovincial routes. In 1981-2 they became subsidiaries of Canada Steamship Lines, Limited (CSL), a former subsidiary of the Power Corporation.

Voyageur advertising, late '90s

In the late eighties Voyageur experienced significant business challenges. Its fleet was old and maintenance costs were growing. It was fighting VIA Rail over reduced one-way summer fares over Montreal-Ottawa and Montreal-Toronto, which promised to seriously affect revenues during the peak travel period. Although Voyageur was successful in having VIA's fares suspended by the Canada Transportation Agency in June 1988, it had something much bigger on its mind – serious labour disputes.

CSN Strike

Voyageur Inc. had suffered the same declines in the eighties as Greyhound under competition from the private car, the deregulated airline industry, and, particularly for the Toronto-Ottawa-Montreal corridor, from heavily subsidized passenger rail. Voyageur needed wage concessions in order to try and control costs in line with falling revenues.

Following unsuccessful negotiations with Voyageur's union, La Confédération des syndicats nationaux (CSN), pickets began to go up on December 7, 1987. Initially the affected employees were mechanics and garage staff, but as other collective agreements ran out and the original strike continued unabated, as of June 10, 1988 the strikers also included Voyageur's ticket sellers and telephone operators.

In order to keep the operation running, Voyageur Inc. locked out the strikers and brought in replacement workers, which caused intense fury among the strikers. The strike lasted almost a year and was marked by violence and vandalism. Al Mezzetta, who began working for Voyageur in 1979, recalls:

I had to go to court twice for the picket lines. We brought in replacement workers to keep things going, had to cross picket lines every day. For their safety we brought the workers in vans with the windows darkened. When you went to work you didn't know when you'd get home.

Twice the van didn't make it in – it was attacked at the gates, trashed with picket signs made with axe handles.

We had 24-hour security at the garage and outside managers' houses. Their windows were broken. Someone planted an explosive in the garage. There was a huge bang and a 45-gallon drum jumped up and hit the ceiling. The police found an explosive device. Pure luck no one was hurt.

The strikes did not end until December 11, 1988. By that time it was estimated that Voyageur had spent almost $5 million on security alone, not including the unrecoverable millions in lost business.

Fire Sale

By 1990 CSL had had enough and started looking for buyers. That summer CSL sold off most of Voyageur's Quebec network to a group of investors led by Serge Mérineau, which subsequently became the very successful Autocar Orléans Express Inc.

CSL then began looking for buyers for Voyageur Colonial's inter-provincial network, and in summer 1993 they began negotiations with Greyhound.

Greyhound could conceivably have purchased all the Voyageur Colonial routes in Ontario and Quebec, but president Dick Huisman was concerned about the French language administrative burden attached to the Quebec-based routes. Earlier, Voyageur had run into trouble with the Office québécois de la langue française as a result of passenger complaints, and subsequently paid to put all non-bilingual Voyageur drivers through a French language certification program.

Due to the cost of installing French-speaking drivers and managers and providing a full complement of translated company forms, advertising, policies and procedures, Greyhound restricted itself to the Ontario routes. In time-honoured fashion, Roger Pike and Voyageur executive Don Haire divided up the routes on the back of a place mat over dinner in a Mexican restaurant in Ottawa.

The Purchase

On February 8, 1994, Greyhound announced it had reached agreement with Voyageur Colonial Limited to:

acquire specific route authorities in Ontario for a purchase price of $10.0 million cash. The agreement is subject to the approval of the purchase by appropriate government agencies.

President Huisman commented, "The strategic value of the acquisition is to further strengthen our operations in Ontario, improving our ability to service our customers across the country."

"This recent acquisition, expected to close in the second quarter of 1994, has improved the Company's opportunities in the most densely populated region of Canada, Ontario, and in particular, southern Ontario. Greyhound is confident that these routes will contribute approximately $14 million in annual revenues . . .

With this acquisition, over 30% of Greyhound's scheduled passenger business was now being generated in Ontario. Bruce Elmore, senior vice-president, finance and chief financial officer commented, "They *(the Voyageur routes)* add immediate value to our shares and will increase our market presence in Ontario."

The Routes

Under the purchase agreement, Greyhound acquired the following routes from Voyageur Colonial Ltd.:

- Toronto-Ottawa Express
- Toronto-Ottawa Local
- Toronto-Peterborough
- Toronto-Belleville
- Toronto-Pembroke
- Ottawa-North Bay
- Ottawa-Pembroke

The highly lucrative Toronto-Ottawa express route was the jewel in the crown, and the main reason for the $10 million payment, which was essentially a goodwill premium for the route authorities. The purchase did not include any facilities or equipment but was strictly limited to route authorities and the operators to drive them. Greyhound had turned down the opportunity to acquire Voyageur's fleet in favour of reallocating coaches from its other operations. Because of the ongoing recession, the company elected to allocate 32 coaches across the system to serve the six new routes, positioning them where they could earn the highest return. According to Bruce Elmore:

> The deal solidifies our infrastructure in Ontario. If we didn't grow, the infrastructure would have become too expensive to support. With both Gray Coach and Voyageur we were able to expand our business base while minimizing costs. With Voyageur, we've only incurred direct operating costs such as drivers.

Operations Commence

Greyhound began operating the newly acquired Voyageur routes on June 28, 1994. The routes were dispatched out of Toronto under Al LaBarge, then general manager for London and Windsor. As part of the purchase, Greyhound received 100 Voyageur employees, including 84 experienced operators as well as non-union administrative staff. 46 of the 84 drivers were based out of Toronto, with the remaining 38 out of Ottawa.

According to Bill Noddle, former president, ATU, local 1415, "They were an excellent group of employees. They understood the business, were 'real' bus drivers, did good work and understood the contract".

A year after the purchase, the Canada Industrial Relations Board ordered that the two groups of drivers, formerly represented by the CAW union, be merged into the ATU agreement. In 1995, 12 of the operators were subsumed under the ATU, local 1374 collective agreement. The remaining 65 were brought into the ATU, local 1415 agreement. Of these 65, 40 were dovetailed into the seniority list effective June 12, 1995, and the balance were end-tailed effective June 28, 1994, the date of the acquisition.

Last Piece of the Puzzle

CSL continued to seek buyers for the remaining Voyageur lines, and in 1996 Ontario operator Trentway-Wagar, then owned by Al Bolton, Ron English and Jim Devlin, bought the Toronto-Montreal route from Voyageur. A number of Voyageur administrative staff moved with the purchase to Trentway, which was seeking to build its market share through this valuable route authority. However, the Ottawa-Montreal route was still on the market.

Following the Laidlaw acquisition in 1997 and subsequent capital infusions, Greyhound was bullish on acquisitions and began discussions with CSL on Voyageur's remaining route authorities and infrastructure.

On November 19, 1998, Greyhound signed an agreement to purchase the operating assets and assume certain liabilities of VCL from CSL Equity Investments Ltd for the purchase price of $15.6 million. The purchase was finalized in February 1999 and effectively made Voyageur a subsidiary of Greyhound under the name Voyageur Corp.

Ottawa Routes

Under the purchase Greyhound received Voyageur's operating licences for Ottawa-Montreal and Ottawa-Kingston, as well as a fleet of 37 vehicles (a mixture of 1990 and 1997 models) and 79 employees. At this time Voyageur was described as operating 3 million miles and serving over 600,000 passengers annually.

The Montreal-Ottawa route was a wonderful buy. In 1996 this route had been estimated as carrying almost half a million passengers a year, enjoying high load factors and utilization. It was considered the second largest route in Canada for passenger ridership, after Montréal-Québec City, and six times larger than Calgary-Edmonton.

Last Integration

The Voyageur drivers were represented by the CAW union, local 4573. As their collective agreement had expired on July 10, 1998, Greyhound began working with the union to schedule dates to resume negotiations but also began looking at moving towards integration. Eventually, the drivers were integrated from the CAW, local 4573 into the ATU, local 1415 union, following a decision from the Canada Industrial Relations Board in February 2000.

At the same time Greyhound had the task of converting more than forty Voyageur agencies to the Greyhound system, which required the translation of contracts, tariffs, policies and procedures and all other administrative materials into French. Many of the agencies had no insurance or signed contracts under the Voyageur organization, and in essence had not been managed or scrutinized under Voyageur as closely as they became under Greyhound.

BREWSTER SPIN-OFF

Brewster and Greyhound became enemies beginning in the late twenties when the company forfeited its Calgary-Edmonton route to Greyhound in 1929 as punishment for poor service. The feud between George Fay and Jim Brewster was life-long, and the companies continued to war until Greyhound purchased the company in 1965, following the death of Jim Brewster's successor, Lou Crosby.

Brewster preserved its identity following the Greyhound purchase. Its tourism activities were diverse: in 1976 Brewster Transport received eight of MCI's specially equipped "skyview" buses and took delivery of two new 41-passenger Snocruisers for its Columbia Icefield Tours. At this time the Japanese tourism market began to take off, and skiing grew in popularity, leading to more business in the "off season." The following year the company tried to extend its mountain tourism interests by acquiring the Jasper Sky Tram, but politics intervened and the federal government blocked the sale.

Brewster president Jack Hayes then personally acquired the Sky Tram. He then left the company and was replaced as general manager by David Morrison, who first began driving for the company as a student and later went on to become controller and vice president of administration. In February 1980 Morrison became president and chief executive officer of Brewster Transport, responsible for its varied fleet of sixty-two sightseeing buses, twenty-four snowmobiles and other pieces of equipment. David Morrison has enjoyed an exceptionally long tenure and is still president and chief executive officer.

Business continued to grow over the years and in 1993 Brewster recorded record earnings, with the Sno-Coach service to the Columbia Icefield and Athabasca Glacier attractions receiving high tourist volumes. Brewster was close to completing a new agreement with Parks Canada to develop new facilities in 1996. At that time Brewster was also responsible for operating Gray Line franchises in Banff, Calgary and Edmonton.

Unfortunately, the culture of competition between Greyhound and Brewster had not diminished since the purchase. Brewster was never integrated and continued to operate as a stand-alone from Greyhound's other operations. Inattention from the increasingly diversified and distracted Greyhound Corporation parent in the States meant Brewster management were not brought to meet margin expectations or enforce a non-compete environment, and the impact was diminishing the bottom line for both companies.

Banff Eviction

Matters came to a head in the early 1990s. Disputes over scheduling between the two subsidiaries led Brewster to evict Greyhound from their terminal in Banff, Alberta. With the support of Peter Armstrong, president of Rocky Mountaineer Railtours, Greyhound began negotiating with CP Rail to get access to their station in Banff and make it a multimodal facility. Brewster called on its deep community ties to try to keep Greyhound out of the town.

Greyhound had to work hard to convince the different levels of government of its case. To show it was committed to supporting tourism and economic growth, the company donated coaches to the College of the Rockies, a technical vocational school in Cranbrook with excellent tourism, heavy maintenance, and driver training programs. With Greyhound's support, the school's highly proficient in-house production company began work on a movie about the Rockies that Greyhound could show on its buses.

This and other endeavours helped turn the tide in Greyhound's favour. The company obtained a one-year non-renewable agreement to use the CP train station in Banff, managing to stretch it out a few more months when the term ran out. At the same time, Brewster was beginning to realize how much money it was losing without Greyhound as a tenant. Morrison finally allowed Greyhound to return to the Brewster depot.

Expensive and time-consuming as the dispute was, it opened the door for other opportunities. One good result was that Greyhound managers Lorne

Anthony and Lew Aldrich developed a relationship with Peter Armstrong that eventually led to Greyhound winning the Rocky Mountaineer contract, which it retains today. Greyhound's efforts reinforced that it was in the community to stay and be proactive. Finally, taking a major piece of work away from Brewster helped opened their eyes and improved relations for the time being.

The Spin-off

Brewster Transport was finally spun off from Greyhound in June 1996, in a move to satisfy the foreign ownership rules impeding Greyhound from launching the Greyhound Air initiative.

According to the terms of the May 31, 1996 separation agreement, the Brewster Transport Company Limited remained a subsidiary of Dial Corp. (originally named The Greyhound Corporation), leaving newly named Greyhound Canada Transportation Corp. to become a bus transportation and courier company with no single, major shareholder or significant U.S. ownership.

Brewster is still owned by the same parent, now called VIAD Corp., and continues to operate its large portfolio of sightseeing and tourism activities throughout the Rockies.

MAVERICK

Greyhound's eventual acquisition of the scheduled service operating authorities from Maverick Coach Lines of Vancouver in December 1998 first began to come together in the late 1970s, when Maverick obtained most of Pacific Coach Lines, a bus company with nine lives.

Pacific Stage Lines

Originally created in 1924 to consolidate B.C.'s intercity bus services, Pacific Stage Lines (PSL) was operated by BC Motor Transportation Corp., a division of BC Hydro and Power Authority, a Crown corporation of the government of B.C. This bus division originally included BC Rapid Transit Co., Pacific Stage Lines, Vancouver Transfer Co., Consolidated Truck Lines, Yellow Taxi, Gray Line, and Triangle Line.

Sometime in the late 1970s Pacific Stage Lines management made it clear that PSL intended to compete with the private sector beyond its mandate to provide public transit and freight services to Vancouver, Victoria, Vancouver Island and the Lower Fraser Valley. It began performing sightseeing and long-distance charter work, and built up its fleet through government grants.

According to a letter from Mr. Tom MacDonald of Trailways to Robert Bonner, chairman of B.C. Hydro, on January 4, 1978:

Pacific Stage Lines Limited, according to published financial reports, has a large deficit each year. This operating deficit is subsidized by the taxpayer. In addition over the past four years Pacific Stage Lines has received over $3 million in outright grants by way of gifted equipment.

Because PSL did not have to recover its costs, unlike private bus companies, which operate without subsidy, PSL used its position to deep discount its rates and undercut the competition.

This generated a hue and cry from the private intercity bus and industry and in March 1978 the Minister of Energy, Transport and Communications informed the Premier that B.C. Hydro had "decided to dispose of Pacific Stage Lines' sightseeing and charter operations by the year end."

However, the problem that remained was that all consumers of BC Hydro continued to bear the burden of subsidizing its large and diverse transportation division. The annual costs required to subsidize BC Motor Transportation Corp. had been hidden for several years in the hydro rates. According to a January 25, 1978 letter from the former Minister of Energy, Transport regarding the "future of government-owned inter-city bus companies",

Pacific Stage Lines Ltd., wholly owned by B.C. Hydro, and Vancouver Island Stage Lines, wholly owned by B.C. Hydro, reporting through the Minister of Municipal Affairs and Housing, together cost the B.C. taxpayer more than $10 million a year.

Following a May 1978 report by the federal government's Select Standing Committee on Crown Corporations in British Columbia, BC Hydro was entirely stripped of its bus transportation division. That July the government created a new Crown Corporation, Pacific Coach Lines Ltd. (PCL). PCL was responsible for interurban bus services in B.C., including Vancouver Island.

Pacific Coach Lines Ltd.

Unfortunately, this new entity soon ran into trouble. In 1983, it was predicted that the Vancouver Island bus line would lose $10 million for that year alone, criticism mounted and the Ministry began looking into privatizing PCL, as per the Honourable Brian Smith (Oak Bay-Gordon Head) in the August 24, 1983 Hansard:

I see no reason why the Pacific Coach Lines routes cannot be taken up by private carriers, very effectively. Greyhound and other private carriers can carry out the major routes of Pacific Coach Lines in a very effective way, just as they can with the service from downtown Victoria to downtown Vancouver.

MR. REID: And save $7 million.

PCL's services and infrastructure were sold off to several private companies effective April 1st, 1984, creating three new entities. As reported in the British Columbia Hansard for March 27, 1984, the recipients were:

• Pacific Coach Lines (1984) Ltd., based in Victoria, licensed to operate in Victoria and Vancouver, which received 33 coaches from PCL's fleet;

• Maverick Coach Lines, Vancouver, operating Vancouver-Nanaimo, Vancouver-Whistler, and Vancouver-Powell River, which received 14 coaches;

• Gray Line of Victoria Ltd. operating between Victoria and Port Hardy, as well as Nanaimo and Port Alberni, which received 26 coaches; and

• Cascade Charter Service Ltd., Chilliwack, operating between Vancouver and Harrison Hot Springs, which received 9 coaches.

Greyhound's involvement at this time was limited to assuming the head lease for the Vancouver bus terminal on Cambie Street at Larwell Park, providing service to the spun-off PCL entities, as well as sales and parcel express service.

The Sale

Fourteen years later, the opportunity arose to pick up the rights on Maverick's valuable Vancouver-Squamish-Whistler and Vancouver-Nanaimo routes from owner Bud Coles. Late in 1998, Greyhound announced it "continues to add to its Canadian operations in both the East and West. In December, Maverick Coach Lines Ltd. providing scheduled service between Vancouver and Whistler, and Vancouver and Nanaimo, British Columbia was acquired." The resolution for Greyhound to purchase the linehaul operations of Maverick Coach Lines Ltd. was signed November 30, 1998.

Dave Leach, general manager, B.C. region led the integration into Greyhound's B.C. network, achieving a very smooth transition. Maverick Coach Lines is still in operation as a charter and tour company. Maverick's other scheduled service routes, such as

Vancouver to Gibsons, Sechelt, Madeira Park and Powell River, are now served by local bus lines such as Malaspina Coach Lines. Greyhound operates an interline agreement with Pacific Coach Lines (1984) Ltd., who continues to operate the Vancouver-Victoria service.

GREY GOOSE BUS LINES

Grey Goose Bus Lines was originally started in Winnipeg in 1924 as a family enterprise by W.R. and Gary Lewis. The company soon acquired a local firm, Royal Transportation created by Allan Ramsay. In 1961, A.J. Thiessen, owner of Thiessen Bus Lines established 1946, acquired the company along with several others during a long period of expansion beginning in 1951, and renamed the combined entities Grey Goose Bus Lines.

Grey Goose Bus Lines (Alberta) Ltd. Luxury Coach Service.

Artist's rendition of one of three MC-9s used by Grey Goose in charter service, ca. 1981. These "Silverliner" coaches held up to 30 passengers in 2+1 seating

Under Thiessen's leadership, Grey Goose went on to acquire several other companies, such as International Transportation Ltd. of Port Arthur, Ontario. Most particularly, in 1969, Grey Goose acquired Manitoba Motor Transit Ltd., based out of Brandon, which pioneered bus routes to Flin Flon and Thompson prior to the purchase. A few years later, in 1974 Laidlaw acquired Grey Goose Bus Lines but left the operations under the control of the Thiessen family.

Rugged Routes

Over the years Grey Goose became the largest provider of scheduled services in Manitoba and Northwest Ontario, linking over 150 communities in Manitoba alone.

Grey Goose routes have included some of the

most isolated, rough driving in the country. The historic Lynn Lake, Gillam and Sundance routes were 657 and 642 miles away from Winnipeg respectively, with much of the road running over bog land heavily silted with limestone dust.

As well, Grey Goose offered service over the highway between Lake Winnipeg and Lake Manitoba, sections of which run for more than 100 miles without a single community. When the highway opened in 1971, Manitoba required Grey Goose to equip its coaches with emergency equipment and radio-phones in the event of a breakdown or other emergency. Cellular phone service is still uncertain in some less-densely populated areas of Manitoba.

Over the years, Grey Goose built a proud tradition of excellent service in demanding weather and road conditions. During severe forest fires in 1989, Grey Goose stepped in to help evacuate entire communities threatened by the fires.

Preferred Charter Carrier

Grey Goose was, and still is, the largest charter operator in Manitoba, offering the latest luxury motorcoaches.

Grey Goose's excellent reputation for charter service was built upon its top-notch fleet of Prevost and MCI coaches, and attention to customer service. In 1989 the company began showing first-run movies on charter runs, and expanded the service to scheduled travel in March 1993.

Package Express

In 1989, Grey Goose bought four specially built MCI 102A3 coaches to support the great demand for package express service in the comparatively isolated north.

In 1993, its 70th anniversary year, Grey Goose took an innovative fleet approach by buying six Ford E350 extended vans with trailers custom-made by Glendale Industries Ltd. of Brandon to serve areas where passenger and courier volumes were declining. The vans were warmly received by the passengers and helped to maintain cost-effective service in less densely populated areas.

Strategic Partnership with Greyhound

Greyhound and Grey Goose began cooperating as strategic partners several years before Laidlaw purchased Greyhound. Starting in the early 1990s, Greyhound and Grey Goose began to streamline their courier express service and improve service levels at shared facilities. Mike Cafferky, then Grey Goose's district director of operations, commented that since implementing expanded pick-up and delivery services in 1991, Grey Goose had seen 43% growth in that area.

Another important step was ensuring compatibility of ticket issuing systems, and Grey Goose soon implemented the pioneer Gateway system developed for Greyhound, introducing computerized ticketing at Thompson, Manitoba in 1994.

Grey Goose coach and driver, late eighties

Integration

Laidlaw made it clear when it purchased Greyhound Canada that it would integrate Grey Goose into the Greyhound operations. At the time of the integration, Grey Goose owned three company terminals located in Thompson, Flin Flon and The Pas, shared four terminals with Greyhound in Winnipeg, Brandon, Dauphin and Thunder Bay, and employed eighty drivers, forty-five of which had over one million miles of accident-free driving.

The integration process took some time to take shape, but thanks to the efforts of Dave Leach, vice president, passenger services, Brent Gibney, general manager, Manitoba, and Miriam Van Essen, director, labour relations, in February 2002 Greyhound signed an agreement with CAW, local 4209 and the ATU. On April 21, 2002, 139 unionized employees were integrated into the Amalgamated Transit Union.

PENETANG-MIDLAND COACH LINES

Penetang-Midland Coach Lines Limited (PMCL) began in 1867 when Joseph Dubeau opened a livery stable in Penetanguishene at 15 Robert Street. Here, "livery, first class, single or doubled rigs were always ready for long or short drives." Joseph was always ready to harness his horses to a carriage and drive the daily stage eight-mile return between Penetang and Midland. The Barrie stage coach took a full day with a change of horses at Hillsdale.

By 1892, responding to high demand, Joseph began operating a stage coach between Penetang and Midland. Harsh winter conditions were challenging, as Joseph's son Arthur, describes:

> Some of the sleighs seated twenty, and many a night would carry a load of passengers, snugly wrapped in buffalo robes, to parties and festivities. Winters were long and hard and often drivers could not tell where the road lay because they were riding on top of twenty-foot snow-drifts. To keep the coaches from going off course, pieces of fence rail were used as markers and it was not unusual to drive by a house and look into the upstairs windows.

One night in March, during the Flu Epidemic of 1918, Arthur had to make an emergency trip in bad weather to Christian Island (an Indian Reserve on Georgian Bay) to bring two nurses to the Chief's House. Many of the Indians were critically ill and dying and medical help was desperately needed. When the sleigh reached the middle of the bay, it ran into a sheet of water so deep that Arthur and the two nurses had to stand on the seat while the water rose up over the floor of the coach.

Following Joseph's death in 1917, his son Albert, 21, took over the business and started a summer jitney service along the Penetang-Midland route using a Model T Ford open touring car. Later Albert became a driver for the late John Roach (former NHL goal tender) who had his own local bus service. The operation was in trouble and Albert soon bought Roach's bus for $1,800. In 1925 he bought a second 15-seater coach and Penetang-Midland Coach Lines Limited was on its way.

In the late twenties, the Department of Highways was not responsible for snow removal, and like Greyhound did in Alberta, Albert often had to plough his own roads to make the scheduled runs between Penetang and Midland. Albert also had to be chief driver, head mechanic, bookkeeper and president of the company. His versatility and commitment paid off and his business remained a success.

Ontario Public Vehicles Act

In 1929 the Ontario government proclaimed the Public Vehicles Act and PMCL received one of the first public vehicle operating licences, No. 42, allowing them to run between Penetang and Midland.

The provisions of the Act required that each vehicle had to be equipped with interior lights if it had a covered top, a working speedometer, a spare tire, skid chains and brakes which could lock the wheels at a speed of 10 mph. Also, drivers had to be of "good moral character," could not smoke or drink while working, were limited to working 10 hours on a shift and could not allow passengers to ride the running board.

Irene Takes Over

Albert Dubeau died in 1938, aged 42, leaving his wife Irene and nine children ranging from 2 to 19 years of age. Although PMCL's fleet only consisted of two coaches worth less than $500.00 apiece, Irene made the decision to continue running the company. Together with her four sons, Laval, Bernard, Lomar, and Murray, Irene managed to keep PMCL afloat during World War II. At the time Irene Dubeau was reputedly the only woman in Canada operating a licensed bus line.

PENETANG-MIDLAND COACH LINES

PMCL's service network and fleet continued to grow and in 1947 the company obtained the municipal transit contract from Midland. PMCL was formally incorporated in 1953. In 1964, Irene Dubeau suddenly died, leaving her three sons, Laval, Bernard and Murray, to run the business. Laval became president with Bernard filling the post of senior vice president. In 1967, with a fleet of 16 buses, Laval Dubeau began employing the fourth Dubeau generation, hiring sons Brian, Michael, James and Terry.

Expansion

Beginning in the late sixties PMCL's network expanded rapidly. In 1968 PMCL extended its service from Midland to Perkinsfield, Elmvale, Wasaga Beach and Collingwood. Their next license in 1969 allowed them to extend service from Midland, Collingwood, Barrie and Wasaga Beach to and from Pearson International Airport.

In 1973, PMCL received authority to operate charter buses from Barrie and to operate routes for and on behalf of Gray Coach and Voyageur Colonial Ltd. The following year the company's passenger and freight services extended to include all of Simcoe County to and from the Pearson International Airport. As well, PMCL received authority to operate charters extra-provincially to other Canadian Provinces, and in 1976 the company won a contract to operate the city of Orillia's transit system.

In 1978 PMCL extended its Barrie service to Hillsdale, cracking the Toronto market in 1979, when it was granted operating authority between Collingwood, Alliston and Metropolitan Toronto. In 1980 the company won the City of Barrie transit contract, constructing a new terminal costing over a million dollars. PMCL has held the Barrie contract for over twenty years.

Charter and Tour Services

At the same time, PMCL branched out in the tourism market, offering motor coach tours across North America. The company also launched very successful bus-and-boat cruises, initially with the ship Miss Midland running a two-and-a-half hour boat cruise among the 30,000 Islands of Georgian Bay. The company also took on school bus contracts through Ontario.

Last expansions

In 1988 and 1989 PMCL essentially completed the expansion of its scheduled services outside its home base of Midland-Barrie-Orillia-Collingwood. In February 1989 it won the right to run over the Barrie-

Owen Sound route alongside Gray Coach. Under the subsequent re-codifying of its licences with the Ontario Highway Transport Board, the company's route structure now consisted of:

- Toronto-Barrie-Orillia
- Toronto-Barrie-Midland-Penetang
- Toronto-Barrie-Collingwood
- Toronto-Barrie-Owen Sound
- Toronto-Bolton-Alliston-CFB Borden-Collingwood
- Barrie-Orillia-Gravenhurst-Bracebridge-Port Carling-Bala
- Toronto-Barrie-Collingwood-Owen Sound-Southampton-Port Elgin-Kincardine-Hanover-Walkerton-Durham

Over the next few years PMCL continued to build its charter and tourism business, upgrading its cruise ships. PMCL was non-unionized with a lower labour cost structure, which allowed it to offer extremely competitive charter rates to its clients.

In 1998, a year after the sale of Greyhound Canada, Laidlaw acquired a 49% stake in the PMCL from the Dubeau family. Two years later Laidlaw acquired the remaining 51% of PMCL. The company was transferred to Greyhound on February 28, 2003, and in May 2004 their operations were integrated.

CHATHAM COACH

Chatham Coach Lines ("Cha-Co") was founded by a Mr. Ivan DeNure on July 15, 1948 in Chatham, Ontario when his transit proposal to City Council was approved and awarded a ten year franchise. The new transit system was served by 6 new Fitzjohn City Liners and three used Twin Coaches DeNure had purchased from Toronto Transit, maintained in a

Ivan DeNure, July 1948

modern Quonset style garage on King Street East in Chatham. The routing he devised was excellent and the service quickly became successful.

In Spring 1949 DeNure expanded the operation and purchased a new 1949 28-passenger Fitzjohn Duraliner Highway Coach as well as a new Fitzjohn City Liner for the local transit. That summer, he expanded again, acquiring the Thames View Bus Lines operation from Raymond Cadotte, adding school buses to the Chatham Coach Lines fleet.

Around the same time, DeNure established a timetable for a Chatham-Merlin line run, which allowed him to run charters, thanks to the operating authority granted by the Ontario Municipal Board (now the Ontario Highway Transport Board). By the end of 1949 Chatham Coach Lines boasted a fleet of 3 highway cruisers, 5 school buses and 10 city buses.

In Spring 1950, Ivan DeNure successfully applied to the U.S. Interstate Commerce commission for charter operating rights in the United States. Located so close to the border, the company's charter business quickly grew. By 1956 Chatham Coach was chartering extended trips, made over 70 school runs and continued its transit operations.

Starting around 1962, Ivan's two sons became involved in the family business by working in the washrack, assisting the mechanics and helping out in the office. By 1966, Ivan's son Reg DeNure was very active in the company. Business was expanding, and Ivan and Reg decided to acquire the property across the street from the existing bus barns to accommodate their fleet. A few years later, in 1969, Chatham Coach Lines developed a tourism wing, "Carefree Tours" to address the long-haul tourism demand from area residents.

In 1989, Gray Coach abandoned its London-Kitchener and Owen Sound–Barrie/Collingwood routes. By agreement Penetang-Midland Coach Lines picked up the latter, while Chatham Coach obtained the London-Kitchener authority. The scheduled service included stops in Elginfield, St. Mary's, Stratford, Shakespeare, New Hamburg, Baden and the University of Waterloo.

To keep up with the expectations from its charter clients, the company was careful to maintain its inter-city fleet and was quick to begin showing onboard movies to its passengers. DeNure's other interests were also doing well. By 1998 Chatham Coach, marketed as "Cha-Co Trails – The Best All-Ways", had a fleet of over 200 school buses, and was providing intercity transit, airport service and day care runs.

That year, a year after the sale of Greyhound Canada, Laidlaw acquired a 49% stake in PMCL from the Dubeau family. In August 2000, Laidlaw Transit Inc. acquired J. I. DeNure (Chatham) Inc. from the DeNure family at the same time as the remaining 51% of PMCL. These two companies were transferred to Greyhound Canada on February 28, 2003, and in May 2004 their operations were integrated.

GRAY LINE ACQUISITIONS AND TRANSFERS

In August 2002, as part of the ongoing Laidlaw Inc. restructuring, Laidlaw Transit transferred to Greyhound Canada the ownership of The Gray Line of Victoria Ltd., Gray Line of Vancouver and Marguerite Tours. This increased Greyhound's franchise holdings in the Gray Line worldwide network, in addition to the existing Gray Line Toronto and Gray Line Ottawa operations.

SOUTHERN ONTARIO COMMUTER SERVICE

Greyhound Canada's interest in the Southern Ontario inter-city and commuter markets originally began in the late seventies when it won the right to operate Sudbury-Toronto and Buffalo-Toronto alongside Gray Coach. This opened the door for the future Gray Coach and Voyageur purchases which made up the backbone of the commuter service.

However, Greyhound began to seriously market to commuters on April 24, 1995 when the company introduced a special one-week commuter pass for Guelph-Toronto commuters. Offered in addition to the monthly pass, this fare product was sold for 8 weeks as a test market, and following its success was established permanently in Kitchener, Cambridge, Guelph and Peterborough.

As these Golden Horseshoe communities grew,

Greyhound expanded its commuter runs, eventually numbering over 120 a day. When local operator Sharp Bus Lines abandoned a short route between Hamilton and Brantford, Greyhound rescued it on March 11, 2002, recognizing its value to the network as a whole.

Improvements in 2002

2002 was a significant year for Greyhound's commuters. On January 3, following extensive customer surveys the previous September, Greyhound Canada announced "substantial improvements to commuter service in Southern Ontario". The improvements included implementing a dedicated commuter fleet of new-model buses, more commuter fare products, and overhauled schedules with better connections and higher frequency.

Greyhound's flexible pass products now included same day return discounts, weekly passes, 20 ride flex passes and monthly passes at up to 50 percent off walk-up fares, to capture occasional commuters. The Flex Pass, consisting of 20 one-way or 10 same-day return tickets, was developed in response to strong customer demand and is perfect for commuters who only work in Toronto 2 to 3 days a week.

Other changes included improved interior maintenance schedules, regular customer surveys, and the introduction of Greyhound's commuter watchdog program, a Commuter of the Month draw, and a special email contact, **commuter@greyhound.ca.**

The commuter watchdog program has been especially well received, as it allows commuters to easily report and follow up on concerns. Volumes have significantly increased in the Guelph, Kitchener and Cambridge markets and customer satisfaction is much higher. Greyhound regularly hosts commuter meetings with senior management, where the responses confirm strong, sustained improvements in service.

Currently, Greyhound is working on a number of initiatives to expand its infrastructure and commuter services in the Golden Horseshoe. Greyhound is committed to developing seamless intermodal travel with all stakeholders and levels of government; through interline partners and intermodal facilities that link bus, rail, air and municipal transit.

CHAPTER FOUR

OUR DRIVERS

Greyhound drivers, or "Greyhounders" are the first link between the public and the company. For the past seventy-five years our drivers have been responsible for creating and upholding Greyhound's reputation for safe, courteous and reliable transportation. From the onset Greyhound drivers have been famous for their friendliness and helpfulness to passengers.

In many cases the Greyhound driver is the only physical link between rural Canada and the rest of the world. Operating in isolation, Greyhound drivers shoulder unique responsibilities and persevere in unusual and demanding circumstances. They are proud to represent the company and provide an essential service to the public.

In the early days, Greyhound drivers not only required excellent driving skills, they had to be their own mechanics in case of a breakdown. Each bus carried tools for emergency repairs. Drivers also changed their own tires in the garage, greased their own buses and cleaned them prior to their run.

The Uniform

Greyhound drivers have always been well known for their distinctive blue-grey uniform. The company has collaborated with LaFleche Bros. of Calgary since the thirties, modifying and adding to the uniform over the years. The first Greyhound uniforms had a decidedly military appearance, consisting of a jacket, breeches, boots, Sam Browne belt and cap.

The Greyhound jacket was quite long and included large flap pockets for carrying tickets, punches, etc. The breeches tapered into leggings coming down over the calf, and were worn with very high boots, called "Daks," which came up over the legging.

YOUR HOST

At the end of a Greyhound trip passengers often pause to express their appreciation for the thoughtful courtesy of their host. His matchless skill is revealed by National Safety Council figures that show Greyhound buses to be seven times as safe as the average motor car.

Greyhound uniform, mid-1930s

Although they were quite warm in the summer, Daks were ideal for deep prairie snow. The uniform was finished off with a standard driver's cap, pinned to which was each man's numbered badge.

Although today our drivers receive a biannual clothing allowance, in the thirties they were responsible for purchasing their own uniforms and boots. Those cost between $15 and $20 – a significant sum in the Depression – and the drivers took very good care of them. This was not easy on the dusty, dirty and gravel roads. Before separate baggage compartments were developed, all large baggage was carried on top of the coach, covered with a tarp. Drivers could quickly become covered with dust as they climbed up to stow or take down luggage from the roof of the bus. Despite the environment, Greyhound drivers were famous for looking as if they had just stepped out of a box.

In 2004 Calgary operator Chris Michiels commissioned LaFleche to recreate the iconic driver's uniform from the thirties, searching out vintage buttons and badges and having replica boots custom-made. LaFleche still had one of the original driver's hats in storage, and from May to October Michiels wore the uniform on his Calgary-Edmonton route.

"In the old days, Greyhound motorcoach operators were respected and identified with bravery and romance," says Sandy Russell, Calgary operations manager. "Many people loved the image so much that they left their farms to become a Greyhound motorcoach operator. The reception that Chris has received on his uniform reflects that this enthusiasm still exists."

Passengers, retired drivers, tourists and even the RCMP have stopped Michiels to admire and ask questions about the attractive uniform. Michiels has put together a fascinating collection of antique badges, shoulder flashes and other memorabilia from busophiles happy to see the emblems of early Greyhound, Sunburst, Canadian Coachways and others on the road again. Perhaps the most touching aspect is the heartfelt response from relatives of Greyhound drivers who have passed away. Michiels is a walking memorial to their service.

FIRST GREYHOUND DRIVERS
Layton Miles

Greyhound's first driver on record is Layton Miles. Born in 1908 at Kamsack, Saskatchewan, Miles spent most of his childhood in Victoria and grew up with the Olson brothers. He signed on to Speed Olson's Kootenay Valley Transportation in June 13, 1929, becoming a Greyhound driver as a result of the Fay acquisition and subsequent November 30, 1929 incorporation.

At the end of his first summer, Miles returned to Victoria, but Olson wrote to him in the fall and asked him to return. Olson's letter, the oldest existing piece of Greyhound documentation, gives a picture of what the conditions were for a driver in the Kootenays at the time:

> Now in regards to a job here, they have done a lot of work on the New Denver rd. then have blown all the sharp rocks sticking out of the road between the new road and Slocan City and have put a grader over it making it considerably wider and have 7 trucks hauling gravel from a conveyor and hopper on the highway gravelling it, they are working from Slocan City to where the new road cuts off. A real job of road work and they will have the new road open on

Operator Chris Michiels wearing the vintage uniform reproduced with company uniform supplier LaFleche Bros.

Nov 1st, Archie and I were up it about half ways it sure is a fine wide road.

Motherwell says it will cut at least a half hour off each way cutting it down to 7 hrs driving time.

Now if this run will interest you at $5.50 a day you can come at once. You can get your board and room for $45 per month or 2 meals and room for $37.50.

Now this road will be open all winter and I have got a dandy heater in the little Reo, it runs real good now.

Now if you will consider taking this for the winter why in the spring you can probably get something better.

Miles did come back to take the job. He remained on Greyhound's active driver list for more than forty years, compiling an enviable record of safety while driving several million route miles.

Some of the other original drivers included Grant Smith, Bud White, R.F. "Blondy" Jacques, Bill Clark, Del Draper, Pat Cleary, and Bud Olson.

Grant Smith

Grant Smith was a native of Moose Jaw who moved with his mother at a young age to Victoria. They lived on Beechwood Avenue close to Barney Olson's home on Hollywood Crescent and Olson often picked the lad up on his way downtown.

Barney Olson was fascinated with travel, and as young Grant was in the merchant marine, Olson was always interested in hearing about the seaman's latest voyage. He frequently promised to teach Smith how to drive a bus someday and when the Circle Tours started he made good on the promise. Grant forsook the sea for the daily drive to Butchart Gardens, becoming one of the company's most reliable drivers.

In 1929 Olson again approached him. Telling him of the plan to start a new bus company, he asked if he would be willing to work in Alberta. Grant expressed some hesitation about driving in snow and ice, but Olson promised that he could come back to Victoria if he didn't like it.

Fortunately, the company start-up in July gave Smith and the other drivers a chance to learn their routes and machines before the onset of the treacherous Alberta winter. However, driving in the spring and summer on the clay and gravel roads in inclement weather was no picnic either.

Smith recalled an early trip to Edmonton where he had to fight his way through a torrential, blinding rainstorm on slick, muddy roads. Reaching a railway crossing, he opened the door and the window of his Y coach checking if he could see or hear anything coming. Unsure, he asked his nine passengers if they could see anything and they all agreed that nothing was coming.

Smith put the bus in gear and crept over the crossing. As the back wheels cleared the rails, a flash went by that just missed the bus – a C. & E. train. It was flying through the rain and darkness without any running lights.

The close call so unnerved Smith that, when he got into Lacombe and made his stop, he was shaking so badly he couldn't pick up a cup of coffee.

Walter Hyssop

Walter Hyssop was from a pioneer ranching family north of Lethbridge. When Greyhound began serving Lethbridge, Hyssop got to know Bud White. One of Greyhound's original drivers, White sometimes took Hyssop along on trips, teaching him how to drive.

In February 1931 Hyssop borrowed $20 to go to Calgary for an interview with Speed Olson, a recommendation from the mayor of Lethbridge tucked in his pocket. He arrived at a perfect time, as Olson had a charter booked to go out the next day but no driver on hand. After giving him a perfunctory driver's test, Olson told Hyssop to be at the garage at 8 a.m. to take the charter, a load of Boy Scouts, to Lethbridge.

It was a memorable first assignment. Travelling to Lethbridge by way of Vulcan, a recently acquired secondary route, Hyssop ran into a severe blizzard. What was supposed to be a straightforward few hours' drive turned into a two day epic as the group holed up to ride out the storm.

Bill Brown

Bill Brown, who would earn a reputation as one of Greyhound's finest drivers, had grown up on a farm west of Didsbury, Alberta. The son of a teamster, Bill didn't like horses and in 1923 he decided to take his motorcycle and go to California. He got as far as Banff where the motorcycle broke down and he ended up driving a truck for the parks department. After this he took a job driving the tramway to the Chateau Lake Louise, which was being reconstructed following a fire in 1924. Brown began his career with Greyhound on January 31, 1931.

Being low in seniority, initially Brown worked out of Fort Macleod driving the run to Cardston, but was soon transferred to Lethbridge and put on the infamous Lethbridge–Cardston mail run, which

Del Draper (left) and Bill Brown (right), at Waterton Lakes, 1934

Greyhound had taken in 1930. The mail contract made very little profit and gave Greyhound more headaches than any other part of its operations, but George Fay believed it gave Greyhound a good public image and he continued to bid on it.

Brown held this run for four years, delivering passengers and mail to Raymond, Magrath, Spring Coulee, and Cardston in winter and continuing to Waterton Lakes in the summer, driving in the first day and back the next.

To honour the mail contract, the service was supposed to run no matter what the weather, which made for some terrible drives. As well, wrestling with the mail sacks was tremendously hard work. In normal circumstances Brown carried passengers as well as mail, but when the mail was especially heavy, as at Christmas, he drove an overload that carried nothing but mail. Early Greyhound employees can remember feeling sorry for Bill, seeing him at the Lethbridge depot with mailbags stacked up twice the height of his bus.

As well, Bill was responsible for making liquor deliveries, in some people's minds an even greater public service than the mail delivery. There were no government liquor outlets in the heavily Mormon-populated district between Lethbridge and Cardston, which left the city as the sole source of supply. Under its freight service Greyhound had an agreement with the government liquor board, which allowed customers to have Brown deliver their liquor permits and

payment to the Lethbridge liquor store.

Brown would pick up the orders before loading the mail and the passengers at the depot. The liquor was usually carried on the wide back seats of the bus and the first-class mail sacks were stacked on top, preventing thirsty passengers from getting at it while the driver was distracted. At each stop Brown had to manhandle the mail sacks to reach the order of the impatiently waiting purchaser. But his customers were grateful for the service and he didn't lack for friends along the route.

Once, when running an overload, Bill drew No. 23, a cantankerous Yellow Y coach. He was coming out of Magrath, watching out for a turkey farm whose 100 turkeys were usually out at that time of day. Coming over a hill, he saw the birds crossing at the bottom and applied the air brakes hard, but to no avail. Picking up speed as he descended the slope, he shot right through the flock before coming to a halt by running the right wheel over the edge of a bank.

Hurrying back to the flock, he picked up two injured birds, but as he was already running behind schedule he had no choice but to slit their throats and hang them on the bus door. At the next town, he wrapped the birds in newspaper and asked the agent to tell the farmer he would pay for the turkeys on his next trip.

The following day the agent told him that the farmer had said the birds would not cost him anything. Furthermore, he appreciated Bill Brown's honesty so much that he was invited to stop for a big turkey dinner whenever he could. Brown's experience was one familiar to every early Greyhound driver, with livestock constantly moving on the roads and highways.

Later in his career, Brown was about to take an afternoon run from Calgary east to Oyen. That morning an elderly couple had come into Calgary from Hanna to do some shopping. At departure time the husband was waiting but the wife was nowhere to be seen.

In such situations the drivers had to use their judgement. Bill realized it was the last bus of the day and knew it would be a hardship for the couple to have to stay over in Calgary. He decided to wait but gently ribbed the man about having to get himself a new wife. Twenty minutes later the lady came puffing up and the bus pulled out, quickly making up the lost time.

During the dinner stop the man thanked Brown for his understanding, predicting "I'm sure you won't have any problem in the hereafter" for his kindness. Incidents like these made Brown one of Greyhound's most popular drivers.

Greyhound drivers have always had a reputation for not only looking after their own passengers but for coming to the aid of other travellers in need. Once, Bill Brown was driving during a severe blizzard near High River. Crawling along in low gear, trying to see through the blowing snow, he spotted a light out of the corner of his eye for a brief instant.

Brown stopped the bus, got out and walked back down the road, intently scanning the ditch. He could just make out the back of a car sticking out of a snowbank. Digging the snow away from the window, he found an unconscious driver at the wheel.

Brown and his passengers dug out the door, got the man out, hauled him into the bus and laid him out on the back seat. A few miles down the road the man regained consciousness. After finding out what had happened he tried to pay Bill $5 for saving his life.

Jack Rajala

A native of Thunder Bay, Ontario who moved to Fort Steele, B.C. in 1925, Rajala worked for various lumber companies in the Kootenays before becoming a driver for Fred's Stages. From 1927 to 1930 he made three trips a day from Kimberley to Cranbrook in a 7-passenger car, before going back to hauling ties and lumber for better money. However, when he saw Greyhound buses running between Nelson and

Jack Rajala with a Kenworth bus at Nelson, B.C., 1936

Fernie, Rajala decided he wanted to become a Greyhound driver.

Fortunately, Rajala knew F.L. MacPherson of Cranbrook, highway traffic and utilities engineer with the B.C. Department of Public Works. MacPherson was personally acquainted with Fay and the Olsons, often meeting with them to discuss the company's licences, and he agreed to write a letter of recommendation for Rajala to Speed Olson.

Early in July 1935 Olson phoned Rajala to come to Calgary for a drivers' test. As it was Stampede time and the company was very busy, he was hired on the spot after proving his skills.

Jack Rajala, September 2, 1988.
Jack began driving for Greyhound in 1935

Pat Williams

H.K. "Pat" Williams was born in 1908 in Edmonton. He studied engineering for a term in the winter of 1926-27, but didn't enjoy university and instead took a job surveying for the Edmonton, Dunvegan and B.C. Railway. In 1928 he served as resident engineer for the line on the Hythe to Dawson Creek section and then went on to work for the CPR, surveying bridge alignments at Lethbridge and Cranbrook.

During the early thirties he replaced timber trestles on the Coquihalla Subdivision of the famous Kettle Valley Railway near Hope and in 1932 spent a season prospecting for gold in the Cariboo. His wife contracted T.B. in the spring of 1934 and was confined to the Sanatorium in Calgary. Back working on the E.D. & B.C., he received a leave-of-absence to go to Calgary to look for a job. In Calgary he got in touch with Jerry Brown, who had worked with him on the survey from 1928 to 1929. Brown was now working in Calgary as a Greyhound ticket agent and agreed to keep his eye open for a job for Williams.

The opportunity soon appeared. Speed Olson was famous for his bad temper and when riled would fire a driver without hesitation. On this occasion he fired a driver on the street in front of the depot, then turned to Brown and barked, "Where is that driver you've been talking about?" Brown asked him to wait a few minutes, then took a taxi to the Sanatorium to get Williams.

Racing back to the garage on 11th Avenue, Brown talked garage manager Jack Deagon into lending him a bus to take Williams on a student drive. Pat had only seen a bus once before and had no idea how to drive one. Brown quickly pointed out the rudiments, taking him up and down the 11th Street hill, demonstrating the double shifting necessary to keep the Y running smoothly on the grade.

Back at the garage, Olson soon appeared and took a nervous Williams out for a test drive on the same route. Suitably impressed with the way he handled the hill, Olson informed him that he was hired. He pointed to a loaded bus that had been waiting for an hour and a half since he had fired the previous driver. "Take 'er to Lethbridge!" he commanded, as he turned on his heel and left.

Dumbfounded, Williams had an immediate dilemma. Not only did he have no idea where Lethbridge was, he didn't know how to get out of the city onto the highway. Sliding into the driver's seat,

Pat Williams' retirement, 1973

he turned around and asked a friendly looking fellow sitting behind him if he could help out.

Fortunately, the man travelled the route often and proved to be a lifesaver. He not only gave him directions over the cemetery hill out onto the gravel road to Lethbridge, but pointed out all the regular stops along the way and instructed Williams how to collect the tickets. He never found out the man's name, but Williams was extremely grateful. Without him his career with Greyhound may have been very short-lived. After three months of driving Williams would use his engineering skills to help design Greyhound's first steel bus, soon moving into a management role. He retired in 1973 in the role of assistant to the president.

Ed Dunn

Ed Dunn was born and raised in Medicine Hat in 1911. In the early thirties he worked at the local Redhead bulk service station and regularly serviced R.J. Duncan's Calgary and Eastern Bus Lines vehicles. After Greyhound bought out Duncan's operation, Redhead began serving Greyhound, and he became very friendly with the regular drivers on the route, Layton Miles and Walter Ritson.

By the spring of 1935, Dunn wanted very much to become a Greyhound driver too, and his friends put in a good word for him with Speed Olson. Olson visited the station and Dunn convinced him to take him on. He was sent to Calgary for training, which consisted mainly of accompanying Miles and Ritson on their run to see how things were done. While Layton Miles took the straight approach, Walter Ritson was more humorously inclined. Ritson told Dunn, "I'll

Ed Dunn (left) with partner Red Townsend on the Alsask-Saskatoon run, 1935

teach you everything you shouldn't do and Miles will teach you everything you should do. Now about smoking cigars. Never let any of your passengers smoke a cigar – unless they give you one first."

By May 15th Dunn had mastered all the finer points of driving from Miles and passenger etiquette from Ritson, and took his first run between Medicine Hat and Swift Current. Over the next couple of years he worked a variety of Saskatchewan routes, including Saskatoon-Alsask, which he remembered as one continuous cloud of dust, and Swift Current-Saskatoon.

On the Swift Current-Saskatoon run, south of Kyle at the South Saskatchewan River, passengers were ferried across the river to a bus waiting on the far shore. When the river was completely frozen the bus simply drove across it (although some passengers preferred to walk), but when it was not completely frozen the passengers were loaded eight at a time into a large basket on a cable and hauled across by a horse on a winch.

In 1937 Ed Dunn graduated onto the "main line" on the Fort Macleod-Swift Current run, and was proud to be asked to drive when Greyhound put its first night bus on the route. His troubles began when he hit the cow near Maple Creek, Saskatchewan. The impact damaged only the bus lights, leaving him with just a spotlight to guide him safely to Medicine Hat.

Unbeknownst to him, some of the contents of the bursting cow sprayed through his half-open driver's window and splashed some of the passengers behind him. When Dunn arrived in Medicine Hat, the girl

who had been sitting directly behind him asked where she could change her clothing. Thinking she was asking about the bus connections, he responded, "No, no, Miss, you don't change here, you're going on."

Upon arrival, Dunn had intended to send the bus through to Calgary for repairs, but to his horror discovered that Walter Ritson, now the depot manager, needed the bus for an overload to Lethbridge. As if

Greyhound passengers in basket ferry over the South Saskatchewan River

this weren't enough, Speed Olson had arrived on one of his periodic visits. He heard Speed Olson exclaim when he saw the damage, "My God, I thought I'd hired a driver."

Certain he was about to be fired, Dunn asked Ritson for his advice. Ritson told him the only thing to do was to jump in the bus with the few overload passengers and take off before Speed got really worked up. Dunn pulled out immediately. As Olson watched the bus depart he said to Ritson, "What's that guy going to do for lights?" Ritson responded, "The same damn thing as he did getting here, run with his spotlight."

Dunn was certain he would be called on the carpet for the incident, but he never heard another thing from Olson. Ritson was not quite so forgetful and began circulating this version amongst the other drivers: "Dunn was driving near Maple Creek and he hit this cow. The cowshit came through the window and when it hit the girl behind him she woke up and screamed, 'My God, the driver's been killed'." Ed Dunn's encounter with a cow thus became a part of Greyhound lore.

WEATHERING THE ELEMENTS

Although spring and summer weather posed their own problems, winter on the prairies was much more treacherous. Equipment was hard to start and often froze up completely. Sometimes drivers had to light fires under the engines to thaw them.

One early driver remembered a late September storm that forced him to hole up with his passengers in the only hotel of the southern Alberta town of Cayley. Draining the radiator so it wouldn't freeze, he watched for two days as the storm piled a gigantic seven-foot drift around the bus.

After the storm broke, Speed Olson arrived to help dig a path for the vehicle. Carrying hot water in pots and pans from the hotel, they filled up the radiator, cranked up the engine and soon were on their way.

The road from Lethbridge through the Crowsnest Pass was particularly bad between Cowley and Lundbreck because of the heavy drifting. Jack Rajala recalled an occasion when he was stranded at the hotel in Cowley and could walk out of the second storey onto a huge hard-packed drift.

During the winter each bus carried two shovels. Company policy allowed drivers to hire a passenger to help with the shovelling. Sometimes passengers helped in return for free passage.

Between drifts, the road was frequently covered by wind-packed snow, forcing the driver to inch along with one wheel in the ditch and one on the road. Sometimes it was easier to abandon the road altogether and take to adjacent fields blown bare of snow.

In the early years, when the conditions forced drivers to put up at a hotel for the night, they were

A "Y" coach at High River, Alberta, 1930

allowed to pay the passengers' expenses but the company did not reimburse their own expenses.

Sometimes conditions became so extreme that the drivers could not drive at all. One immutable law, recognized by every Greyhound driver, kept them going – if you didn't drive, you didn't get paid. Jack Rajala recalled that the winter of 1937 was particularly bad. The westbound drivers "didn't turn a wheel for six weeks", as the roads were completely blocked.

During winter blockages or spring thaws that made the roads impassable, most drivers turned to temporary work, often finding a job with the Department of Public Works getting the roads open again.

Working in the Kootenays in B.C. was scarcely easier, thanks to the ferries on some runs. Ferry schedules were erratic in winter, and the drivers didn't receive time or mileage while onboard. Loading the buses onto the ferries was a difficult, tricky job that required careful manoeuvring and a steady hand. On more than one occasion a bus trying to back up an ice-covered ramp would find itself sliding right into the lake.

Greyhound bus on Kootenay ferry, ca. 1937

Ross Nichol

Decades later, despite improved equipment and better roads, driver Ross Nichol found that prairie weather could still make things miserable. Spring storms in particular can be vicious and catch people unprepared.

In spring 1952, while operating the Calgary-Oyen run, Nichol left Drumheller for Calgary at 5 pm. Melted snow was running down the streets and he expected to have a comfortable run.

As the bus passed the Carbon Corner, a heavy snowstorm reduced visibility to almost zero and the bus's motor began to miss at the slow speed. Nichol realized he was very worried. He had eighteen passengers on board, two of them women wearing light dresses and nylon stockings, and a third who was feeling ill.

He handed out mitts and scarves from the emergency bag, then stepped into the blizzard to check the engine compartment. It was completely encased in ice and snow, and the wind drove in snow as fast as he could dig it out. He went back inside the bus and tried to start the engine several times, but it failed to catch.

Recognizing the danger of trying to go for help at night in a storm, Nichol reluctantly advised his passengers they would have to settle themselves in for the night.

In the morning they were awakened by someone pounding on the door, a farmer whose car had been stranded nearby. He and Nichol decided to go for help even though the storm was still raging. Keeping to the road, they eventually reached a farmhouse, which they found packed with other stranded people and without a telephone.

Tied together with a piece of rope, they then made for a nearby old bachelor's farm where there was food and a team of horses. Unfortunately, the horses would not set foot in the storm, and the two men were forced to backpack blankets and some food back to the stranded passengers.

Realizing his passengers' peril, Nichol decided that his duty was to get help at any cost. Knowing the road as well as he did, he set out for a gas station three miles down the highway where there was a telephone. It was a gut-wrenching, freezing walk further improved by the fact that he had to go to the bathroom but couldn't because his zipper was frozen shut.

When Nichol telephoned the shop in Calgary, they told him conditions were so bad that it could be days before the roads could be ploughed enough to bring his passengers relief. He slowly trudged back to the bus trying to figure out what to do.

Happily, while Nichol was off on his trek, the farmer had been able to coax his horses out of the barn and sleighed the passengers to his house. They waited for three more days before the storm subsided enough to clear the road.

When he finally arrived at the depot, he got no sympathy from his supervisor. "What happened, Nichol?" he shouted as the driver stepped down. "Had some gas trouble," a tired Nichol retorted. "Gas trouble, eh? You ever let that happen again and you might as well put on your snowshoes and head for the Arctic."

COACHWAYS GRIT

Drivers working on Canadian Coachways' far northern routes had experiences no less gruelling than Greyhound had undergone for the North West Service Command during the Second World War. Acquired by Greyhound in 1970, Coachways had its share of pioneers, as shown by a 1960 *Edmonton Journal* interview with operator Clyde Berryman:

Six times a month, Clyde climbs into the driver's seat of a Canadian Coachways bus at Peace River, puts the motor into gear and starts on a 400-mile journey down the Mackenzie Highway to Hay River, N.W.T. It is the only bus service operating into the Northwest Territories.

The run, to hear Clyde tell it, has no equal anywhere on the continent. "After a few months most runs get monotonous, but not this one," he says. "This is a run with personality. No two trips are the same; you never know what's going to happen next."

Clyde and the bus he drives are a familiar and welcome sight to the people who live at scattered points along this twisting gravel road that pierces the wilderness. However, Clyde is more than just a bus driver to them.

He is the mailman who distributes about 30 bags of mail per trip among communities north of Hotchkiss; he is the man who brings them their daily newspapers and delivers parts for a disabled tractor needed on a construction project, and the man who agrees to pick up a birthday card for a woman living at a lonely wayside point. Above all, he is their friend . . .

The drive to Hay River is a hard, eleven-and-a-half hour grind over a narrow highway that is

Coachways provided important passenger and express services to the developing north

dusty when it's dry and greasy when it's wet. The bus leaves Peace River at 9 a.m. on Monday, Wednesday and Friday and arrives in the Great Slave Lake community at 8:30 p.m. the same day. The following morning at 10 a.m., it heads back . . .

Humour, excitement and the unexpected ride the bus to and from Hay River . . .

He says he will never forget the time the water pump gasket blew out at about mile 150. Clyde says he canvassed his passengers and ended up with an assortment of bubble gum, chewing gum, soap, sugar and even some tar.

"We mixed everything together, boiled it until it became a sticky goo, then spread it on the pump joint and prayed it would serve as a makeshift gasket until we reached Hay River," he recalled. "Well, to tell you the truth, it stuck so well we did not have to install a regular gasket for three weeks!" . . .

Two years ago, he stopped the bus at Indian Cabins for the regular 15-minute stop and was checking the tires when he heard someone moaning inside the bus.

He looked inside and saw it was a woman who had boarded the bus at Steen River. "I asked her what was the matter and she replied: 'I'm going to have my baby.' Man, you could have knocked me over with a feather right then," Clyde said.

"I rushed into the cafe, bellowed 'Let's go' to the rest of the passengers and I got the bus rolling in no time flat. That was one of the fastest 90 miles I've ever made with a bus. I pulled up in front of the nursing station and got the woman inside. Ten minutes later, she was the mother of a bouncing baby boy."

The Coachways drivers were a tremendously dedicated group. Operating long runs with towns hundreds of miles apart, where a breakdown could mean disaster, they carried duffle bags full of clothes, a toolbox and extra parts, fixing the bus on the side of the road and building fires in the bus to keep the passengers warm.

RETIREMENT

For many Greyhound drivers, the company is "in their blood". Despite the job's challenges, they rack up decades of seniority, and when they retire, they choose a good run to close on.

In the past, the favourite route for many older drivers, including Bill Brown, was the Rogers Pass route from Calgary to Revelstoke. This route had two great advantages – infrequent stops, about three hours apart, and no need to shovel in winter, thanks to the avalanche control provided by the National Parks Department. Brown would describe his last five years on this route as the most enjoyable of his career. He retired in 1966 after thirty-five years behind the wheel.

Bob Borden, Bill Brown and Lorne Frizzell
after Brown's last run, 1966

Layton Miles, who drove the first bus through the Rogers Pass, also held the run for several years before his retirement in 1973. And Jack Rajala spent the last seven years of his career on the Trans-Canada Highway prior to retiring in 1977. Jack especially appreciated the smooth mountain driving after many years driving in the Crowsnest Pass area.

Walter Hyssop was operating the Fort Macleod to Medicine Hat run when he retired in 1972. A new bus was sent down from Calgary for the occasion, and two of his best friends got on at Lethbridge enroute to Coaldale to deliver a speech to the passengers extolling Hyssop's virtues as a veteran Greyhound driver and a kind human being.

Hyssop collected congratulations throughout the run. A police escort accompanied him into the city of Fort Macleod, where a crowd was waiting, including the mayor, the press and several company officials. That night he attended a special party staged by his friends and received a commemorative saddle blanket emblazoned with the Greyhound logo.

Ed Dunn used his last trip in 1976 for a vacation. Knowing that a month-long charter tour to Florida was coming up during his last six months, he surprised everybody by signing up as spareboard driver. When the trip came up on the board his seniority assured he would get it. His wife went with him and they had a wonderful time, especially because the tour conductor, Doc Evans, was a former Greyhound driver. After lunch each day, Evans would tell Dunn to park the bus and have a little nap, or took over the wheel himself while the driver found out what it was like to be the passenger.

Today, retiring Greyhound drivers are acknowledged in a corporate function and receive a large plaque commemorating their years of service. Many drivers come back for summer driving work, and keep up their friendships through company golf tournaments, regional Christmas parties and other functions. To commemorate Greyhound's 75th anniversary, all current and retired drivers received a package of memorabilia specially designed by the Marketing department, including pins, key chains, commemorative stamps from Canada Post, etc.

UNION BROTHERS AND SISTERS

During the Great Depression jobs were at a premium. Although a driver's income at Greyhound could vary wildly depending on the run, the money was good for the times. Initially, new drivers were usually assigned to a particular run, which were limited by the number of licences the company operated at the time. But as the routes and connections multiplied, the fleet grew and the company began to pick up charter business, it became necessary to have spare drivers.

Spare Board

To share out the work, the company created a "spare board", now the standard method all bus companies use to assure a driver is always available. Spare boards are part of the seniority system. Jack Rajala was put "on the board" when he was hired in 1935, joining a group of three other drivers. The spare board worked on a first-in, first-out basis; that is, the driver in longest from a previous trip drew the next trip that came up on the board.

This meant uncertain and erratic schedules for the drivers on the spare board, as they were never sure, day or night, when the next call to take out a bus would come. Additionally, they could not predict the amount of their monthly paycheque since they never knew how many – or how few – trips they might take nor how long they might be. Later, minimum guarantees were established to ensure that spare drivers received base pay in the event that the board was slow, with furloughing also an option.

Under the seniority system headed by Greyhound's first driver, Layton Miles, the most senior drivers could secure the routes they wanted through the bidding system. Bid sheets listing the company runs were put out every six months. Since most runs required two drivers, they were usually bid in pairs. As seniority determines the winning bid, the most senior pair would get the run they wanted, the next most senior got their second choice, and so on until all the runs were bid.

The remaining drivers without runs would go on the spare board, but even there the seniority system continued to function. Here, the spare board's first-in/first-out process was modified by the right of senior drivers to take or refuse a trip when their name came up, passing it down to a more junior driver on the board without losing their own position on the board.

Because Greyhound operated in two regional divisions, Nelson and Calgary, and added other divisions, Edmonton and Regina, as the decade progressed, the seniority system was portable from the outset. A driver transferring divisions took his seniority with him and was given seniority in the new division according to his years of service in comparison to those in the division.

Obviously, because senior drivers tended to hang onto their preferred routes, younger drivers were stuck with the unpopular routes. For example, drivers working in the Kootenays tended to earn less than drivers working on the prairies, simply because the routes tended to be shorter. Nelson-Trail was the best run as it had service several times a day, allowing the driver to earn about $5 driving them all.

Early Working Conditions

Before World War II, labour problems had not played a significant role in the company's history. The only recorded "strike" dated to when some of the company's first mechanics walked off the job for a few days in 1930. Fay put this action down to "red influence" and soon solved the matter. During the Depression most employees were happy to have a job at all, and Fay, himself on short shrift, told them he would be happy to pay more if the company could afford it.

On occasion a driver would get fed up with the 1.5 cent a mile rate and complain about his pay cheque. Bill Brown recalled an instance when Bud White, one of the company's original drivers, received a cheque for $6.00 and was so mad that he tore it up, made out a ticket to Vancouver for himself and disappeared on a two-week "holiday."

Things improved by the mid- to late thirties and drivers were receiving 2.25 cents a mile for some trips. However, other working conditions had not changed. Drivers still had to pay for expenses incurred during layovers due to mechanical failure or weather conditions. If a bus blew a tire or broke down outside the range of company maintenance facilities, the driver had to pay for the repairs out of his own pocket and then requisition it back from the company later.

Labour Relations

With generally more enlightened employer-employee relationships developing in the years after the war, the company was involved in negotiating better salaries, benefits and working conditions with its employees. The first move in this direction came in 1944, probably as a result of the recommendations that various Greyhound Corporation committees were making in terms of benefits for its employees.

That year the company's board passed a resolution adopting a pension plan "satisfactory to the employees" that took into account past as well as future service. The same year Greyhound entered into negotiations with the Metropolitan Life Insurance Company for a contract to cover life, accident, sickness and hospitalization insurance for its employees. This Group Insurance Plan came into effect on May 21, 1945.

While these benefits went a long way to improving conditions for employees, salaries were still the most important issue. The company would negotiate its first union contract in 1946.

First labour negotiations

In the late thirties a union known as the Amalgamated Association of Street, Electric Railway and Motor Coach Employees of America successfully organized the employees of numerous Greyhound Corporation affiliates. Probably because of World War II, the union did not begin to organize on the Canadian scene until the mid forties.

Post-war Canada was extremely pro-labour, reflecting the large numbers of enlisted men returning from overseas. The union's first efforts in Winnipeg found fertile ground, and it soon applied for the right to bargain for drivers throughout Canada. Certification was granted by the Wartime Labour Relations Board (National) in April 1946.

Although it opened negotiations with several companies, the union targeted Greyhound as one of the largest. Fay was decidedly not pro-union, but he could see the writing on the wall. He obtained advice from the Greyhound Corporation on how to write a labour contract and what points had caused trouble in the American contracts. Bargaining was assigned to Duncan Robertson, Lorne Frizzell and Bill deWynter, district superintendent in Calgary. They went head-to-head with the union's bargainer: a huge, tough union man from Portland, Oregon named George Herbert, president of the new Canadian Division, 1374.

First contract

Despite hard-nosed stances on both sides, the first contract was agreed upon fairly quickly and ratified by Greyhound's board on December 31, 1946. Signed on January 4, 1947 with a one-year term, the agreement became the model for subsequent one-year, and later three-year, contracts.

This contract had four articles, the first defining the sections applying to all company employees, such as grievance procedures, suspensions and dismissals, probationary periods, etc. One of the more interesting sections laid out seniority rankings under which employees from acquired companies would be dovetailed into the Greyhound seniority list. It stated:

> such employees as are taken over with the operation will be merged, according to their occupational classification and in order of their actual

Nelson mechanical staff, 1936. Greyhound's increasing staff of drivers, mechanics and depot workers were not unionized prior to the war

service with either company, with the seniority lists of the company in the seniority district or districts into which the acquired operation is merged.

A unique feature of the contract was free transportation for employees and their families, as per the following: "Free transportation for all employees and wholly dependent members of their immediate family will be granted subject to the rules and regulations of the company."

Classifications

The remaining three articles discussed the salaries, benefits and working conditions of the three identified categories of company employees. These categories were the mechanical department, terminal employees and motor coach drivers, each divided into sub-classes using various criteria. In the mechanical department, for example, there were class "A" employees, or specialists, which included "any employees having exceptional skill in any occupation as required by the company."

Mechanical Department

The mechanical department included mechanics, machinists, welders, electricians, bodymen, painters, upholsterers, batterymen and radiator men. The starting rate for 1st class men in these positions was 84 cents per hour, rising to 89 cents per hour after one year and 94 cents per hour after two years. Other classes of employees in the maintenance department included service employees, shop clerks, storeroom employees and other garage employees (stenographers, file clerks, etc.). These were mostly paid on a monthly basis with salaries ranging from a starting rate low of $57 per month for a junior clerk to $147 per month for a chief stores clerk.

Terminal Employees

Terminal employees were divided into far fewer classifications than were mechanical department workers. There were basically three classifications:

Ticket clerks – Grade 1. Their duties were "selling tickets, billing and handling express, travel information, billing and handling baggage, dispatching coaches, making reports, supervision over depot employees and general responsibility for operation of depots in the absence of higher designated authority";

Ticket clerks – Grade 2. Their responsibilities were much the same except with less of a supervisory role; and

Baggage and express employees, whose duties included checking and handling baggage, express,

newspapers and mail, billing express shipments, making out reports, accounting for all cash collected and giving out information.

Salary rates for the three terminal classifications were tied to a classification system based on the type of depot they worked in. Class "A" depots included Calgary and Edmonton, class "B" depots were Lethbridge, Saskatoon, Moose Jaw and Brandon, and class "C" depots included Nelson, North Battleford, Swift Current, Medicine Hat, Ashcroft, Princeton, Vernon, Kelowna and Penticton.

Class "A" depots starting salaries were 50 cents per hour for grade 1 ticket clerks, 47 cents per hour for grade 2 ticket clerks and 45 cents per hour for baggage and express employees. Maximum salaries were 70 cents, 67 cents and 60 cents per hour respectively for those with over four years of service. Employees in class "B" and "C" depots received three and six cents per hour less for the equivalent positions.

Driver Classifications

Drivers were divided into five classifications, ranging from class "A" to "A-4". New drivers were placed in class "A". They had to remain in the class for one year or such longer period of time as it took to drive 60,000 miles (45,000 in the Nelson district and 50,000 in the Penticton district) before moving up to the next class. Rates of pay ranged from 3.3 cents per mile for class "A" drivers to 4.1 cents per mile for class "A-4" drivers.

Other compensatory clauses covered the rates for deadhead driving (equal to those for driving), non-driving deadheading (called "riding the cushions", or "cushioning" today), which were equal to half the rates for driving, and charter trips, where the driver could choose to be paid by the hour or by the mile.

Other Clauses

The other sections of this first collective agreement were mainly focussed on the rules of seniority and bidding for runs. Other items covered the previously contentious matters of accommodation and uniforms. Greyhound agreed to provide regular drivers with rooms at lay-over points away from their home terminals and spare board drivers with a room each time they were required to stay away from their home terminal. Each driver in class "A-1" or higher was to be refunded half of the cost of any part of two uniforms per year.

Bargaining in the 50s

Greyhound's increasingly good financial performances in the fifties encouraged the union to seek more concessions and higher wages. President Bob Borden had helped negotiate several previous collective agreements, which stood him in good stead in the current situation with the now-named Amalgamated Association of Street Railway & Motor Coach Employees of America.

The union negotiator was George Morrison, formerly of British Columbia Electric. Morrison was a tough bargainer and a strong labour man, but honest and not radical. Borden was also a tough negotiator. Many of their contracts required long drawn-out bargaining sessions that went to the twelfth hour before a settlement was finally reached. However, neither side wanted a strike and through many contracts they always avoided one. By the end of the fifties these contracts were normally ratified for a term of three years.

Cost of Living Allowance

As Greyhound earnings increased, salary increases awarded in 1960 through to the end of 1962 were accompanied by a new cost-of-living allowance (COLA) clause that pegged wage rates to changes in the cost-of-living as computed by the Dominion Bureau of Statistic's Consumer Price Index. Whenever the cost of living rose by 0.7 per cent, a driver's salary rose by a half mill per mile while other employees' salaries rose by 1 cent per hour.

With the addition of cost-of-living increases to the new wage rates settled by the contract, class A drivers in the Calgary seniority district now received 9 cents per mile at the beginning of the contract and 10 cents at its end, while class A-4 drivers received 9.8 cents at the beginning and 10.8 at its end.

Mechanical department and terminal employees received similar increases. Starting salaries for class A mechanical department employees went from $2.175 per hour at the beginning of the contract to $2.385 per hour at its end, while those with two year's experience went from $2.31 to $2.54.

Ticket clerks in class "A" depots now received $1.78 per hour as a starting wage at the beginning of the contract and $1.955 per hour at its end, while those with four years of experience earned $1.99 at the beginning and $2.185 at the end. Classifications and rates varied slightly for the employees of Eastern Canadian Greyhound, who had their own contract.

1981 – First Strike

Following recent record company profits, in early 1981 the union demanded a 36% wage increase over

Len Munter, president, ATU, Local 1374

three years plus continuing the cost-of-living allowance. Reflecting the reality of Canada's inflationary spiral, management offered 27% over three years while insisting on dropping the cost-of-living clause that had been part of the contract from the early sixties. The value of the company offer was calculated as $20.1 million over three years compared to the union's demand of $34 million.

Following unsuccessful last-ditch efforts, 1,400 Greyhound employees went on strike for the first time on April 22nd, 1981, disrupting transportation across the country. After ten days a tentative settlement was reached. Wages would increase 10% a year over three years, or 30% over the life of the contract, and the cost-of-living allowance was retained but with conditions.

Top drivers now received 39.88 cents per mile in 1981, representing a salary of $28,000, based on average annual miles of 70,000, plus a 4% meal allowance. First class mechanics would receive $12.20 per hour, ticket clerks $10.20 per hour, and coach cleaners $9.47 per hour. The only other significant gain was a driver's guarantee of twenty-four hours off duty at home in any week.

Second Strike

A few years later, poor economic conditions beginning with the recession in the early eighties made it increasingly important for Greyhound to bring its continually rising labour costs under control and in line with the stagnant business climate. Unfortunately, the company sustained a second short strike in 1987, which affected its reputation for reliable service.

Concessions

Under president Dick Huisman, in 1989 Greyhound management launched regular labour-management meetings to help resolve issues and gain support for upcoming changes. With both sides well aware of the company's financial challenges, collective bargaining yielded significant union concessions on driver wages to help make the company more viable and competitive.

Company management, such as Art Jackman, Bruce Thiessen and Bev Mundt, played key roles in these negotiations, achieving agreements without labour stoppages. However, the attitudes between the company and union (now named the Amalgamated Transit Union, or ATU) were sometimes unnecessarily combative and corrosive to the relationship.

Improving the Relationship

In 2000 the company and the union sent large groups to the George Meany Center in Washington, D.C. for labour-management training. This labour school, taught by labour instructors, was very beneficial in bringing both sides together and marked a new era in collaborative bargaining.

Further sessions at the Center in 2001 and 2002 have gone a long way to establishing real communication between the company and the union and resolving adversarial attitudes. Greyhound continues to develop its relationship with the ATU, conducting monthly labour-management meetings and attempting to resolve issues through consensus.

In particular, the 2002 George Meany Center sessions focussed on the concept of "interest-based bargaining," which is being actively applied. In addition to the agreements it holds with the ATU, Greyhound

Gary Dorion, president, ATU, Local 1415, November 2001. Photo courtesy Bill McCarthy

also maintains relationships through subsidiaries with other unions such as the Teamsters, the CAW and OPEIU. Greyhound is committed to using these techniques to build consensus and trust in all its union relationships. The key truth is to realize that union and management objectives are not mutually exclusive after all. We look forward to continuing our strong labour-management relationships.

CHAPTER FIVE

OUR FLEET

THE 1930S
First Coaches

Although Greyhound Canada's fleet today numbers over 500 coaches, mostly from Motor Coach Industries, in 1929 the company had a tiny fleet of just four buses and some 7-passenger touring cars. These were sufficient for Greyhound's three Nelson B.C. routes, but once the southern Alberta franchises were in place and the decision was made to operate the Calgary-Edmonton run, Greyhound needed to expand its fleet. As a former General Motors salesman, Fay naturally turned to G.M.'s Yellow coach division, placing an order in January 1930 for three 20-passenger model Ws. That March the three new Yellow coaches were put into service.

These coaches were 24 feet long and 90 inches wide with a 185-inch wheelbase, featured dual rear wheels and a 36.6 horsepower engine, and were painted a light blue colour with a white top. As a public relations gesture, Greyhound offered free rides from its depot to the Armouries for a few days before assigning them to the Lethbridge run.

The Pontiac Run

Fay also ordered eight new Yellow model Y 29-passenger buses from the General Motors plant at Pontiac, Michigan. Features of the Ys included the luggage racks for regular baggage, while larger pieces and trunks were carried on a quarter-deck on top. As well, the seats were constructed of wicker covered with leather.

That May Speed Olson and eight Greyhound drivers (three from Victoria, B.C., the rest from Alberta) drove to Pontiac to pick up the new buses. The plan was to drive them to Detroit and then

Greyhound and Yelloway "Y" coaches at plant in Pontiac, Michigan, May 1930

Convoy of "Y" coaches enroute to Calgary, May 1930

straight west through South Dakota into Montana, and then up into southern Alberta.

Once the buses were signed over, Speed Olson was anxious to get them to Calgary and into service as fast as possible. Up and away at 6 a.m., the convoy pushed hard, driving late at night, until fatigue resulted in an accident.

At 11 p.m. Victoria driver Grant Smith was driving behind the other buses, which had already crossed a river in South Dakota. Smith could see them on the other side, but he misjudged the distance on a sharp, steep curve and his vehicle turned over. The damage was essentially limited to a broken windshield caused by the hammer kept with the driver to check the tires and it did not slow the convoy down. However, Smith feared he would lose his job and made the rest of the drive in much trepidation.

The convoy reached Calgary on May 22, 1930, two and a half days after leaving Pontiac. Much to his surprise, instead of being given a ticket home to Victoria, Smith was told he would be driving one of the new buses to Edmonton the next morning at 7 a.m.

Canadian-Made

Unfortunately, the original Ys and Ws were too heavy for the rough roads in Alberta and B.C. The poor suspension made for a difficult ride, and the coaches were difficult to start.

To resolve these problems, Fay approached J.C. Scott, head of Hay and Harding, Blacksmiths and Waggon Builders, located at 14th Street and 10th Avenue S.E. in Calgary. Fay asked Scott to build buses similar to the Yellows, but on a smaller chassis and lighter in weight. Scott and his staff of thirty set to work, producing Greyhound's first three Canadian-

built coaches from 1932 to 1933.

Structurally the new coaches were very similar to the Yellows. The basic body was made of wood with wooden posts supporting wooden roof bows that in turn supported the roof. The roof itself was made of canvas stretched over wooden slats, oil treated and painted, unlike the roofs of the Yellow coaches which were made of light sheet metal. The wooden sides of the vehicles were covered with twenty-gauge body steel that was nailed in place.

Hay and Harding bus built for Greyhound, 1932-33.

An Accident

Greyhound's first years of operation were carried out on this original fleet of Ws, Ys and the Hay and Harding coaches. However, Fay worried about the safety of the industry's wooden coaches on the hazardous roads, and in October 1933 his worst fears were realized.

On October 29, 1933 during a trip from

Lethbridge to Calgary, a Y with twenty-five passengers on board had a terrible accident.

Fay's report to the Department of Public Works described the circumstances:

This Bus operates between Lethbridge and Calgary, and on the above date it left Lethbridge at 2 p.m. enroute for Calgary and reached High River on time at 5:50. It left shortly afterwards enroute for Calgary, with a load of 25 passengers, exclusive of the driver, Walter Hyssop, who has been in our employ since April 1931, and who has operated continuously without previous mishap.

When about 2 miles north of High River, and while proceeding at a speed estimated to be between 30 and 35 miles per hour, Hyssop observed the bright lights of an approaching vehicle, and in due course he swung to the right to pass this vehicle, which proved to be a truck owned by the Alberta Transport Company.

He had no sooner swung to the right than a parked truck loaded with oil casings loomed up before him and he immediately swung the bus again to the left, but the right side of the vehicle failed to clear the projecting oil casing on the left side of the truck, with the result that a collision occurred and the oil casing struck the bus at the door and cut through the right side to the rear, with resultant injuries to six passengers sitting next to the window, four of whom were killed, and two of whom sustained serious injuries.

Although Hyssop was blameless, the fatalities deeply affected Fay and he began to seriously consider how to build a better bus made of metal that would be much safer than the wooden ones. With pictures and specifications of General Motors' latest "cab-over-engine" model in hand, he again approached J.C. Scott, and Hay and Harding built a bus emulating the American one.

Unfortunately, the additional weight of steel and aluminum proved too heavy for the chassis and the front axle broke on the vehicle's maiden trip.

As his forte was mechanics and metal work, Fay then set out to design his own bus but without success. Although he knew what he wanted, he just could not get it down.

First Steel Bus

Happily, in 1935 Greyhound hired a driver who solved the problem and went on to have a long career, making a significant contribution to the company's future – H.K. "Pat" Williams. Trained in engineering, Williams drove with Greyhound for three months and probably would have continued to do so had it not been for a passing remark ticket agent Jerry Brown made to Fay.

Fay was lamenting his inability to get his idea for a steel bus down on paper when Brown told him he had an engineer on staff who might be able to help out. Fay asked Brown to send the man up to his office immediately. When Pat arrived, Fay explained what he had in mind and showed him what he had tried to draft up. Williams asked for permission to take the material home overnight and give it some thought. Fay quickly agreed, and added that if he needed any drafting material he could charge what he needed at Calgary Drafting Supply across the street.

Sensing a chance for advancement, Williams decided to grab the opportunity by both horns. He arranged with a friend at Calgary Drafting to open the store at 6 a.m. the next morning, then went home and began translating Fay's thoughts into a set of detailed plans and drawings.

Working through the night, he produced eight pages of drawings that included everything from general body design to detailed profiles. Then he hustled down to Calgary Drafting at 6 a.m. to meet his friend. They spent the next two hours turning his drawings into blueprints. As a finishing touch, Williams included a title page that announced in bold letters that these were drawings of an all-steel bus designed by George B. Fay.

When Fay came to work that morning, Williams waited a few minutes and then went up to his second floor office. The president asked him if he had given any thought to his ideas. Handing him the portfolio, Pat replied he'd "done a few sketches." Fay took the package over to his drafting table and began to leaf through it. Williams, watching for signs of reaction, didn't wait long.

As the material sank in, "Fay's eyes all but bugged out of his head." Before him lay the reality of the vision that had distracted him so long. He went through the plans several times, and then told Williams to go down to the restaurant and charge up the biggest breakfast he could eat. Williams happily complied.

While he was eating he noticed that Speed Olson and Jack Deagon went up to the office. Waiting for what seemed an eternity after finishing breakfast, Williams finally went back up and was invited into the office. Fay asked him point blank if he could build the bus. Pat protested that he had no experience in that field. Fay retorted that he had enough to suit him and the matter was settled on the spot.

No. 25 – "Two-bits"

Greyhound's first steel coach, No. 25 (familiarly known as "Two-bits") was built in the summer of 1935 on a Hayes-Anderson chassis with a Hercules engine, bought in advance by Fay and stored in the loft of Greyhound's garage. The project team included Hank Carlson and Ray Fulson among several others. Under Williams' direction they soon understood what he wanted and even suggested improvements.

The 21-passenger bus had the same fundamental design as a conventional wooden bus, with a hood on the front like a car, but it was more aerodynamic, particularly the sloping back. This helped to prevent water from accumulating on the roof, a problem of the earlier flat-roofed G.M. models.

Unlike earlier buses, No. 25 had a true baggage compartment with a large door, making baggage handling much easier for the driver. The posts and ribs were now made of steel, and the building team had to design a special tool capable of bending the ribs in a complete arc from floor to floor. The siding of the vehicles was also completely steel, of a heavier gauge than previous buses, and it was riveted on instead of nailed.

Finally, drawing from American influences, the team developed a new type of seat made of steel tubing instead of wicker, making them more comfortable, durable and safer.

This new bus fully justified all expectations. Sometime late in 1935 it was assigned to a new route between Fernie and the border at Kingsgate, the major connection for travellers to the United States and the Canadian west coast. Route operator Jack Rajala found the bus warm and comfortable for winter driving, although the brakes tended to grab a little more on the front than on the rear.

Hope Justified

While driving to the border one afternoon in February 1936, Rajala came around a bend on an icy, rut-filled road near Moyie Lake on a slight hill. In the other direction were three American wrestlers heading for a match in Calgary. They were late and driving too fast. When they saw the bus approaching, the driver hit the brakes and the car slid into the front end of the bus.

The collision pushed the bus through a 2x4

No. 25 after accident, 1935

guardrail and down a hundred-odd foot embankment. The bus landed on its roof on the railway track.

But the bus's steel frame roof did not cave in. Of Rajala's thirteen passengers the only ones seriously hurt were an elderly couple from Saskatchewan. Rajala severely injured his knee and was laid up in the hospital for three months. The bus had saved lives. The concept was sound.

No. 25 was taken to Nelson and turned over to Pat Williams and John Learmonth for rebuilding using the increasingly popular cab-over design.

Western Steel

Meanwhile, Fay had decided on further developments for the metal bus and negotiated an agreement

Bus built on Ford chassis by Western Steel in Calgary, ca. 1936.

Paving of western Canadian roads began in the late thirties

with Western Steel to build a few. Speed Olson came up with the idea of building these units on Ford chassis stretched to accommodate the length of the 17-passenger requirements.

Under Pat Williams' supervision, in 1936 Western Steel's Calgary plant produced three units with conventional front ends, incorporating a number of improvements over No. 25.

However, Fay needed an alternative source for new buses. Production was slow and with only twenty-five buses, the fleet was simply not large enough to handle the demand. As well, many prairie dirt roads were being graded and receiving their first coat of gravel. Greyhound needed a bus that would ride well on the improved roads and with greater capacity than the earlier 17-passenger to 29-passenger vehicles.

The "Pusher" Bus

In the United States the Greyhound Corporation was working with General Motors' Yellow Coach Division to develop a revolutionary new bus, the Yellow 719, which featured a raised platform floor allowing the engine to be mounted in the rear and the baggage to be stored underneath. The vehicle promised a smoother, quieter, vibration-free ride, increased headroom, a reclining seat for comfort on long journeys, a footrest and roll-down window shades.

Unfortunately, the new vehicle was so popular that none could be spared from the Greyhound Corporation companies. The rest of the market had to content itself with Yellow's more prosaic model 732. It was less streamlined and not as comfortable, but did have a version of the new rear-mounted engine and Westinghouse air brakes.

The company decided to try out four of these "pusher" buses in late 1936 and immediately ran into problems. The coaches were heavier than expected –

19,700 pounds with 145 gallons of gasoline. Special permission from Alberta's Department of Public Works was required for the large balloon tires the "pushers" used, and the company had to promise to pull them out of service in the spring when the roads were soft.

As well, drivers assigned to the vehicles constantly complained they lacked power for prairie conditions and a couple soon blew their engines. Because of the weight factor and what Fay described as other "unsatisfactory mechanical details," the company returned these coaches to G.M. in April 1937.

Hayes and Kenworth

With this failure Greyhound was forced to turn to other coach suppliers, focussing on 29-passenger Hayes-Andersons from the Hayes Manufacturing Co. in Vancouver and Kenworths in Seattle.

In July 1937 Greyhound purchased two Kenworth 32-passenger coaches and a Ford coach. Kenworth had its sights on G.M.'s popular Yellow 719s and the new 743 "Super Cruiser", the new darling of the Greyhound Corporation. To compete, Kenworth developed the steel T-32 bus in partnership with the Tri-Coach Manufacturing Co. who built the bodies. This model had a very long spring in its suspension, which gave a smoother ride, a rear-mounted underfloor Buda engine, and a very comfortable, smart-looking Tri-Coach 33-passenger capacity body.

These were painted with the new "streamlined" colour scheme the company started copying from Greyhound Corporation around 1936 – a blue body, white roof, and an imaginative white stripe which ran down the side and swept up over the wheel wells, capped by the running greyhound dog and a sign reading "Greyhound Lines" set in blue against a wing shaped white background.

FORT GARRY MOTOR BODY
AND PAINT WORKS

By this time some of Greyhound's original Yellow "Ys" purchased in 1930 were reaching the end of their useful life, the bodies deteriorating and the engines wearing out. Lacking capital to buy new buses, Greyhound took them for repair to Fred Sicinski and Harry Zoltok's Fort Garry Motor Body and Paint Works.

Harry Zoltok was a Polish Jew who immigrated to Montreal after World War I. After establishing his engineering credentials on a series of temporary jobs, in 1928 he moved to Winnipeg and soon began a partnership in the auto body repair business of

Harry Zoltok

J.R. Horne and Company. In 1932, despite the Depression, he convinced a group of associates to invest in a new company, Fort Garry Motor Body and Paint Works Ltd.

With Fred Sicinski as president and Zoltok as vice president, the new company established itself in a 5,000 square foot plant on Fort Street. Initially Fort Garry concentrated on auto body repairs and manufacturing custom-built car bodies, but by 1933 it produced its first "bus," an 11-passenger vehicle built on a Packard chassis with individual doors for each row

Fort Garry's first bus, 1933

of seats. From there the company went on to manufacturing real buses on truck chassis, a common practice in the thirties.

Barney Olson met Harry Zoltok not long after he moved to Winnipeg in 1935 to begin Trans Continental, and sometime in 1936 or 1937 Fay met him at a bus operators' convention. The two immediately liked each other and struck up a friendship, leading to the work contract in 1937.

Fort Garry took a couple of the Ys that were in better condition and completely rebuilt and streamlined the bodies, fitting them with rebuilt engines and thoroughly impressing Fay.

Fresh from the bad experience with the Yellow "pushers" and looking for a coach that had the same features and appearance as the Super Cruisers but cheaper than the Kenworth imitations, Fay asked Zoltok to consider creating his own version. Zoltok agreed and came up with an excellent imitation – the model 37-UM.

Fort Garry's Model 37-UM

Modelled after the Yellow 743 "Super Cruiser", the conventional-style bus's body was to be of rigid construction mounted on a truck chassis and fitted out with a standard Hall-Scott pancake engine. The thirty-seven passenger capacity would make it much larger than previous company coaches. Fay insisted on steel construction and the highest attention to safety, and Zoltok and Pat Williams spent a lot of time working on the plans.

Construction was slow while the team found ways to avoid the shortcomings of the Yellow 743 model. Only after Fay and Zoltok were assured that these problems had been overcome did production go ahead. During development, in January 1938 Greyhound purchased four 33-passenger coaches from another source, possibly from Kenworth, to keep the fleet going.

The first two model 37-UMs were ordered in September 1938 for service on Trans Continental's lines. As development was still going on when the order was placed, an estimated cost of $15,000 was quoted. Greyhound ordered four in November 1938 at $15,600 per unit, and another soon afterward.

Model 150 "Supercoach"

Almost before Greyhound had broken in the first five 37-UMs (numbered 106-110), Fort Garry was busy developing an improved coach, the model 150. Copying the aluminum siding treatment of Yellow's "Silversides" PDG series, the coach featured a new

Greyhound's late-thirties advertising copied U.S. campaigns for the Yellow 743 "Super Cruiser"

aluminum siding treatment that imitated the popular railway car design, offering protection against corrosion.

Greyhound ordered ten of these 150s (numbered 150-159), and was very proud of its new "Supercoach," advertising it in spring 1940:

These new highway cruisers, now in regular service on all principal lines throughout the country, are up-to-the-minute in design, performance and appearance.

The new-type motor is installed under the floor in conformity with the best and most modern automotive practice, and its smooth, vibrationless operation, with plenty of power for all emergencies and all types of highway, is a tribute to the men who design the country's automotive equipment.

The motor cannot be seen nor heard. Exhaust fumes are left far behind, and there is no vibration to cause passengers annoyance.

Super-coach passengers are afforded an uninterrupted view of passing scenery due to the raised seat-deck, and wide, safety-glass windows are provided.

Real comfort can be enjoyed in these new high-

way cruisers. The seats are in reality arm chairs, with five positions of the back, so that the passengers can recline at any angle they wish.

Soft, diffused lighting is provided, through frosted-glass tubes, and ventilating and heating systems are provided to add further to the comfort of travellers.

There is a new and luxurious spaciousness about the supercoach that is unique. The seats are wider than those of conventional-type buses, and are placed further apart, to ensure ample leg room. Easily adjustable footrests are provided in front of every seat, to add their bit to perfect comfort.

The interior of the supercoach, like the exterior, is streamlined, with all unsightly non-essentials removed. Overhead is a streamlined luggage-rack, where passengers may place their hats and smaller personal articles of luggage, while suitcases and other larger articles are placed in waterproof, dustproof compartments located under the seat deck. These compartments are locked in transit, and thus the safety of passengers luggage is assured.

Two Major Innovations

As attractive as they were, these advertising claims did not point out the two main features that made the 150s so revolutionarily different from Greyhound's previous coaches. These features were aluminum construction and climate control.

Using aircraft manufacture techniques, Fort Garry built the 150 out of aluminum, making it stronger, safer – and two tons lighter than conventional buses. The coaches achieved high fuel economy, while the driver could handle the vehicle more easily and stop it more quickly.

The other radical change was in the bus's climate control, which had been a constant problem with earlier vehicles. Fort Garry installed one large heater instead of the five or six smaller ones typical of earlier buses, and circulated the warmed air using a series of vents, uniformly heating the entire vehicle. In the summer, the system was switched from heat to cool air – a new cooling feature for hot weather travel that had never been attempted before.

THE 1940s

The 1940 Fleet

In mid-1940 Greyhound had a fleet of sixty-seven vehicles worth $1.1 million, consisting largely of old Yellows, Kenworths and Hayes-Andersons along with seventeen almost-new Fort Garry coaches, including the two from Trans Continental.

Greyhound continued to place orders for additional model 150s, ordering twelve on November 16, 1940 and eight more on January 8, 1942, although this second order was cancelled at the suggestion of the wartime transit controller.

In 1942 Greyhound would use modified model 150 buses on the North West Service Command where the rugged and frigid conditions proved a true test for the vehicle's ability to stand up to the wear and tear of Canada's north.

Motor Coach Industries (MCI)

Fort Garry was doing so well that Sicinski and Zoltok renamed and recapitalized it to meet the growing demand. Fort Garry was renamed Motor Coach Industries (MCI), and capitalized at one million shares selling at a par value of 25 cents each. Sicinski and Zoltok each bought approximately one-third of the shares and five other investors bought the remaining one third.

MCI immediately moved to a new 20,000 square foot plant at Erin and St. Matthews Streets.

Unfortunately, Greyhound would not be able to place another order until May 1944, as Canada's minister of munitions and supply, C.D. Howe, soon had MCI producing an array of military vehicles to support the war effort, which slowed bus production to a trickle.

Despite the diversification, Zoltok constantly thought about how to combine the body of the bus and the chassis from two separate units joined together in the building process into a single module.

The Courier 100

With support from Greyhound, MCI produced and introduced its new bus in 1945, the Courier 100. Under Zoltok's guidance, his plant engineers developed a design that would revolutionize bus building: an integral tubular steel alloy welded bus frame in one complete unit covered by an aluminum alloy body shell. The 33-passenger deluxe intercity Courier 100 model was 29 feet 10 inches long, 96 inches wide, 118 inches high, weighed 16,600 pounds and was powered by an International IHC Red 450-A, 6-cylinder, 451 cubic inch rear-mounted engine instead of the old Hall-Scott pancakes.

MCI's launch advertising described the Courier's five outstanding features as follows:

• Ease of Maintenance – Too many costly hours are spent in overhaul and service and operators

know from past experience that a reduction in these hours is most profitable. It can be safely stated that the Courier Coaches show savings in service and maintenance costs as high as 50% over other coaches. Within a matter of six hours complete new mechanical units may be installed. This means that less than a day in the coach's operating time is lost on overhaul periods.

• Economy – The 100 Courier is economical in operation with gasoline consumption averaging 7.25 to 7.5 M.P. G. This means 900 miles of operation per tank of gasoline. This fuel consumption is an outstanding record for a coach of this size and type.

Balance – A perfect balance ratio of 1:2 is maintained, one third of the weight to the front and

Motor coach travel was becoming increasingly comfortable by the forties

two-thirds to the rear. Contingent upon this balance is the life of the tires. Tire life has been increased by 25-50% thereby cutting costs of tire replacement and service even under adverse operating conditions. This perfected balance more than doubles brake lining life and gives smooth and equalized braking.

• Springs – Springs of carbon chrome steel are suspended in transverse rubber torsion tubes mountings. The leaves of these springs are shot-blasted on the tension side. This, together with the rubber mounting arrangement, is responsible for an increase in spring life of 100 to 300%.

• Steering – The advanced steering geometry and installation of the touch control steering (M.C.I.

patented features) and its shock-free characteristics is a contributing factor in combatting driver fatigue.

The Courier 100 was the first of many Courier models, each new model making improvements over the previous. Its appearance was followed in 1946 by the Courier 200, a 37-passenger version.

Fleet Refurbishment

During the war, Greyhound had not purchased many new vehicles, although it obtained several used ones through company acquisitions. In the post-war period Greyhound took steps to build up and modernize the fleet. The Courier model met the company's stringent standards and in October 1945 Greyhound purchased twenty Courier model 100s.

By this time Greyhound's credit with MCI was so good it was able to get these vehicles on a time payment plan, depositing 15% of their cost as a down payment and paying the balance in quarterly instalments over a five-year period with annual interest of 2%.

In August 1946 Greyhound ordered twenty more model 100s and twenty model 200s, and in September 1947 ten of each size again. These cost $17,550 and $19,975 per coach, f.o.b. Winnipeg, plus sales and excise taxes. To finance them Western Canadian borrowed $265,000 from The Canada Trust Company and issued equipment trust bonds bearing 3% interest to secure the loan.

Because Greyhound was MCI's major customer, the relationship between Fay and Zoltok grew in the post-war years, leading to a very important opportunity. Zoltok confided to Fay that he was growing restive with his partners in the business.

Acquiring MCI

Diversification was the post-war business trend and Fay saw a chance for Greyhound to control its vehicle supply and avoid restrictive duties on imported American coaches. It also seemed likely that MCI would not be able to grow fast enough on its own to supply all of Greyhound's needs. MCI was then producing a coach about every two weeks.

However, because the potential cost to buy MCI made the earlier bus line acquisitions pale by comparison, Fay would have to sell the idea to parent company the Greyhound Corporation, which had acquired his company in 1940.

The Resolution

Apparently he was very convincing. On July 14, 1948 a meeting of the Corporation's board of directors passed a resolution approving Greyhound to acquire controlling interest in MCI. The resolution read in part:

Resolved, that this board does hereby recommend that Western Canadian Greyhound Lines, Ltd. enter into an agreement with Harry Zoltok for the purchase from him of 353,314 shares of the capital stock of Motor Coach Industries Limited . . . of which 3,314 shares are to be purchased immediately for a price of 25 cents per share, and the balance of 350,000 shares are to be purchased in instalments as and when requested by the vendor within 30 days after receipt of audit of the financial condition of said company at the end of its fiscal years ending each of the years 1949 to 1957, at prices equal to the book value of said shares at the end of the last fiscal year preceding the time of purchase, plus 10 cents per share, which agreement is to provide that certificates representing the shares to be so purchased are to be deposited in escrow pending delivery of the same, that no dividends may be paid by Motor Coach Industries Limited prior to the close of the fiscal year ending in 1955, and is to contain other provisions for the protection of Western Canadian Greyhound Lines, Ltd., deemed advisable by counsel.

To finance the purchase, Greyhound had to pay roughly $130,000 up front and assume some $100,000 of MCI's outstanding liabilities. Greyhound's U.S. parent, The Greyhound Corporation, had to guarantee these funds to make the deal possible.

Other provisions arranged for a purchase of part of the stock held by one of Zoltok's partners, Philip Kurtz, and for all of the stock held by the other five shareholders on basically the same terms. Fred Sicinski immediately retired and Zoltok took over the presidency.

THE 1950s

Greyhound's fleet was in an admirable position in 1950. Its refurbished fleet was almost entirely composed of post-war MCI vehicles, mostly Courier 100 and 200 models with 33-passenger and 37-passenger payloads. This new, modern 129-vehicle fleet was worth $2.71 million.

The new MCI equipment that came into service after the war made life considerably easier for Greyhound drivers. Improved seating and suspension resulted in far fewer back ailments, new power steering eliminated the "wrestling" required in older

Motor Coach Industries' assembly plant, ca. 1950

buses, and improvements in heating and ventilation made the coach a much more tolerable work place.

MCI was prospering. Under Zoltok's leadership, MCI now had two plants in operation, each capable of producing a vehicle in less than a week. This was a vast improvement over the two weeks required to produce just one vehicle in the early 1940s.

As well, MCI was diversifying its product line. After the war, as Canada began to upgrade and pave its road systems, the company began to fabricate road-building machinery. MCI followed this up by developing a whole line of pole line hardware, such as streetlight and overhead powerline standards, extruded aluminum window frames for both commercial and home use, and metal grain boxes. Later the company acquired subsidiary National Porcelain of Medicine Hat, which made electrical insulators.

However, the company remained first and foremost a bus builder, and Zoltok was constantly considering improvements. MCI soon developed an advanced bus with several improvements over the Courier 100s and 200s – the smaller, lighter weight 50-85 series. Greyhound immediately began to try them out, ordering four 37-passenger models at a unit cost of $25,380 in 1950.

That November, Greyhound completed the MCI acquisition begun two years ago in 1948, acquiring the remaining 20,000 shares in Philip Kurtz's hands.

Bringing Brewster into the Fold

During 1950 MCI was involved in helping former Greyhound rival and now subsidiary Brewster Transport rebuild its fleet. Unlike Greyhound, Brewster had suffered a major blow during the war because of regulations forbidding the use of buses for sightseeing purposes. Brewster eventually sold off much of its fleet, and after the war it moved strongly to re-equip.

Following the European trend, Brewster decided to use the "skyview roof" in most of its new equipment, eliminating the need for buses with convertible roofs. Made using Plexiglas panels in the arched ceiling of the coach, the skyview allowed magnificent views of the Canadian Rockies scenery.

At first, Brewster went to Zoltok's foremost Winnipeg competitor, Western Auto and Truck Body Works, for the first skyview roof coaches. Western Auto's coaches were cheaper than MCI's but used the old system of separate bodies and chassis.

In 1950, with its post-war financial recovery in hand, Brewster turned to MCI's more expensive model 85 vehicles, purchasing two "Courier Skyviews" for $17,635 each. Brewster would go on to buy many more MCI coaches.

MCI produced two Courier Skyviews for Brewster Transport in 1950

Dieselization

The development of the diesel engine promised lower fuel consumption and fuel cost than the conventional gasoline-powered motor. In Europe, where fuel costs were high, diesel engines began to be adopted in the late thirties. However, it was initially rejected in North America because of the roughness of the engine when running at low speed and the strong smell of the exhaust.

The Greyhound Corporation's engineers identified some improvements, and in 1939 General Motors produced the corporation's first diesel engines. These achieved fuel economies of up to 40 per cent, and by the end of the war Greyhound affiliates had more than 1,500 diesel coaches and was placing orders for 1,500 more. The war itself made diesel the universal motive power for military equipment on land and sea.

In contrast, dieselization in western Canada was delayed by the post-war discovery of Alberta oil and the resulting relatively cheap fuel costs. It wasn't until 1951 that MCI offered its first diesel bus for the Canadian market. The coach was a model 85 equipped with a Cummins diesel engine and listed $2,000 cheaper than the regular model. That October Greyhound purchased one to try out on an experimental basis.

George Mermet with a Courier 85, 1954

Courier Model 95

MCI's production and repertoire were expanding and its customer portfolio was growing with it.

In 1952 MCI entered a contract with the Department of Defence Production to manufacture 1,275 quarter ton cargo trailers. It also accepted an order from Provincial Transport Co. of Montreal for fifty buses costing a total of $1.25 million payable at 25% down with the balance in monthly payments over five years, the balance due bearing 5.5 % interest.

During 1952 MCI also sold up to eight buses to SMT (Eastern) Ltd., one to Cities Bus Services Limited, Sarnia, and five model 95s to New England Greyhound Lines, Incorporated, marking MCI's first sale to a Greyhound affiliate in the United States.

The model 95 Courier was designed especially for use with diesel engines – one of the first such buses in Canada – while delivering a new level of luxury and comfort. Powered by a four-cylinder General Motors diesel engine (a first for MCI), the model 95 had increased room for baggage storage, larger windows, modern styling, and a better heating system. The 95 was designed to carry 37 passengers, but MCI also offered a thirty-five foot extended version that carried forty-one passengers.

In December 1953, Greyhound placed an order for nineteen 37-passenger model 95s at a base cost of $26,332. The order was worth more than half a million dollars. Greyhound went on to purchase eighteen model 95ADs in November 1954 at a base cost of $26,332 and twenty model 95REs in November 1955 at a base cost of $29,149.

Air Suspension

In the late 50s MCI finally replaced its highly successful model 95 with the 96. The 96's most outstanding feature was the introduction of air suspension.

This new system featured air springs, a type of heavy rubber bellows, mounted on the axles of the vehicle. Each air spring received its supply of air from a reservoir pressurized at 100 psi. The air suspension kept the level and height of the bus constant as the passenger load increased or decreased pressure on the air springs. This gave a smooth, comfortable ride whatever the payload. Greyhound ordered twenty-nine model 96s in 1957.

MCI Purchased Outright

In August 1957, under the reorganization that created Greyhound Lines of Canada, Zoltok's remaining 350,000 shares were purchased for $500,000. It was a far cry from the book value of 25 cents plus a 10-cent profit originally offered him in 1948.

Greyhound now owned MCI outright, almost a decade after first acquiring controlling interest in 1948.

Answering the G.M. Challenge

MCI was keenly aware of and eager to challenge General Motors' position as North America's largest coach manufacturer. During the fifties, GM introduced two models, the 4104 and the 4501 Scenicruiser, setting the stage for fresh competition.

GM's 4104 model was the first to feature large picture-style tinted windows rather than individual passenger windows. More importantly, the 4104 was one of the first coaches to offer onboard toilet facilities, an important break-through in passenger comfort.

The 4501 Scenicruiser offered the same advantages in a raised level passenger compartment. GM heavily promoted this unique design as providing improved passenger comfort and sightseeing potential, hence the name "Scenicruiser".

THE 1960s

MC-1 Challenger

Realizing that MCI could not challenge both GM models, Bob Borden, Lorne Frizzell and Harry Zoltok decided MCI should emulate the 4104 and build it better than the competition. In 1959 MCI introduced the MC-1 Challenger.

The MC-1 was the first to use stainless steel for the bus's lower structure as well as the exterior panels, giving complete corrosion control. MCI soon released other models in the Challenger series, and in 1961 Greyhound purchased ten MC-2 buses with V-6 engines and washrooms at $42,000 each. Greyhound Corporation's subsidiary, Eastern Canadian Greyhound, purchased six at the same time. And in November 1961 Greyhound bought ten of the MC-3 model.

In June 1962, Greyhound used the latest Challenger buses to inaugurate the new Trans Canada service. Fresh off the MCI production line, the thoroughly modern buses made an impact:

> The buses will be Greyhound's recently introduced "Challenger" buses equipped with restrooms, picture windows with shaded glass, adjustable seats, individual lighting and ventilation. Many will be air-conditioned.

While the early Challengers certainly could not dislodge GM's control of the North American market (only 189 units of the MC-1 to MC-4 models were built), they did achieve their purpose. The Challenger proved that MCI could make a more durable, longer-lasting bus with a superior maintenance record to comparable GM coaches.

Switching Loyalties

At this time the Greyhound Corporation's fleet was almost exclusively made up of thousands of GM coaches. If the Corporation could be convinced to switch from GM, subsidiary MCI would have a shot at the big leagues of bus building.

With this strategy in mind, Greyhound continually brought MCI and the Challenger's performance record to president Frederick Ackerman's attention and the Corporation began to take notice. But MCI's lower production was an obstacle.

To get around this, Greyhound proposed to the Corporation to have the coaches built in the United States rather than in Canada. In February 1961 Greyhound Lines of Canada's board resolved to build an assembly plant in Pembina, North Dakota, just across the border south of Winnipeg, and to enlarge the present MCI production facilities in Winnipeg. The facilities investment was budgeted at $425,000.

The enlarged Winnipeg plant would concentrate on producing bus shells. The shells would then be trucked to Pembina and assembled for sale in the States. Even though the Greyhound Corporation owned the Pembina plant, MCI managed the entire operation from its Winnipeg headquarters. It was an innovative approach that worked well and eventually helped make the MCI coach the Greyhound Corporation's bus.

MC-5 Breakthrough

After working out Challenger's bugs through models MC-1 to MC-4, the company began producing a new coach, the MC-5, in 1964. This bus would lead the breakthrough in the American market that Borden, Frizzell and Zoltok sought when they pushed for the Pembina plant.

The upgraded Winnipeg plant, now employing 503 workers, more than double the previous staff of 233, could now turn out a bus shell a day. Some 200 per year were sent to the United States plant for assembly, while the remainder were finished in Canada.

Greyhound ordered its first eighteen MC-5s, complete with washrooms and air conditioning, in November 1963 at a unit cost of $52,575. The following summer, Borden requested authority from the board to purchase eighteen more, pointing out that only fifty-six coaches in the fleet had air-conditioning, a feature the travelling public now considered a necessity. These thirty-six MC-5s cost almost $2 million, which the company partially offset by selling twenty older coaches for $200,000.

Trucking bus shell from Winnipeg to Pembina, 1968

Thanks to the MC-5 and MC-5A series, MCI achieved phenomenal growth. Almost every year the plant expanded and production increased. In just two years plant capacity doubled to two bus shells per day and MCI added another 300 employees.

Greyhound continued to buy the MC-5A Challengers, ordering twenty-two in late 1965, four of which were intended exclusively for the rapidly growing highway tours business. Greyhound's fleet was now 167 strong, seventy-nine of which were air-conditioned. This trend continued and in 1966 Greyhound bought thirty-eight buses and in 1967 a record forty-four.

Meanwhile, some of Greyhound's older buses went to Brewster Transport for conversion into sight-seeing buses. Seven used MCI model 96 Couriers were sold to Brewster in 1966, who had Beverley Bus and Truck Body in Winnipeg install the Plexiglas tops. These converted coaches were so successful that ten more used units were purchased from Greyhound in 1967 for conversion. By 1980 MCI had sold 2,000 MC-5s.

MC-6 Supercruiser

In 1966, MCI celebrated the completion of its 1,000th MC-5 coach shell. However, the industry now wanted a larger vehicle than this thirty-five foot model.

Back in 1963 MCI had started work on an experimental bus initially called the X-6. Designed to challenge GM's popular, but smaller Scenicruiser in the long haul market, the X-6 was a monster: forty feet long, twelve feet high and 102 inches wide, at a time

Greyhound brochure for the MC-6

when the maximum permitted coach width was 96 inches.

Unfortunately, problems soon arose. First of all, the size of the bus forced MCI's engineers to research every engine made in North American and Europe before settling on a Detroit Diesel V-12, beginning an enduring association.

Secondly, to accommodate production of the new coach, now named the MC-6 Supercruiser, MCI undertook an extensive and expensive building and remodelling programme on its plants. In 1966, MCI built a $1.4 million addition to the Winnipeg plant as well as a new 157,000 square foot plant in suburban Fort Garry for $2.6 million.

When the new coach came off the assembly line in 1969, it was an absolute wonder with many features not found on any other contemporary bus. These included an entirely stainless steel framework; rear suspension supports at full body width providing an extremely comfortable ride; separate air conditioning, heating and defrosting systems in the driver's area; and a power operated sedan-type entrance door.

In May 1969 Greyhound put its fifteen new Supercruisers into service on the Toronto-Vancouver

The MC-6 in production

and Edmonton-Calgary runs. Press, government and industry representatives were invited to receptions in nine major cities to view the beautiful new bus.

This public relations effort was backed by a national advertising campaign that featured popular Canadian singer Tommy Hunter in a cross-country concert tour. During the tour Tommy cut a 45 single, "Nowhere Bound with Greyhound", with "I Can't Find a Place to Park my Car" on the B-side.

Regulatory Problems

Unfortunately, although the public loved the spacious and comfortable new coach, U.S. regulatory agencies were not so enthusiastic. Design and production had gone ahead on the assumption that maximum coach height and width restrictions would be relaxed, but this was not the case. Although the coach was free to operate in Canada, in the United States operation was severely limited to certain western states and to the Pennsylvania Turnpike and New York Thruway in the east.

Additionally, the coach's size and engine made it very fuel inefficient. In the U.S, the engines were eventually replaced with V-8s and automatic transmissions. After the years of development and capital invested in the MC-6, production was halted at 100 units.

MC-7 Challenger Scenicruiser

While the MC-6 prototype was being developed, Greyhound management hedged its bets and MCI began developing and testing the MC-7 coach. This was a forty-foot long version of the MC-5 with some of the MC-6 improvements and took less than a year to finalize. In June 1968 the first units rolled off the Fort Gary assembly line.

The 47-passenger MC-7 Challenger Scenicruiser was MCI's first three-axle, forty foot coach, featuring several industry firsts. These included high level seating, larger luggage compartments, a two-level roof line, optional automatic transmission, in-station heating, air conditioning and lighting, flush-type lavatory and sealed double-glazed sash. The high level seating avoided wheel-well intrusion into the passenger floor and also permitted baggage compartments under the bus. For the first time anywhere, MCI also introduced a 100,000 mile one-year warranty with its new model.

Greyhound purchased its first fifteen MC-7s in May 1968 and would acquire many more in the succeeding years. The bus was immediately accepted in the United States and firmly established MCI's reputation in the American market. In October 1972 the 2,000[th] unit was completed and that same year the first offshore sales were made to Australia and Hawaii.

The MC-7 established MCI's reputation in the American coach market

THE 1970s
MC-8 Crusader

MC-7 sales probably would have gone to sell many more than their eventual 2,550 but for the introduction in 1973 of the successor model, the MC-8 Crusader. Like all other MCI coaches, the Crusader was promoted for its style, comfort and safety:

The Crusader is a big, bold, contemporary bus with clean, uninterrupted lines. Fads and frills have been avoided. The anodized aluminum black window treatment underlines a look of great distinction and provides a sunglass effect for passengers.

Inside: more legroom, more view, more cushioned comfort and a quieter ride. Sculptured lines, spirited colors and the soft glow of concealed lighting give total harmony.

Safety features are tailored to increase driver efficiency. Controls are in the most natural, reachable positions. The driver has separate, adjustable air-conditioning to maintain alertness. Audible warning signals and automatic transmission enable the driver to keep his eyes on the road, his hands on the wheel.

The overall result is a unique bus – "the Best Bus ever Built."

Obviously the industry agreed, and between 1973 and 1978 a total of 4,475 MC-8 Crusaders were built. At the same time, in 1973 MCI bought Frank Fair Industries, a bus parts manufacturer in Winnipeg, to further control its supply chain.

Management Changes

By 1969 Harry Zoltok had reached Greyhound's mandatory retirement age, but there was no one at MCI sufficiently trained to succeed him. As a result Zoltok was asked to stay on so successors could be groomed to fill out the management team.

For personal reasons, Zoltok retired in 1971 and Bob Borden had to take over the presidency of the company as an interim measure. George Mason, former chief engineer, was appointed vice president and general manager and after two years he was named MCI's new president and chief operating officer. A t the same time Borden became chairman of the board and chief executive officer.

In late 1969, Lorne Frizzell left Greyhound after thirty-one years in maintenance and operations. Ever conscious of the need to keep his machines on the road, Frizzell was responsible for Greyhound's fine record of minimal time lost with equipment down for repairs. As well, he took a very active role in deciding the requirements as MCI developed each new coach.

Frizzell's desire to protect Greyhound's image of dependability led to the circulation of a possibly apocryphal story. Apparently a Greyhound bus broke down just west of Banff and was parked by some trees just off the highway. When Frizzell learned of the breakdown, he immediately hopped in his car, drove to the site and cut down some dead trees to cover the bus so that it couldn't be seen by the passing public.

MCI Goes on Strike

MCI workers were first unionized in 1943 by the Motor Coach Workers Union, Federal Local No. 147, an affiliate of the Trades and Labour Congress of Canada. In 1950 this union was replaced by the International Association of Machinists, Red River Local No. 1953 for MCI's hourly workers.

Bargaining with this union was traditionally tough, but agreements had always been reached over the years without a single strike. This record was broken in late October 1970 when the workers went on strike for two-and-a-half months.

A settlement was finally reached ratifying a three-year contract, and the company naturally hoped that future negotiations would avoid such disruptions. The annual report pointed out that despite the strike MCI had experienced one of its most successful years ever, achieving record production levels, and predicting that by 1971 the company would be producing three bus shells a day.

Unfortunately, MCI was back on strike three years later when the contract expired. This strike lasted for almost three-and-a-half months and the contract that ended it was very expensive. Again, Greyhound's annual report cited record earnings despite the strike. To illustrate its faith in MCI's future, Greyhound also reported that MCI had acquired a subsidiary, Frank Fair Industries Ltd., a Winnipeg bus components manufacturer.

Unfortunately, these two very serious strikes had taken their toll in increased operating costs, poor labour-management relations and lost confidence. Greyhound's parent, the Greyhound Corporation, decided to dilute the risk.

New Roswell Plant

At the board meeting on July 1974, James Kerrigan, the Corporation's executive vice president for transportation, presented a contract between the company and a newly-organized subsidiary of the Greyhound

Corporation. Named the Transportation Manufacturing Corporation, this subsidiary would build MCI buses at a new plant in Roswell, New Mexico.

Citing MCI's recent problems with labour, resulting in the most expensive settlement in its history, and the fact that the Canadian government had recently conducted a very successful raid on key MCI employees, Kerrigan said the Corporation had decided that it was necessary to have a secondary facility available outside Canada to protect the future interests of Greyhound Lines, Inc., the major purchaser of MCI products.

Initially, the parts for the TMC buses would be built in Canada and shipped to New Mexico for assembly, but it was indicated that TMC would begin fabricating its own parts and components as soon as possible. TMC would equip itself by purchasing idle jigs and machinery from one of MCI's two Fort Garry assembly lines, allowing it to produce one bus shell a day.

The Canadian response indicated that while they were not particularly pleased with this development, they recognized that "there was no question about the propriety of establishing another facility in the United States." However, they tried to make the best deal possible for the public shareholders, obtaining an agreement for TMC to pay cost plus 8% for all component parts and assemblies and even a royalty of $750 for each MCI bus TMC manufactured.

Somewhat taken back, Gerald Trautman pointed out that it was most unusual for a Greyhound subsidiary to pay a royalty to another subsidiary, but "he would approve it in this case in deference to the opinion of the Canadian directors that the royalty is necessary in the interest of the minority shareholders."

Brewster's Columbia Icefield Operations

Greyhound subsidiary Brewster Transport continued to convert used Greyhound coaches for sightseeing. In fact, 1974 marked Brewster's first purchase of new sightseeing equipment in many years, three MC-5Bs.

As well, Brewster needed equipment for its expanded winter operations, particularly its high-altitude Sunshine Village ski service. Sightseeing buses were inadequate for this task, so in 1973 the company purchased seven new Taylor school buses, which delivered high performance on steep grades. However, Brewster's most unusual service was its snowmobile operation.

In 1952, a Jasper businessman obtained a government concession to offer snowmobile sightseeing tours on the Columbia Icefield. He built up the oper-

A Brewster Foremost snowmobile, 1971

ation over the years, and in 1968 it included fourteen Bombardier vehicles and a staff camp housing seventy-five summer employees.

That year he gave Brewster Transport an option to purchase, and Jack Hayes managed to convince his board that the service would fit in well with Brewster's existing Columbia Icefield Chalet operation. The new subsidiary, called Columbia Icefield Snowmobile Tours, Ltd., initially used the Bombardiers, but as the tours grew in popularity the fleet began to run short of demand.

Hayes then approached Foremost, a Calgary-based company that manufactured tracked vehicles for oilfield use, and got them to design a passenger-carrying body fitted on their vehicle's chassis. Two were built in 1970-71, one for 28 passengers, the other for 40 passengers, and they soon went to work carrying tourists over the deeply-creased ice of the Athabasca Glacier.

In 1976 Brewster provided Foremost with two model 96 Courier bus shells to mount on their chassis, creating 40-passenger snowmobiles. Columbia Icefield Snowmobile Tours now boasted total seating capacity of 308 in answer to the growing demand to see the icefield.

More MCI Innovations

In 1976, MCI began building new "skyview" sight-seeing buses based on its MC-5 and MC-8 models. The same year it delivered ten new "Combo" 30-passenger buses with large freight capacity to Greyhound.

This was a similar adaptation to the one practised by Canadian Coachways in 1951 on some MCI Courier 85s. Because Coachways depended so heavily on its package express service to cross-subsidize its lightly-populated northern routes, it bulk-headed two 85s to create a large express area behind the passenger compartment, reducing the seating from thirty-seven to twenty-nine.

MC-9 Crusader

In 1977 MCI introduced an updated version of the MC-5, the MC-5C, a 39-passenger coach designed especially for airport and charter service. The MC-5C replaced the MC-5B, which was built from 1971 to 1977. Then, in 1978 MCI introduced a new model, the MC-9 Crusader II, which offered many improvements over the MC-8. These included tall picture-frame passenger windows four inches higher than the MC-8 windows, and new parcel racks with passenger reading lights and public address speakers.

Continuing its fleet replacement program, Greyhound took delivery of thirty-five MC-9s. These coaches cost almost $150,000 each, a far cry from the MC-7's $65,000 price tag twelve years earlier.

In fact, the MC-9 was so popular that almost the entire 1979 production was on order before the end of 1978. MCI finished the decade with an unprecedented production of 1,450 shells in 1979, and would go on to sell almost 10,000 over ten years. It became the best selling coach in North America.

MCI also moved to address the specialty market, selling two buses a month to companies, entertainment groups and private individuals, as well as enjoying strong offshore sales with a contract to sell fifty MC-5s in Taiwan and 197 in Saudi Arabia in 1978.

THE 1980s

The Recession Hits

MCI's growth came screeching to a halt when the recession hit in the early 1980s and dried up the North American market for new buses. Production figures plummeted from a high of 1,600 bus shells in 1981 to 1,000 in 1982 and just 766 in 1983. Gross revenues sank $95 million in 1981 to $75 million in 1983.

However, despite the softening of the travel market Greyhound remained committed to keeping the average fleet age under six years. Forty new MC-9s were ordered in 1981, forty more in 1982 and twenty in 1983.

Model 96A3

After celebrating its 5000th MC-9, MCI developed the model 96A3, a new futuristic-style bus, 96″ wide with 3 axles, released in October 1984. The 96A3 and the two-axle 96A2 were based on the MC-9 but with considerably more glass. Greyhound ordered twenty-five in February 1985.

MCI's new 96A3, 1984

102 Series

In 1985 MCI produced the 102A3, 102″ wide with 3 axles, to satisfy the growing demand for roomier coaches. Along with the greater width these coaches included more luxury detailing and customizable options. The 102A3 became MCI's biggest seller until the 102C3 was introduced in 1988.

Developed for the tour market, the fully-paintable 102C3 featured higher headroom, greater

Coach #810, an MCI 102A3 used in Expo '86 service, at Point Gray Park. In the background are Grouse Mountain (left) and North Vancouver (right)

forward visibility, optional galleys, video and stereo systems and conference seating. It was so popular it represented 37% of MCI's total coach production in its 1st year.

The 102C3 was followed in 1989 by the 102C3SS, a stainless steel version which became the overall sales volume leader in the industry. These three models – the 102AE, 102C3 and 102C3SS – represented 75% of MCI's production in 1989. That year MCI controlled 70% of the North American market and sold 1200 coaches.

Market Control

In 1986, the now very diversified Greyhound Corporation sold off the American Greyhound operation while retaining Greyhound Canada and MCI. This unexpectedly cut the ties between MCI and the U.S. Greyhound company, for decades its largest customer. However, two years later, General Motors sold their bus division to MCI. It had accomplished the goal it set in 1959 when it launched the MC-1 Challenger against GM's 4104 – virtually complete control of the market.

RENEWED COMMITMENT

1989 was a very important year for the Greyhound fleet. Under a new president and management team crackling with energy, the company undertook several major infrastructure, operational and attitudinal initiatives to improve the quality of the business and increase customer satisfaction. This strategy included upgrading the fleet.

52 coaches worth $13.5 million were ordered. Delivered from MCI in time for the Christmas rush, the new "jet-like coaches" included wider, plusher seats, increased legroom, upholstered walls, personal headphones and movies. The company even experimented with an on-board refreshment galley and personal attendant.

To help deliver the best experience for the passenger, senior vice president of marketing John Munro asked the five largest bus seat manufacturers in the world to sell Greyhound their research on bus seats. He wanted to identify the most comfortable seats for short- and long-haul travel, such as 3 hours vs. 12 hours. Munro had to go to extraordinary lengths to convince the manufacturers to engage in the research and provide samples for testing, but the end result was a better, more ergonomic seat.

The new fleet made an immediate impact and passengers responded with praise and enthusiasm. The movies were so popular that Greyhound commit-

Coach #593, an MC-9, travelling on the Icefields Parkway below the Sawtooth Range near Banff, AB, ca. 1989

ted to outfit 25% of the fleet within two years. 97% of passengers said the video made the trip shorter and more enjoyable.

The following year Greyhound spent $7.6 million to purchase another 40 new coaches. These fleet renewals brought down the age of the fleet, helping reduce maintenance and out-of-service costs.

102DL3

In 1990 MCI produced its first 45-foot prototype coach, the 102DL3, "L" referring to its length. The following year restrictions on coach length were relaxed to 45´, and MCI began production in 1992. Popular for long-haul runs and the charter market, its 102˝ width provided extra side room for passengers and has since become standard.

At the same time, MCI was working on a wheelchair-accessible coach. With financial help from the Canadian federal government, a fully accessible prototype was developed based on the 102C3 and was presented in the summer of 1990. Able to accommodate two wheelchairs onboard at a time, the coach included a wheelchair lift designed to be stored in the baggage bay during transit, and a fully accessible washroom.

More Fleet Upgrades

Greyhound continued the fleet upgrades in 1991 with a purchase of 30 new coaches that came into service just in time for the Christmas travel period. In 1992 the company renovated eighty coaches, adding amenities such as video capability, headphones and better seats. This was followed by another purchase of 10 coaches in December 1992.

At the same time the company installed a new computerized maintenance system to track breakdowns, campaigns, inspections, etc. This injected much-needed reliability into the maintenance accounting function, helping remove uncertainty and facilitating the budget process.

MCI Spin-Off

In late 1993 the Greyhound Corporation, now called the Dial Corporation, began the process to spin off its MCI subsidiary. The Corporation had become more involved in consumer and food products beginning years before and continued to divest its now non-core transportation assets.

Dial created a separate corporation called MCII (Motor Coach Industries International), incorporating MCI, TMC, and other companies, including Custom Coach Corp. and Hausman Bus Sales. This was announced on December 29, 1992, approved by the shareholders on February 4, 1993, and was effective April 30, 1993. The spin-off included a legacy program committing Greyhound Canada to acquire 75% of its new coach requirements from MCI from 1993 to 2002.

MCI and Prevost Coaches

In 1995, Greyhound bought 35 new MCI coaches, allowing the company to retire more of its older equipment, and in 1996 the company planned to buy 10 new Prevost coaches, bringing the total Greyhound fleet to 370 coaches. The MCI purchase included fifteen 45-foot 54-passenger video-equipped coaches with greater under-belly luggage and courier express room, and twenty 40-foot 44-passenger coaches with the same amenities. Fourteen of the coaches were equipped with wheelchair lifts.

In 1997 the company's annual report proudly related that "a substantial portion of Greyhound Canada Transportation Corp.'s fleet of 359 buses have our new plush interiors and onboard entertainment systems, such as video movies and audio channels all with the convenience of headsets."

Safety manager John Coombs and driver Ross Mark demonstrating the wheelchair lift on coach #986, 1999

Going Forward

Today, Greyhound Canada is upgrading and replacing its fleet with MCI's new G4500 55-passenger model launched in 2001. The G4500 offers a quieter ride, excellent fuel economy, a wheelchair-accessible option, and increased baggage capacity for the long-haul market.

To support its fleet, in 2003 the company implemented a new Total Quality Management program (TQM) to enhance the maintenance process. Under TQM, through training and concentrated assignment of work, Greyhound's mechanics become experts on specific coach systems, such as air conditioning, powertrain and electrical/video. These and other changes will help us better manage and reduce out-of-service levels and improve the overall condition of our buses over the long term.

As well, Greyhound is investigating a range of special amenities and e-services for implementation in our corridors. These could include laptop plug-ins, satellite Internet/email connections, work and meeting tables, audio-visual equipment and other services, depending on the market served. Maintaining and improving our fleet is key to our service, and we will continue to provide an attractive, comfortable and safe travelling environment that fulfills the needs of our passengers.

CHAPTER SIX

GREYHOUND COURIER EXPRESS (GCX)

Greyhound Canada has provided courier service to Canadians since its inception in 1929. We have hauled everything from newspapers and farm equipment parts to flowers, whisky, baby chickens and blood donations.

Today our modern fleet of 93 pup trailers delivers same-day, next day, station-to-station and door-to-door services to hundreds of communities across Canada. We also provide international service from major hubs in Vancouver, Calgary, Edmonton, Winnipeg and Toronto, and in August 2003 we launched a domestic air service providing overnight air service between these hubs.

Greyhound Courier Express is a important part of Greyhound Canada's operations and is very well known particularly in Western Canada.

First Paper Route

Initially, Greyhound's parcel service was extremely fragmented, an informal sideline. Aside from errand work for local farmers, Greyhound's first formal service was for the newspapers. In return for delivering the paper along several rural routes, Greyhound received free advertising during its formative years. While this was good business, the early drivers considered it a nuisance, disliking having to slow down at each farm to throw the paper. Later, a spring-loaded launcher attached to the coach window helped make the task a little easier.

Cardston Mail Contract

In the late 1930s Greyhound took on a contract to deliver the Royal Mail to Cardston, Alberta from the Lethbridge depot. This contract became an expensive, frustrating burden during the infamous winter of 1937. That January and February the harsh road

Winter conditions near Lethbridge, 1937

and weather conditions made running the service almost impossible, and a complaint to the district director of postal services elicited the following reports from Greyhound superintendent R.F. "Blondy" Jacques, one of the company's original drivers.

Jan 1st-12th: O.K. both ways.

Jan 13th: Both trips cancelled. No one carried mail.

Jan 14th: (mail came in on train) Incoming Coach 23 left at Spring Coulee broken rear spring. Driver came in with Cooper's truck, took over 8 hrs.

Jan 15th: O. K. both ways.

Jan 16th: O.K. coming into Lethbridge. Outgoing went out 15 miles and to turn back on account of blizzard.

Jan 17th-18th: No trips. All cancelled.

Jan 19th: No incoming trip. Out-going carrying all mail with Chev sedan overloading. Had to come back from 12 miles out, held mail on bus overnight.

Jan 20th: O.K.

Jan 21st-29th: No trips. Train started carrying mail on Jan. 22nd.

Jan 30th: Outgoing O.K. to Magrath. Carried mail as far Magrath. No incoming.

Jan 31st: Run only to Magrath.

Similar interruptions in service occurred until March 9th when the weather problems ended. In his report, Jacques summed up the extra expenses the company incurred in trying to sustain the service:

1st day we had 8 men shovelling snow digging out road Magrath south so's to get the bus running to Cardston. Paid these men $2.00 per day and bought them meals. 50 cents per meal – $24.

2nd day had 6 men at $2.00 per day and a meal – $15.

Run co. Chev sedan 7 round trips Leth to Magrath to inspect road and help with shovelling out highway.

3 R.T. with #3 hauling men to work onroad.

Round trip and V2 train fare Leth to Cardston. Driver riding train with mail.

Around about $15.00 phone calls concerning roads, mail etc.

Roughly $7.00 paid for meals for passengers while bus was held up on Highway or in towns.

Besides these expenses, Greyhound had to bear the cost to have trucks pick up the mail at the railway station and deliver it to the post office.

Growth in the Late 60s

Aside from local contracts such as these and a steady flow of ad-hoc work on the rural routes, Greyhound's parcel express service did not become a significant division until the sixties. It took on a higher profile in 1962 when the Trans-Canada Highway opened. Canada was experiencing interruptions in mail service due to the Canada Post strikes, and Greyhound's ability to deliver parcels throughout most of Canada on the highway made the service much more marketable.

In 1965, Greyhound's package express revenues generated a 24% increase over the previous year, and in 1967 they increased another 12%. That year Greyhound introduced "Greyhound International Package Express", a complete customs brokerage service for companies shipping packages into Canada from the U.S. Greyhound's express services. Originally begun as a convenience to its customers, it had grown to the point where they were competing with the railway on small freight.

More Canada Post Strikes

Canada Post's labour unrest continued, and in 1975 the union went on strike for 42 days. Faced with continued high demand, Greyhound set up parcel express offices at its terminals. In 1977, the company recorded $14.8 million in parcel express sales, making it Greyhound's second largest revenue source ahead of charter and tours.

Another 40-day postal strike in 1981 helped increase Greyhound's parcel express revenues by 16%.

In 1984 Greyhound introduced freight trucks in British Columbia

*Package express conveyor system in
the new Calgary depot, 1986*

The following year, perceiving increasing competition in the inter-city courier market, Greyhound implemented a pick-up and delivery service for the residential and commercial markets.

Despite the recession that followed, parcel express revenue continued to grow. The company entered an interline programme with Air Canada to provide better service between major cities and rural communities. As well, in 1984 Greyhound bought four specially designed freight trucks to serve the major freight routes in British Columbia. These were designed to carry sixteen lightweight aluminum containers with a total load capacity of 1,900 cubic feet.

The business continued to quietly grow until 1989, when the adoption of a revolutionary business model turned the business on its head.

The Loomis Business Model

Greyhound's freight business had become a serious revenue source but it wasn't professionally handled. Tracing packages was very difficult and the company didn't have a solid system for handling overloads.

In 1989, president Dick Huisman brought former Loomis executive Ron Parker onboard as senior vice-president and general manager of Greyhound Courier Express. Considering the size of the Greyhound network, its 24-hour, seven-day-a-week operation, and the built-in cost structure, Parker felt the time was right to build parcel express into a separate product line.

He hired compatriots Ken Quirk, Randy Motley and Murray Glass, and began turning the parcel express service into what some called "Loomis II".

Infrastructure Improvements

That year, Greyhound began a massive $14 million program of facility, equipment and service improvements, including new "cross-dock" terminals and storefronts, as well as a new Calgary call centre.

Ron Parker designed the new cross-docks, using the "hub" concept developed by then U.S. courier giant Federal Express, to facilitate fast and easy sorting of parcels between trucks using a system of conveyor belts and docks. Cross-docks were built on Pegasus Road near the Calgary airport and in Vancouver, with more planned for Edmonton, Winnipeg and Toronto.

*Greyhound and Air Canada formed a package
express interline agreement in the early eighties*

*Greyhound Courier Express.
Calgary cross-docks, March 1990*

*New Greyhound Courier Express look, ca. 1990
McLeod Trail agency, Calgary*

Door-to-Door Service

In 1989 Greyhound also introduced its first door-to-door service, in addition to the company's traditional depot-to-depot and city-to-city service, and supported it with a complete rate sheet touted as the "simplest matrix in Canada".

To accommodate the freight overloads as the business grew, the company hired owner-operators to deliver the freight at the local level using their own equipment.

One of the Greyhound Package Express transport trucks

1989 Results

With this new operating plan, volumes grew very quickly. That year Greyhound Courier Express (GCX) grew sales by 25% and moved 7 million parcels across the 18,500 mile network. It was ranked as the 5th largest Canadian courier operator, "holding 50% of the depot-to-depot market and a small percentage of the door-to-door market".

In early 1990, Greyhound entered interline agreements with Ontario, Quebec and Maritime carriers, expanding the company's reach and making it possible to provide coast-to-coast courier service. These included an agreement with Gray Coach Lines, Limited on February 1, 1990 and an exclusive ten-year agreement with Voyageur Colonial Limited in spring 1990.

The same year Greyhound brought on 19 Kenworth tractor-trailers as well as some five-ton trucks to handle the overflow from the increased business. Described as "high-cube" units, the tractor-trailers and trucks were intended to accommodate the "new linehaul containerization program that operates from Toronto to Vancouver".

To increase customer convenience, Greyhound opened storefronts in Regina, Saskatoon, Toronto and Vancouver and planned to open eight more in Vancouver, Calgary, Edmonton, Winnipeg and Metro Toronto by the end of the year. These storefronts were in addition to the 38 company depots and more than 500 commissioned Greyhound agents across the country.

In Vancouver, the main courier express facility was moved to the bus terminal location at the Grand Pacific Railway Station. As a result, GCX was now the only overnight parcel ground service providing next day delivery or pickup between Vancouver, Calgary and Edmonton.

Day of Reckoning

Ron Parker had gone to a lot of trouble to build a separate, parallel Greyhound Courier Express organization with its own infrastructure, management and sales force, following the Loomis business model. Unfortunately, the decision to grow the express business using trucks and tractor-trailers run by third parties dramatically increased the costs and lost the inherent synergies of running on the bus bellies.

The company had added millions of truck miles and built highly expensive infrastructure to achieve growth they ultimately couldn't afford to maintain. Although the cross-docks worked, their deliberate

*"We're Moving All The Time" – Greyhound bus, transport and van.
The additional truck miles were unsustainable*

separation from and subsequent difficulty coordinating with the bus terminals meant schedules were often missed, resulting in service failures and customer churn.

Cross-subsidization Effect

Greyhound's unhappy experience with the cross-docks underlined the importance of the "cross-subsidization effect". Essentially, this is the company's built-in ability to provide four distinct service products within the same network:

- Multiple city pairs (Origin & Destination or O&Ds) such as Calgary-Edmonton, Calgary-Vancouver, Toronto-Ottawa, etc.
- "Flow-through passenger output" outside the primary city pairs, feeding the network.
- Courier express services riding under the bus, and
- Charter work/sightseeing work, ensuring maximum fleet utilization.

This mix of services generates synergies, protecting the core route network and enhancing the efficiency and effectiveness of the carrier as a whole, by allowing the same overhead costs to be shared between multiple sources of revenue. This maximizes long-term profitability.

Subtracting the courier express business from this highly sustainable model, and then building separate stand-alone infrastructure for it dramatically increased costs and decreased efficiency. In contrast, the cross-subsidization gained by keeping courier express and passengers on the same vehicle helps support and often encourages service frequency, creating better connectivity for rural areas.

This holds particularly true in Western Canada, where population densities are often low but demand for courier express is high. The resulting volumes of courier express business make some routes profitable instead of marginally profitable or unprofitable.

In 1991 Ron Parker and the other Loomis imports left Greyhound. The company began to reintegrate the courier express business and shed the unsustainable infrastructure while developing new standard operating procedures complementary to both lines of business.

Grey Goose Partnership

In a move that foreshadowed the future integration of then Laidlaw-owned Grey Goose Bus Lines into Greyhound, in 1991 Greyhound Canada and Grey Goose began working together to streamline their package express services and introduce expanded pick-up and delivery.

Approved by Ron Parker prior to his departure, the joint initiative was based on a business plan contributed by Lorne Anthony, whose interest in creating a shared Greyhound-Grey Goose delivery operation dated back to college. Lorne Anthony later became Director, Greyhound Courier Express, a position he held until his retirement from the company in 2003. As part of the plan, the two companies split the costs to open the Stevenson Road courier express facility in Winnipeg.

Following implementation, Mike Cafferky, Grey Goose's then district director of operations, commented that "the higher level of service has resulted in growth of up to 43% per year."

1993

Thanks to strong growth in the commercial shipping market, in 1993 Greyhound experienced a 4 per cent increase in overall shipping volumes.

That year Greyhound introduced its own "COD" product. This allowed shippers to send goods on a cash-collect basis, with Greyhound collecting the money and remitting to the shipper within a specific time. In the annual report, president Huisman remarked, "Many customers have found this to be a valuable service since there is no alternative option to ship goods this way to the many Canadian locations served by Greyhound."

The company also expanded and upgraded its proprietary point-of-sale (POS) network, automating the courier express waybill transactions and making it possible to capture 90 per cent of all system courier express revenue transactions each day. This was a huge step forward for the company's ability to track and trend the courier express business and produce meaningful business information.

PUP TRAILERS

Recognizing that the attempts to increase capacity by laying on trucks and tractor-trailers could not take advantage of the bus network's inherent synergies, in 1992 Dick Huisman turned to the example of Greyhound Australia, who had begun pulling trailers behind their buses. This represented a major change for the bus industry and would require significant effort, both with the designers and with the different provincial regulatory bodies.

Roger Pike was tasked with obtaining the regulatory approvals, while Harry Fraser, who had joined Greyhound from Calgary Transit in 1991 worked with Intercontinental Truck Body (ITB), a local trailer/truck box manufacturer located in Coaldale, Alberta, to build a prototype. At the same time, MCI studied whether its frame stiffener retrofit kit would be adequate to support the pull of the trailer.

Testing the Prototype

Once the first test trailer was ready, Roger Pike made a presentation for a group of engineering and regulatory representatives from Alberta Transportation and Utilities.

The presentation included a picture of the bus and trailer in front of Castle Mountain on the Trans Canada Highway, and it went well, except for one unanswerable question: "How did you get a bus and trailer picture on a highway without a permit?" Much laughter ensued as Pike stumbled to find an answer.

Following the presentation, a temporary permit was issued specifically for testing the prototype trailer with the specific bus type. The bus and trailer were then taken to Red Deer for the Alberta Engineering group for view and testing.

The reviewers followed behind as the bus with trailer was driven on a remote stretch of highway by drivers Cliff Callaghan and Flo Gilbert. The bus and trailer were deliberately thrown from side to side during the drive to demonstrate the safety of the combination. At its conclusion the senior engineer from Alberta Engineering commented, "follows like a little puppy, don't she?"

Alberta Approval

Several further tests to determine whether the loaded trailer would exceed the gross vehicle weight when in service were so conclusively negative that Greyhound was soon granted an exemption from having to visit weight scales. After this hurdle was crossed, Alberta granted Greyhound a temporary permit to operate the trailer in live service.

Greyhound soon began operating two trailers running two trips a day between Calgary and Edmonton. Drivers were initially concerned, but as they were trained and got over the extra length, many commented that the bus/trailer combination was more stable than the bus alone. Live testing continued and in 1993 the Alberta Highway Transport Board granted its approval.

The company was very serious about the trailer project and had high hopes that it would successfully reduce truck miles. According to the annual report:

> Ultimately we envision that these trailers will replace the need for the truck operations which now transport freight which cannot be accommodated on the coaches. The associated operating savings will allow Greyhound to reduce general operating costs . . .

In 1994 Greyhound added three additional trailers from 2 different manufacturers, and finally chose one prototype from ITB to be the standard. Over 1994-1995 courier express volumes grew to the point that the division now generated almost 32% of the company's income. Since most of this was station-to-station from small shippers, no one account could have a major influence on revenues, reducing risk.

Trailer Analysis

In addition to the live testing, Greyhound commissioned a study from the National Research Council of Canada (NRC). Completed in 1995, from the abstract for the "Analysis of a Bus/Pony-Trailer Combination," "the results obtained indicated that a bus could tow a pony-trailer without degradation of the general safety performance standards of the bus. This may lead to increase of bus productivity by transporting more payloads."

Other Provincial Approvals

Using the Alberta approval as a precedent, along with the NRC analysis, Greyhound began approaching its other operating jurisdictions – British Columbia, Saskatchewan, Manitoba, Ontario, Yukon and the Northwest Territories – for their approval. Greyhound had four more trailers built with modifications based on the testing in Alberta. The process was very slow – over two years for British Columbia – but eventually each province approved the bus/trailer combination, dependent on the continuation of the temporary permit issued by Alberta.

Because Greyhound's operations at the time were focused in the west, at first there was no urgency to implement the trailers farther east than Manitoba. However, in review the numbers showed that the company was experiencing significant less-than-truckload (LTL) rentals from Manitoba to Ontario, and approval was sought in Ontario as well. By the fourth quarter of 1995 Greyhound had pup trailer operating authorities in all its jurisdictions except for Ontario, whose approval was expected in 1996. As the 1996 plan put it:

> Over the past two years we have developed a new type of pup trailer for use with coaches instead of the traditional tractor trailer combination. This new approach will allow us to increase the freight handling capacity of our system without adding any additional miles . . .

One issue with the trailers concerned the brakes. Initially, the test trailers were equipped with surge brakes. Both B.C. and Ontario had issues with this. British Columbia preferred electric brakes, which the driver could apply independently from the bus brakes, and Ontario wanted hydraulic brakes. After several years and much frustration, the provinces agreed to air over hydraulic brakes. Later, following the 1998 Voyageur purchase, the company would also successfully obtain approval to run the trailers in Quebec.

1996

In June 1996 Voyageur Colonial sold its Toronto-Montreal scheduled service route to Trentway-Wagar. This caused problems, as the terms of the sale included a promise that Voyageur would not accept Montreal-bound freight from Toronto. Greyhound felt this conflicted with the terms of the ten-year exclusive freight interline agreement it had signed with Voyageur in 1990. As Greyhound didn't want to interline with Trentway-Wagar, the company sought an injunction in August 1996. It was unsuccessful in gaining an interim injunction and instead of going to trial Greyhound abandoned the action in October 1996.

Door-to-Door Product Emerges

In 1996 Greyhound achieved courier express revenues of $59.4 million. Meanwhile, in response to competition from small niche-player courier companies in British Columbia, Dave Leach, then general manager of B.C., and members of the courier express team developed a true door-to-door courier product, eliminating add-on charges for pick-up and delivery. They also developed a new zone pricing structure that would later be adopted across the country.

In order to deliver the new product, Dave Leach successfully negotiated and implemented a new compensation structure for the agency network. Results were almost instant and market share was regained. B.C. results for 1997 showed a yield increase of 5% and volume gains of 2%. A postal strike the following year also helped boost volumes.

In 2000 and 2001 the new door-to-door product was implemented nation-wide by Dave Leach, now general manager, National GCX. Driven by a motivated sales team led by Ivan Wannamaker and Anthony Milonas, and supported by the new zone pricing and agency compensation structure, the new product helped the Greyhound Courier Express division achieve a 15% increase in revenues and an 8% increase in volumes from 1999 to 2001.

International Service/Domestic Air

In 1998, Greyhound launched an international service, in response to an opportunity through the Vancouver International Airport. Working with local agent ICS Courier for Alaska Air/Horizon Air, the new international service initially served the West Coast of the United States, with Vancouver acting as the hub.

As revenue grew, opportunities arose to service the entire United States and expand the international service to points around the world. A new arrangement was made with a major international air carrier to provide service from major hubs in Vancouver, Calgary, Edmonton, Winnipeg and Toronto.

In response to the success of the international service, in August 2003 the company launched a new "domestic air" service. This courier service offers overnight air service between the major company hubs, with feeds from the national agency network. Domestic Air continues to grow in popularity.

Current Initiatives

Greyhound has continued to expand its trailer fleet to support its healthy courier express division. In December 2003, the company ordered 25 pup trailers, allowing it to make more daily deliveries between Toronto and Winnipeg while eliminating truck costs. Today, Greyhound operates a fleet of 93 pup trailers from B.C. to Quebec. All Greyhound trailers are manufactured by Intercontinental Truck Body (ITB) in Coaldale, Alberta.

At the same time, Greyhound is moving to revolutionize its courier express information handling. In the near future we look forward to implementing state of the art web-based track-and-trace, bar coding and hand-held point-of-sale technology to our courier express services. These initiatives combined with our increased range of service products will make us even more accessible and allow us to deliver a higher level of customer service.

G-4500 Model, coach #1245, and pup trailer, Winnipeg, Manitoba, ca. 2003

CHAPTER SEVEN

BEST PRACTICES

75₀ ver the past seventy-five years Greyhound Canada has played a major role in developing the "best practices" in transportation, particularly in the areas of safety and accessibility. Greyhound is very proud to represent the most environmentally sound mode of travel, as identified by government studies.

Greyhound is also a leader in the Diversity arena and participates in a number of initiatives to enhance employment equity. We are committed to delivering superior customer service, and are making significant capital and technological investments to improve our passenger, courier and charter and sightseeing products. Greyhound is a major charity sponsor and is involved in a number of community outreach initiatives.

SAFETY

Safety has always been Greyhound Canada's first responsibility. Acting as the link between rural and urban Canada, we provide nation-wide access to Canadians safely, reliably and comfortably, achieving millions of accident-free miles and setting the standard for the industry.

Three principles affect every passenger trip: driver quality, coach quality and company philosophy. Our safety record is anchored in the quality of our driver training, the mechanical fitness and design of our coaches, and our corporate attitude.

Greyhound and ATU, Local 1415, Driver Recognition Ceremonies, November 2001
Photo courtesy Bill McCarthy

George Mermet and "Brassy" Ball receiving safe driving award from John Learmonth, 1951

Driver Training

Greyhound Canada has the most demanding driver-training program in the world. Our drivers undergo seven weeks of classroom and practical behind-the-wheel training with our experienced driver instructors.

To become a Greyhound driver, applicants must:
• Have a minimum grade 12 (or equivalent) education;
• At least five years of driving experience, with no more than two moving violations in three years, or three violations in five years;
• Pass a background check, including a police background check;
• Be able to enter the United States; and
• Be able to pass a pre-placement health screening including drug and alcohol testing.

In the classroom drivers receive instruction on everything from geography and ticketing procedures to safety and courtesy, while the on-road training consists of a minimum of 60 hours driving. To complete the training, drivers return for winter training before driving in adverse weather conditions.

Drivers are evaluated regularly and receive additional training as needed. Our driver instructors attend annual safety conferences, where they must successfully pass a written exam and driving course prior to being re-certified. Greyhound also employs "ride-checkers", who randomly ride schedules and evaluate our drivers based on their driving ability and customer service skills. Hundreds of Greyhound

Canada drivers go on to achieve 20 to 35 year safety awards for remaining accident-free.

Greyhound Canada was the first coach operator to be unconditionally approved for the Partners In Compliance (PIC) program initiated in Alberta, which recognizes safety. As well, Greyhound has represented the coach and school bus industry by participating in the Fatigue Management Program pilot project – phases I and II – in Alberta.

We are sharing our proprietary training program and procedures with the Motor Carrier Passenger Council of Canada (MCPCC) to develop programs to professionalize the bus driver vocation, raise the profile of the industry and open the door to new bus drivers.

Motor Carrier Passenger Council of Canada (MCPCC)

The Motor Carrier Passenger Council of Canada (MCPCC) is a national not-for-profit organization funded by Human Resources Development Canada (HRDC). It was founded in January 1999 to "initiate and coordinate human resources programs and initiatives nationally within the motor carrier passenger industry", including the motor coach, school, inter-city and para-transit sectors.

These programs include National Operational Standards for Professional Bus Operators, a National Driver Certification Program, and a Disability Awareness Program – the "Special Needs Rider" program, based on the Greyhound accessibility program. Through these initiatives, the MCPCC and Greyhound hope to:
• Professionalize the bus operator vocation and raise the profile of the industry;
• Stabilize operator staffing through effective recruitment practices that attract qualified new entrants;
• Reduce both short- and long-term human resources costs; and
• Improve skill development, safety and customer satisfaction, thus ultimately increasing ridership.

As reported by the Canadian Urban Transit Association (CUTA), in October 2003 the MCPCC "launched a national multi-media campaign that opens the door to an industry with attractive opportunities and a solid future. It spans urban, inter-city, tour and charter, school, and accessible service segments of the industry. Key audiences include young people between 16 and 9 years of age who are still in secondary school, and 18 and 25 who are entering the work force."

The Council also hopes to help standardize national apprenticeship programs and licensing to help eliminate differences and allow for movement between provinces during an apprenticeship, an important consideration for Greyhound Canada's national operations. Greyhound applauds the Council's work, which is receiving international recognition from bodies such as the U.S. Federal Transit Administration.

Our Fleet

We have consistently taken the lead in introducing safety improvements to our coaches and facilities, and we continually upgrade our fleet to ensure a safe, comfortable and accessible ride for our passengers. This vigorous attitude dates back to 1935, when Greyhound founder George Fay with engineer H. K. "Pat" Williams pioneered the first steel bus, No. 25, known as "Two-bits".

Built in response to a bad accident, at a time when buses had wooden frames and roof bows covered with canvas or light metal siding, the new coach's steel frame with riveted heavy steel siding was revolutionary. "Two-bits" would survive a crash and tumble down a 100-foot embankment, landing on its roof on a railway track, with its frame intact and no passenger fatalities.

Since then, Greyhound has worked diligently with Motor Coach Industries (MCI) to improve coach safety as well as comfort and accessibility. Buses are tough and protective and preserve their integrity even in severe head-on collisions. The overall structure is augmented by devices such as roof escape hatches, emergency windows, seats that lock into the coach floor, secure overhead compartments, and insulated engine compartments, as well as fire extinguishers, first aid kits and cell phones for emergencies. Coaches are equipped with governors to limit speed to within highway limits.

Greyhound's maintenance program exceeds provincial and federal requirements. The company continually examines and modifies its maintenance campaigns and procedures to ensure the road worthiness of its fleet. Beginning in mid-2003, Greyhound implemented a new Total Quality Management program (TQM) to enhance its maintenance process.

Under TQM, through training and concentrated assignment of work, Greyhound's mechanics become experts on specific coach systems, such as air conditioning, powertrain and electrical/video. These and other changes will help us better manage and reduce out-of-service levels and improve the overall condition of our buses over the long term.

Corporate Commitment

Greyhound's management philosophy is driven by the safety of our passengers. In most cases Greyhound safety management personnel are promoted from within. Most Greyhound driver instructors are former drivers themselves, with long safety records and extensive on-road and customer experience. This has allowed us to build a strong corporate culture for safety.

Pat Williams

An outstanding example of this corporate mindset was Pat Williams, long-time director of safety, claims and personnel. Williams finally retired in March 1973 as assistant to the president after almost forty years with Greyhound.

Under his direction, employees attended numerous seminars and workshops to learn about safety procedures. Many drivers remembered Williams' more in-depth training sessions that began with a big steak dinner at a hotel and carried on with films, lectures and discussions. Williams centered his training on the concept of defensive driving. Greyhound relied on this training technique for many years before it became popular. During Williams' tenure the company's safety record significantly improved, and Greyhound won several awards.

For example, in 1963 Williams proudly accepted the Marcus A. Dow Memorial Award – for the fifth time. This award was given in honour of the first president of the U.S. National Safety Council in recognition of the best improvement in accident-free miles over a three-year period.

The same year Greyhound was awarded the William F. Grant Trophy for the second consecutive time in recognition of the best safety performance of the year.

Williams was also responsible for programs such as Greyhound's "lights on for safety" campaign. Under this program Greyhound buses drove with their lights on at all times, reportedly decreasing sideswipes by 20% or more and winning high praise in the media. This practice soon spread throughout transportation and is now recommended as standard safe driving policy for all drivers, private or commercial.

Upon his retirement Williams was replaced by George Savage as general manager, safety, claims and personnel. Savage was followed by Mel Little, who retired in 2000 and was succeeded by Lorraine Card,

Greyhound's present director of safety with an excellent record on accessibility and safety issues and strong industry presence in Canada and the United States.

Industry Policing

As an industry leader, Greyhound plays an important part in helping police the industry. Greyhound submits objections when unsafe carriers request operating licences from the provincial regulatory boards, and rogue operators are reported to the enforcement bodies for investigation.

In addition to the company's long-term work in many industry associations, Greyhound and the Amalgamated Transit Union are working together with Transport Canada and Labour Canada to identify and address safety issues within the public transportation network.

We are also working to build a joint initiative to lobby for legislative changes in Canada and the U.S. that will impose harsher punishments for violence in the transit sector and make it harder for those who might consider such attacks in the future, and we strongly support the federal road transportation security funding initiatives implemented in the United States over the past two years.

Safety Research

Federal research studies in both the United States and Canada consistently find bus travel to be the safest mode of transportation. In 1995, the United States Federal Office of Road Safety found that bus travel averages .07 fatalities per 100 million kilometres travelled, less than all other modes.

In its 1998 Review of Bus Safety Issues, Transport Canada said "Buses provide passengers with remarkably safe travel compared with other road vehicles and other modes of transport." Greyhound Canada's own accident rate has been calculated as ten times better than the trucking industry standard.

Over the years Greyhound drivers and equipment have continued to bear out this excellent record of safety and reliability, despite poor weather or road conditions. The 1998 Ice Storm in Eastern Canada and the 2003 Eastern Seaboard Blackout failed to halt the steady parade of buses, while air and train travel were grounded.

Awards

Not surprisingly, Greyhound Canada has been the recipient of many awards for safety both in Canada and the United States.

Besides the many corporate awards we have received, Greyhound is proud of drivers such as:

- Louis Welch, who in 1989 won the Ontario government's driver of the year award for the third time in a row;
- Thunder Bay operator George Selagi who saved all his passengers from a bus fire and received a police commendation and a citation from the Ontario government for his heroism;
- Toronto-based Walter Kiskunas, who won the Ontario Motor Coach Award for Driver Excellence in 2003, and
- 31-year operator Graham Leech, who received the Colonel Robert Hardie Award of Lifetime Achievement in June 2004.

We offer our congratulations to these and many other Greyhound drivers who have gone above and beyond to ensure a superior, safe, and comfortable travelling experience for our passengers.

Special Events

Thanks to Greyhound Canada's reputation for safety and courtesy, heads of state such as former Prime Minster Brian Mulroney, major sports organizations such as the Harlem Globetrotters, the Olympics and many others have chosen Greyhound for their Canadian transportation needs.

Over the years Greyhound has served many special events, including G7, G8 and G20 summits; the Manitoba Winter Games; the 2002 World Youth Days and Papal Visit to Toronto, Ontario; the Queen's Royal Jubilee Visit to Toronto, the July 30, 2003 Rolling Stones Toronto benefit concert to combat SARS and many others.

We provided transportation to the 1988 Winter Olympics and are a member of the Transportation Committee for the Whistler 2010 Olympics. We also regularly provide political campaign service at all levels, most recently for the Global/National Post Decision Canada cross-country election tour, as well as for former Ontario Premier Ernie Eves, and federal Conservative leader Stephen Harper.

ENVIRONMENTALLY SOUND

According to Transport Canada's study, "The Canadian Intercity Bus Industry" published in March 2000, the bus is by far the most fuel-efficient and least polluting way of travel compared to all other modes, including train, air and the personal automobile. Other studies in the United States have produced similar results.

On June 6, 2001, former federal transport minister David Collenette told the Senate Standing Committee on Transport & Communications that the bus achieves the best fuel consumption per passenger-kilometre (110 passenger-kilometres per litre of fuel as compared to 22 passenger-kilometres per litre for train) and has the lowest level of greenhouse gas emissions of all passenger modes.

As the most fuel-efficient mode, bus travel achieves 385 passenger miles per gallon. Improvements in diesel engines continue to reduce vehicle emissions and increase fuel efficiency, which ongoing fleet replacement will make ever more apparent. Greyhound efficiently cross-utilizes its fleet to provide courier express and charter services using the same fleet, creating further environmental and fuel savings.

Kyoto Treaty

The environmentally friendly characteristics of bus travel are an asset that will help Canada meet its obligations under the Kyoto Treaty. Signed in 1991 by 119 nations, the Kyoto Treaty commits to an 8% reduction of greenhouse gases by 2010 over 2000. As transportation is responsible for 20% of greenhouse gases, the far greater energy efficiency of bus travel makes it an attractive and affordable alternative to the private car.

Low Cost, High Flexibility

These outstanding environmental benefits are further magnified when one considers the relatively low costs to build and maintain bus transportation networks as opposed to fixed rail or air initiatives. In addition, Greyhound and other members of the inter-city bus industry operate profitably without subsidy, an important advantage in comparison with rail and air.

As well, the bus is inherently flexible and can adapt and respond to changing population density and land use needs by simply changing the route and bus stop, as opposed to building new rail track or a landing field. Buses can use the existing road network without causing additional infringement or damage to protected or endangered natural habitats.

Greyhound Canada is committed to the principles of effective land use, and whenever possible seeks to build intermodal facilities in partnership with other travel modes. Offering service to more than 1,100 communities across Canada, compared to fewer than 70 commercial airports for the airline mode, Greyhound believes that intermodalism is critical for Canada's tourism and transportation industry.

Combatting Congestion

The bus's superior capacity (up to 54 passengers per bus) is another factor that makes bus travel an environmentally sound choice. Removing the equivalent number of cars from the road directly reduces highway gridlock, reduces pollution and assures efficient energy consumption.

The increased affordability of personal automobiles (without considering skyrocketing insurance, fuel or maintenance costs) has resulted in steadily increasing traffic volumes on Canada's highways, particularly in Ontario's Golden Horseshoe centering on Toronto.

Congestion is not new to Toronto. In the late 1920's future Greyhound acquisition Gray Coach offered service from North Toronto to downtown Toronto on the prestigious "Hill Route" bus at premium rates. According to the Gray Coach history published in 1987, this "helped alleviate the clogged downtown traffic of the day, since most patrons were motorists who had formerly driven the trip".

Today, addressing gridlock is a provincial priority. In July 2004 the province held a series of public consultations regarding initiatives to reduce congestion and improve the transportation infrastructure network. Greyhound welcomes these initiatives.

Commuting in Southern Ontario

Over the past several years Greyhound has worked to improve its commuter service to Toronto from Guelph, Kitchener, Cambridge, St. Catharines, Peterborough and other cities, as well as Barrie and Orangeville following the acquisition of Penetang-Midland Coach Lines (PMCL). If commuters can rely on safe, effective, reliable and comfortable public transportation, they will be able to leave their cars at home, thereby directly reducing gridlock, greenhouse gas emissions and lost productivity. Currently, Greyhound transports more than 1 million commuters a year to downtown Toronto.

Our commuter service is a distinct product separate from our scheduled services. Greyhound works in conjunction with passengers to review and enhance service through two channels of communication: surveys and public meetings. In Ontario, we have instituted the following:
- schedule changes
- improved interior maintenance schedules
- created a dedicated commuter fleet
- introduced a commuter-of-the-month rewards program
- developed a commuter watchdog ambassador, and

A dog-gone smart way to commute.

Experience the ease and convenience Greyhound Canada has to offer
with our special commuter fares available to and from:
Kitchener-Toronto, Kitchener-Guelph, Guelph-Toronto and Guelph-Kitchener.
Greyhound Canada offers same day and advance purchase fares, as well as monthly passes.
We also boast frequent schedules for our commuter customers.

Sit back, relax and leave the driving to us.®

In 2001 Greyhound launched a comprehensive commuter recognition program, including a dedicated fleet, rewards program, and watchdog ambassador

• assured easy passenger communications through dedicated email support that quickly responds to commuter issues and helps drive service improvements.

We are also investigating a range of e-services, special coaches and new on-board amenities to serve the commuter market.

Finally, Greyhound is developing a number of infrastructure projects that will enhance the commuter network in Southern Ontario and encourage more commuters to make the modal switch from private car to public transport.

Riding the bus helps directly reduce highway gridlock, reduce pollution and assure efficient energy consumption. Riding the bus is an environmentally sound choice that will assist Canada in meeting its Kyoto objectives.

ACCESSIBILITY

Greyhound Canada is very proud of our record on accessibility. Our services include wheelchair accessible coaches, seeing-eye/hearing-ear accommodation, and preferential senior and companion fares for the

disabled community. We have instituted company-wide operating policies and procedures, purchase accessible coaches through our fleet replacement program, and conduct facility audits. As well, we provide sensitivity training to all front-line employees, including drivers and management staff at all terminal and agency locations.

In fact, one customer with a disability was so impressed with the service he received, he travelled from Vancouver to Calgary on Greyhound just so he could meet the customer service staff and thank them in person!

First Accessible Coach

Recognizing the need for diversified services that address the needs of all passengers, in 1990 subsidiary Motor Coach Industries (MCI) received $960,000 in Canadian federal funding to build a 45-foot coach for the handicapped.

Based on the 102C3, the fully accessible prototype was presented in the summer of 1990. The coach included a new-design wheelchair lift that stored below in the baggage bay, a fully accessible washroom, and room for two mobility aids at a time. In 1992 Greyhound conducted a demonstration project with the prototype on selected runs in Alberta, but operational issues sent it back to the drawing board.

Accessible Service Launched

Over 1994-1995, Greyhound introduced ten wheelchair accessible coaches into service, retrofitted with a Ricon lift device and equipped with cellular phones, Braille signage and repositioned call buttons. The service was launched on major routes in four provinces and passengers could reserve space with 24 hours notice. These routes were:

• **British Columbia:** Vancouver-Hope, Vancouver-Kamloops, and Vancouver-Kelowna.
• **Alberta:** Calgary-Edmonton
• **Manitoba:** Select schedules on the Winnipeg-Brandon and Winnipeg-Dryden-Kenora routes.
• **Ontario:** Toronto-Hamilton-London, Toronto-St. Catharines-Buffalo, Toronto-Guelph-Cambridge-Kitchener, and Toronto-Niagara Falls.

Greyhound made its position clear in its press release: "We're very committed to offering accessible service," said John Munro, executive vice-president of Greyhound Lines of Canada. "Greyhound believes that access is a right, not a privilege, and that everyone, including the elderly and people with disabilities should have the right to travel in comfort."

Greyhound further expanded the service in

January 1996, adding wheelchair-accessible service to ten more routes, purchasing 14 new coaches with Ricon lift devices and implementing new telephone services for hearing impaired customers. Improvements and additions have continued to date.

Today Greyhound has two elevator platform systems in use on its accessible coaches. The Ricon system is still in place on the older coaches, with dimensions of 31.8˝ wide by 48˝ long, while the newer accessible G-models have a Stuart & Stevenson platform with dimensions 40˝ wide x 68˝ long. Both elevator systems can accommodate a maximum weight of 600 pounds.

Intercity Bus Code of Practice

Not long after the accessible services launch, Greyhound helped develop the Intercity Bus Code of Practice, which sets out best practices for providing services in a safe and dignified manner to travellers with disabilities. Championed by Transport Canada's Advisory Committee on Accessible Transportation (ACAT), the Code was developed over two years by a group of industry stakeholders and consumer representatives.

The Code was launched by then federal transport minister David Collenette in Toronto on July 9, 1998. Collenette praised the sub-committee's efforts and highlighted the fact that the Code is a "voluntary statement of commitment based on consensus between industry and consumers". The bus industry is a leader in this field. No other form of public transportation has developed such a code.

Under the provisions of the Code of Practice, disabled persons providing advance notice of travel (24, 48 or 72 hours, depending upon the service required) are guaranteed accessible bus services. Disabled persons who require the assistance of a personal aide may bring their companion free of charge.

Passengers who experience barriers can initiate a 3-step complaint process with ultimate recourse to Transport Canada. Complaints are extremely rare, even though accessible coach bookings are increasing rapidly for this growing market. Greyhound is very responsive to concerns and vigorously pursues all accessibility complaints.

Preferential Fare Programs

As early as 1959 Greyhound began providing reduced fares to members of the Canadian National Institute for the Blind, their escorts and service animals.

Additionally, seniors receive a 10% fare discount

and special excursion fares. In the early 1990s the company lowered the eligibility age from 65 to 62.

Supporting diabetes research, the "Ken McColm's Incredible Journey" tour went all over Canada in 1992

Usage Statistics

Reservations for accessible coaches continue to climb. In 2003 bookings increased 17%, with the total number nearly double the number just five years ago. As passengers become more aware of our advan-

Greyhound seniors discount advertising

tages, they call Greyhound's Passenger Sales Centre at 1-800-661-TRIP to make reservations. Currently 10% of our fleet is wheelchair accessible.

Awards

Greyhound Canada has been honoured with several awards for our accessibility efforts. On February 10, 2001, Greyhound Canada received the 2001 Corporate Award from the Canadian Foundation for Physically Disabled Persons at the Foundation's Seventeenth Great Valentine Gala. This award recognized Greyhound Canada's many contributions in assisting persons with physical disabilities, particularly by developing programs that actively support their needs.

Also in 2001, National Transportation Week selected Greyhound to receive an Award of Achievement for contributions to accessibility for persons with physical disabilities.

In June 2003, Greyhound received an Award of Achievement for Significant Contribution to Transportation in Canada. Bestowed by the annual National Transportation Week Awards, the award was given in recognition of our accessibility training program. Later that year Greyhound's brand-new Coquitlam terminal in British Columbia received a 2003 Accessibility Award from Coquitlam Mayor Jon D.H. Kingsbury's Committee for People with Disabilities. The award was granted for constructing a terminal that eliminates barriers for people with disabilities in the Coquitlam community.

National Transportation Week again recognized Greyhound's accessibility program in June 2004. This program was developed by Lorraine Card, director of safety, who has been recognized by the National Transportation Agency for her efforts on behalf of accessibility.

The Motor Carrier Passenger Council of Canada (MCPCC) has created a "Disability Awareness Training Program" based on that developed by our Safety Department. The MCPCC "Special Needs Rider" program has been translated into French and is now being packaged for sale to the industry, to include licensing, trainer certification, and materials.

Greyhound is also an active member of the Advisory Committee on Barrier Free Transportation in the province of Alberta.

DIVERSITY

In 1987 the Employment Equity Act was enacted in Canada with the aim of "achieving equality in the workplace so that no person shall be denied employment opportunities or benefits for reasons unrelated to ability." To this end the Act targeted four specific groups that historically have been under-represented and have been given fewer opportunities for advancement in Canadian workplaces. These four groups are:

- Women,
- Aboriginal Peoples,
- Visible Minorities, and
- Persons with Disabilities

At Greyhound we view employment equity as more than just a legal requirement – it is the right thing to do and ultimately good for our business and the communities we serve. All Employment Equity and Diversity plans, policies and initiatives at Greyhound reflect the spirit of the law and are developed in conjunction with the principles found in the Human Rights Act. Through the information and experiences garnered from the four designated groups, Greyhound ultimately ensures that our employment practices are fair to everyone and that every employee or potential employee is given an equal opportunity to succeed at Greyhound.

Diversity Initiatives

Greyhound Canada was audited by the Human Rights Commission and in June 2003 was found in compliance with all statutory requirements identified in the Employment Equity Act. To put this success into perspective, in audits conducted since 1997, as of

Greyhound driver Norma Edwards

January 2004 only 27% of the 500+ private sector companies covered under this legislation have successfully completed this requirement. One highlight from the audit report was recognition of the "forward looking managerial approach and underlying of the principles" displayed by senior management's commitment to diversity at Greyhound.

Greyhound has also participated in a number of diversity initiatives, including an agreement with the Assembly of Manitoba Chiefs with initiatives geared towards employment and opportunity for the Aboriginal community, which strives to achieve a 3% Aboriginal new hire rate at Greyhound, a target we yearly surpass.

Another such program is our involvement in work experience programs such as the Bow Valley College Immigrant Program in Calgary. This allows professional immigrants the opportunity to gain valuable Canadian work experience. Greyhound has benefited greatly from this and other work experience programs that have resulted in a 30% hire rate for participants either acquiring permanent or contract work with Greyhound.

Other Partnerships
Greyhound also maintains partnerships with organizations such as the National Aboriginal Achievement Foundation's annual Blueprint for the Future Aboriginal Youth Fair, Treaty Seven Aboriginal Futures and Champions – an organization that assists persons with disabilities to obtain meaningful employment. Through our industry partners such as the Canadian Bus Association and the Motor Carrier Passenger Council of Canada, and special interest groups such as the Congress of Aboriginal People, Greyhound strives to encourage young people to stay in school and to foster an interest in the bus industry and in trades.

Internal Initiatives
Internally, Greyhound has implemented a number of organizational initiatives to ensure diversity is at the top of the agenda. These include:

• An employee advisory committee comprising of union, non-union and designated groups which meets quarterly to review and to make recommendations on policies, procedures and process that impact employment.

• A senior management working committee, which meets quarterly to review and considers the recommendations prior to implementing new initiatives regarding employment practices.

• Employee diversity training including Aboriginal sensitivity delivered to new employees.

• The appointment of a national Aboriginal Co-ordinator who participates in Aboriginal events such as National Aboriginal Day and represents the Aboriginal population on the Employee Advisory Committee.

• An annual strategic diversity plan, also submitted to the Employment Equity Commission, that assists Greyhound to identify and review areas where there is under representation of qualified individuals and is used to formulate initiatives to remedy the situation. Greyhound not only strives to meet representation but to exceed representation, especially in areas where representation of qualified individuals is low compared to the working population of the designated group.

All these initiatives have shown Greyhound to be a leader in the Diversity arena. In recognition of our contributions, Greyhound was invited to share its successes at an International Diversity Conference held in Toronto as an example to other organizations implementing diversity practices.

CUSTOMER SERVICE & TECHNOLOGY
Greyhound Canada continually reviews and makes investments to improve our level of customer service. Some of our more memorable initiatives, such as the "Dinner in the Washroom" gambit, have been spurred by John Munro, senior vice president, marketing, who attacked systemic problems with keen creativity and got results.

For example, to improve seat comfort, in 1989 Munro approached the five seat manufacturers Greyhound dealt with on a world-wide basis, asking them for research so the company could perform a study and identify the most comfortable seats. The five declined. Munro then asked them to provide Greyhound with samples of their best seats, for a four-month pilot project, so the passengers could cast a vote. Again, all five declined. Munro wrote back and promised Greyhound would never buy another seat from them. They all changed their minds, and the passengers benefitted.

Top Ten Companies
Following the implementations beginning in 1989 totalling millions of dollars in infrastructure, fleet and customer service improvement initiatives, Greyhound's efforts were rewarded. In November 1991, International Quality Month, the Royal Bank acknowledged Greyhound Canada as one of the top

ten customer service-oriented companies in Canada whose operation met international standards. The ten companies were profiled in a video, which was subsequently shown on all Air Canada flights. Corporate education centres still sell this video today.

New Policies

An important part of Greyhound's customer service is consistency. In 2002 Dave Leach, then vice-president, passenger services, led a full review of company policies and procedures to make them more customer-accountable.

These new policies, combined with regular contact with our customers through surveys and onboard research, will aid Greyhound in providing superior customer service. Greyhound is proud to have implemented Privacy policies in accordance with the new PIPEDA Act that came into effect January 1, 2004, which protects the personal information of customers, employees and third parties.

Technology

Greyhound Canada first implemented point-of-sale technology in its terminals and agencies beginning in 1986 through 1987, in partnership with Gateway. This multi-million dollar project made it possible to quote electronic, up-to-date fares from sales kiosks, launching the move away from paper-based schedules and tariffs. Upgrades to the company technology have continued and recently Greyhound migrated to a mileage-based fares system. The company is also upgrading its courier express technology to include state of the art web-based track-and-trace, bar coding and hand-held point-of-sale technology.

Self-Guided Tour

In his role as general manager for British Columbia, Dave Leach developed a value-added package of services and attractions that could be sold as an add-on to a regular bus ticket. The Self-Guided Tour brochure included commentary and unique facts on selected day schedules in British Columbia as well as a self-guided tour for each leg of the trip.

The product was tested on our Whistler, B.C. corridor and worked well, and the sales materials are in use by our Greyhound Travel Services division. Although not yet fully implemented, the Self-Guided Tour has immense potential nationally and will continue to be pursued.

COMMUNITY OUTREACH

Greyhound Canada sponsors several recognized charities, including The United Way and The Children's Wish Foundation. Greyhound particularly

supports youth-oriented charities, such as Operation Go Home.

One of the company's accomplishments is the establishment of a scholarship contest for high school graduates, "Travel is Educational Too!" which annually gives away more than $70,000 in cash and free transportation to qualifying graduates. The company has also created contests such as "Win a Year on Greyhound" giving university students free travel and shipping for a year.

Operation Go Home

Through the Canadian Bus Association, Greyhound Canada has supported Operation Go Home for the past 34 years. OGH provides services to youth in crisis through their Youth Alternative Centres and Outreach and works to brings kids off the streets. In 2003, Greyhound was responsible for providing tickets to 77% of the qualifying youths identified by OGH, bringing them home and off the streets.

"Travel is Educational, Too!" (TIET)

Beginning in 1997, Greyhound Canada initiated a high school academic reward program, "Travel is Educational, Too!" (TIET), designed to encourage and reward the scholastic achievement of grade 12 students across Canada. TIET provides qualified students with the opportunity to win exciting and enriching travel prizes as well as scholarships to help further their education.

The annual contest, now in its seventh year, also provides an opportunity to win dozens of other prizes from participating sponsors, which in recent years have included Motor Coach Industries (MCI), Hostelling International, Goodmans LLP, Watson Wyatt & Company, Petro Canada, Choice Hotels and many others.

Only those Grade 12 students who achieve a GPA of 80 percent or higher on their spring transcript or unofficial final transcript are eligible to win. To enter, students simply drop off a copy of their transcript with their contact information at any Greyhound depot in Canada. The draw is held in May, with up to 50 prizes being awarded.

On May 11, 2004, 20 Canadian students won TIET scholarships plus a prize package worth more than $1,100 following draws held at Greyhound Canada depots. Thirty other students won prize packages, and all qualifying entrants whose names were not drawn received a $20 Greyhound travel voucher. More than $65,000 in prizes was won.

Student Discount Programs

As part of the company's youth outreach, in September 1998, Greyhound launched a major student discount program, "Choose Freedom". Offering 25% discounts via a special discount card to Western Canada and special city-pair fares to Eastern Canada, this initiative focussed on the flexibility, reliability and convenience of travel by Greyhound, announcing "The Bus is Better".

The highly successful print and television campaign was anchored by the appearance of Gracie, a young greyhound dog and the company's new star.

Greyhound student discount advertising

"Gracie"

A purebred grey and white greyhound, Gracie was adopted from the Calgary Humane Society when she was ten months old. Beautiful, energetic and "zany" Gracie competed against nine other greyhounds to be selected for the television role in the company's new student travel campaign launched in 1998.

Gracie was warmly received by passengers and went on to appear in many other Greyhound spots, along with Arvin, another greyhound. In 2001, she was featured in the critically acclaimed, "Dogs with Jobs" television series. The fifteen-minute segment explained how she won the "Spokesdog" job with Greyhound and followed her on a typical working day. Gracie has also appeared in *Dogs in Canada* magazine.

Although she is now semi-retired, Gracie still makes occasional visits to the Calgary Depot at Christmas to visit with staff and help see passengers off on their trips. She is well loved and appreciated by everyone.

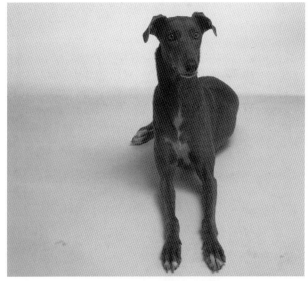

Gracie, the Greyhound

"Win a Year on Greyhound"

Senior vice president Dave Leach conceived the idea for this web-based promotion, which gives college and university students a chance to receive free travel and shipping for one year. The contest received 2,500 entries upon its launch in September 2002, at the time Greyhound's most successful Internet promotion. The winning student, Jolienne Hussick, won travel for a year on Greyhound between her hometown and her university plus two free shipments.

This new promotion complements "Travel Is Educational Too!" and our ongoing student discounts of up to 40% off regular adult fares.

As quoted by Dave Leach, "Greyhound is a huge supporter of post-secondary education, and about 25 percent of our customers are students. We try to create new opportunities for students to enhance their education through travel programs."

In 2003, Leanne Holowach of Penticton, B.C., attending school in Calgary, Alberta, was chosen as the lucky winner.

One night I was a little homesick, so I thought I might go to the Greyhound Web site and look up some bus fares. I saw the Win a Year on Greyhound contest and decided to enter. Before I knew it, I got a phone call telling me I won. Greyhound is an awesome way to help out students because we all know how expensive post-secondary education can be, and with Greyhound it's just a quick bus ride back home. I would like to thank everyone at Greyhound for making my first year at college this much more enjoyable.

Western Hockey League (WHL)

On October 22, 2003, Greyhound Courier Express signed an agreement with the Western Hockey League (WHL) to sponsor its 15 Canadian teams during the 2003-2004 hockey season. The agreement names GCX as the official courier of the WHL, and has been extended to the 2004-2005 season.

The agreement includes a nightly GCX promotion at each of the teams' home games, one promotional display per WHL Canadian venue, advertising in the official WHL pocket schedule, a weekly GCX/WHL player of the week sponsorship and season tickets.

GCX also will assist the league with their "Home Town Connections" program. The program matches current players' hometowns with Greyhound terminals, where their photographs and hockey statistics are posted to keep local residents informed of their achievements.

Greyhound is proud to support these and other community and youth-related projects. We encourage other corporations to examine how their core business can add value to the lives of Canadians.

CHAPTER EIGHT

FACILITIES AND INTERMODALITY

Greyhound Canada is committed to the principles of effective land use, and whenever possible seeks to build intermodal facilities in partnership with other travel modes. Offering service to more than 1,200 communities across Canada, compared to less than 70 commercial airports for the airline mode, Greyhound believes that intermodalism is critical for Canada's tourism and transportation industry.

Recognizing that a passenger's ultimate destination is not a bus terminal or an airport, but a home or a vacation spot, Greyhound first formally presented its intermodal position to the Royal Commission

for Transportation in 2010 in the late 1980s. Greyhound's paper proposed the increased use of intermodal transit to make it easier for travellers to shift among air, bus and rail carriers. Greyhound has since pursued intermodal and interline agreements with Air Canada, VIA Rail, Rocky Mountaineer, municipal transit authorities and other transportation partners.

Perhaps the best example of an intermodal terminal in Canada is Pacific Central Station in Vancouver, B.C. Originally built around 1945, the terminal had fallen into decay. Working together, Greyhound, with partners VIA Rail and CN Rail, completely refurbished and repaired the facility. In March 1993 the station was re-opened.

Vancouver, B.C. garage, 1988. The Pacific Central Station,
which Greyhound would soon help rejuvenate, is just visible in the background

Today, Pacific Central Station serves more than 1 million passengers a year, with connections to Rocky Mountain Railtours, Pacific Coach Lines and other carriers, including a rail link to the Vancouver airport, making Pacific Central Station Canada's first, and very successful, intermodal terminal.

Such public-private relationships help make the transportation network more effective and more accessible to passengers.

HISTORIC TERMINALS

First Depot – Calgary, 1930

Greyhound's founders were initially too preoccupied obtaining the necessary route authorities and completing the company's incorporation to worry much about permanent terminal facilities. Following the first Calgary-Edmonton run, Greyhound secured temporary depot and office facilities in Calgary at a location opposite Eaton's department store on 4th Street West just off 5th Avenue South. Without a garage, the buses were parked on the street, and the company's office was Fay's apartment in the nearby Findlay Block. This makeshift solution was soon replaced by more adequate headquarters in a twenty-five foot bay of the ten-storey Southam Building, and signs went up announcing "Motor Coach Depot, Passengers and Express Services."

Located on the corner of 7th Avenue South and 1st Street West, the surprisingly elegant space had been occupied by Black's jewellers for sixteen years. The decor in the depot was remarkable. Crystal chandeliers hung from the ceiling and teak panelling adorned the walls, making it to many people one of the most outstanding depots in North America, although its passengers were picked up outside on the street.

Around the same time the company acquired its first garage on 11th Avenue South and 7th Street West in Calgary. Fay and Olson created a new company to operate these facilities, "Motor Coach Terminal and Garage Company, Ltd." The majority of its stock was subscribed by Canadian Greyhound Coaches on May 5, 1930, making it essentially a subsidiary company.

Southam Renovations

In 1940, the Southam building underwent a major renovation and expansion, and was proclaimed "one of the finest (terminals) in the world" by the *Calgary Herald*. Built under the direction of Pat Williams, a neighbouring confectionery store was demolished to build a driveway, allowing buses to park off the

Kenworth and Hayes Anderson buses at Greyhound's renovated depot, 1940

street. The terminal also received a covered arrival platform, giving passengers protection in inclement weather. Inside the building, the floor of the area that had once housed the *Calgary Herald*'s printing presses was lowered and two new levels were built.

The completed depot included a large coffee shop, a barbershop, larger ticket, baggage and waiting room areas and a mezzanine floor that housed new company offices. Although the renovation was expensive, involving cutting out concrete floors with compressed air tools, taking out steel and concrete vaults and steel beams with acetylene torches and lowering floors, the end product was worth the effort and the company was proud of it.

In celebration of the opening of this new depot, Greyhound purchased a special section in the *Herald* on March 1, 1940 describing the new premises as well as recounting the history of the company and bus transportation generally in Alberta.

Post-War Expansions

After World War II ended, Greyhound scrambled to develop the physical plant necessary to keep the growing company operative. In its early years, the company concentrated on providing depot and garage facilities only in the larger centres, using hotels as pick-up points in smaller centres and contracting maintenance work out to local garages.

Once the war had ended, the travelling public demanded not only greater comfort during trips but also pleasant depots in which to wait. At the same time, Greyhound's growing and increasingly sophisticated fleet of coaches needed more up to-date facilities to keep them in good working order.

Looking for land

Despite the 1940s renovations and expansion of the Southam property on 11th Avenue, Greyhound soon found itself in a squeeze for mechanical and servicing space. The search for a Calgary property on which to build a new Calgary headquarters garage began in 1944. President Fay hoped to buy a property in the area immediately surrounding the existing facility, contemplating "that the company would construct a garage on part of the property and ultimately construct a new station on the property."

Red Bus Lines shared Greyhound's Calgary depot facilities before it was bought out in 1944

However, Greyhound was embroiled in a series of major bus line acquisitions, which delayed the search for a headquarters garage site. In the meantime, in 1945 the board of directors decided that the search for garage properties should go ahead in other major centres served by the company.

On October 2nd, 1945, the Board resolved "that the President be, and he hereby is, authorized to proceed with a program for the acquisition by this company of property to be used as sites for a bus depot in Regina, Sask., a bus depot and garage in Saskatoon, Sask., a garage in Winnipeg, Man., and a bus depot and garage in Edmonton, Alberta."

Most of the purchases were complete by May 1946. These included:

• a garage property in Winnipeg consisting of six lots located directly in front of the Fort Garry Hotel on the north side of Broadway for $15,000;

• a depot and garage property in Edmonton con-sisting of five lots at the northwest corner of the intersection of 102nd Avenue and 102nd Street opposite Eaton's for $50,000; and

• a garage property in Regina for $31,500.

As well, the Calgary search had revealed a worthy site, now intended for a new general office and garage complex, instead of a depot and garage. The site was not near the old garage but it was a good one, adjacent to the downtown area in the Eau Claire district near the Bow River and next door to a planned Calgary city bus garage.

Eau Claire Property

The property consisted of 6.02 acres owned by Eau Claire Sawmills Ltd. between First Avenue and the Bow River and between First and Second Streets West. It was acquired at the incredibly low price of $1,000 an acre, or $6,020. Greyhound also acquired properties adjacent to its bus depot in Lethbridge and at Kingsgate to serve the increasing flow of cross-border traffic.

Saskatchewan Chagrin

Despite the spate of property purchases, developments in Saskatchewan threw a monkey wrench into Fay's building plans. As a result of the Saskatchewan government's decision to nationalize the province's bus industry, several of the newly acquired properties instantly became redundant. These included the

New Edmonton depot, 1949

Regina property as well as a depot and garage purchased in Prince Albert. These now had to be sold off at a loss, the sales netting $67,000 compared to book values of almost $73,000.

However, expansion continued elsewhere. In April 1947 the company made the following capital commitments:

- $296,000 to build a new garage and bus depot in Edmonton;
- $107,000 to build the garage in Winnipeg;
- $29,000 for the depot and garage in Kingsgate,
- $22,000 for a property in Banff to build a depot, and
- $7,000 for renovations to the Macleod depot.

Calgary Construction

Meanwhile, work was going ahead on the new Calgary garage and office building, as Greyhound had committed $300,000 to a design that would give it the most up-to-date facilities in the country. However, Fay proved a tough bargainer with the designers.

For example, the architect, J.M. Stevenson of Stevenson, Cawston, Stevenson, had to take a reduction in the basic 5% fee specified under the Architect's Act, allowing .5% for a basic layout the company had come up with, .5% for providing "data from other projects which will lessen the engineering problems," and .5% for Greyhound's engineering department collecting all necessary information on "pits, air lines and small engineering problems," leaving a total fee of 3.5%. Similarly, contractors submitted bids on the usual "cost plus 5% basis". However,

Fay wanted to fix the construction cost if the building went over the $300,000 budget, and signed a contract on June 5, 1946 with the Hurst Construction Company for a flat fee of $15,000.

Construction began in summer 1946 under the supervision of Pat Williams, but the specifications were a moving target under constant revision. One such change concerned the new washing system to clean buses. Having studied information from Teche Greyhound Lines in the United States, Williams suggested a sprinkler system be suspended from the ceiling in both lanes of the wash rack area. This would allow the washers to completely wet down the coaches prior to scrubbing, and to rinse them off afterward.

Williams also recommended that a well be drilled to supply water for the washing, costing approximately $2,000 including a pump. Water needs were calculated. Giving a good picture of the expected demands, Fay commented:

> As discussed with you it appears that our present scheduled arrivals and departures would total approximately twenty coaches. Allowing ten minutes to wash each coach, this would amount to 200 minutes of washing time. The water consumption amounts to 120 gallons per minute so our monthly consumption, based on these figures, would be 200 minutes x 120 gallons x 30 days or 720,000 gallons.

Using these figures, Williams estimated a $1,411 savings each year if using a well compared with paying existing city water rates.

Drawing for new Calgary depot

The company's insurance brokers suggested that the garage have the most up-to-date technology, a sprinkler system. Duncan Robertson made the case. The building would cost about $225,000 and would contain about $200,000 worth of contents at any given time, therefore a sprinkler system costing $12,500 would be a worthwhile investment, particularly when it would reduce insurance premiums by $2,250 annually.

Because the building was already approaching cost overruns, Fay consulted with Greyhound Corporation president Orville Caesar. Caesar gave the go-ahead, and Fay's file noted, "Caesar advised in view of savings considered advisable to install sprinklers."

Over Budget

Not surprisingly, the costs of the building escalated. On February 26, 1948 the contractor supplied new estimates showing the building would cost $487,750 due to the added costs, which also included changes to the drivers' dormitory, special garage service facilities and increased costs of labour and materials.

The same day an executive committee authority for expenditure allowed for such costs in excess of the original $300,000 as were necessary to complete the building. This was justified on the basis that the improvements would pay for themselves in the long run and would extend the life span of the building.

Nothing could have been truer. The garage and office facility, which officially opened in October 1949 remained Greyhound's administrative and maintenance headquarters for the next thirty-seven years. Fay built to last.

Buying the Southam building

The plans to build a new depot in Calgary were laid to rest by another development. In September 1948, Fay's discussions to buy the entire Southam building came to a conclusion with Greyhound obtaining an option to purchase. The executive committee promptly gave authority for the company to incorporate a wholly-owned subsidiary under the name of "The Greyhound Buildings Limited" having 750,000 common shares of a $1.00 par value. It also authorized the company to tender a cheque for $250,000 in full payment for one-third of these shares, with the funds then available being used to provide the down payment on the total building cost of $600,000. Part of these funds was raised by selling Greyhound's old garage property.

The new company was registered on October 12,

Calgary garage facilities, ca. 1950

1948 with Fay, Borden and Robertson as the temporary directors. The latter two were replaced by Greyhound Corporation executives Orville Caesar and Ralph Bogan the following year. Fay then began to plan changes that would allow the Southam property to meet Greyhound's growing depot needs and make it more attractive to potential tenants.

Renovation Scheme

In December 1949 Fay presented the board of directors with a renovation scheme that would provide new restroom facilities, baggage rooms and retail space in the basement, and, thanks to the office relocation to the new Eau Claire facility, enlarged restaurant and retail store areas on the ground and mezzanine floors. Total cost: $67,000. These improvements ensured that the public's demands for better facilities were substantially met, and the new garage and office continued to serve the company well for many years.

Food Services

From the beginning Greyhound incorporated restaurant facilities in its buildings as a service to the travelling public. These were leased to independent operators, and many of the arrangements worked out quite well. For example, Mickey Conti ran the lunch counter in the Edmonton depot for decades. And when the Calgary depot was renovated in 1940, the restaurant lease went to Lyman Porteous who opened the fourth in a string of "Koffee Kounters." Porteous took his advertising cues from Greyhound bus advertising, and a careless reader might have thought the writer was talking about the latest transportation equipment rather than a lunch counter:

> Every bit of space has been utilized. The counter stools have been especially built to provide restaurant comfort. Of rose-ochre shade, the stools have an air-conditioned seat and are padded with soft rubber material.
>
> The attractive colour scheme for the new room is white and soft creamy buff. The upper part of the walls is covered with a velvety white and the rest is of a light buff colour, with strips of chrome separating the two colours. Chromium is lavishly used in the remainder of the furnishing throughout the room.
>
> One of the outstanding features of the counter is the fact that small compartments have been built underneath the counter so the patrons may place their cases or small parcels. This is an entirely new innovation and will undoubtedly prove very popular.

Following completion of the intense building program, the value of Greyhound's company structures grew from $109,400 at the beginning of the decade to $1.73 million at its end.

SIXTIES EXPANSION

During the mid-sixties, strong company growth created a need for enlarged and improved depot facilities and more and better bus equipment. In 1962 Greyhound committed itself to upgrading and modernizing its public facilities. Two of the largest metropolitan areas it served, Edmonton and Winnipeg, were particularly in need of attention.

Edmonton, Alberta – 1962

Edmonton's terminal at 102nd Avenue and 102nd Street no longer could handle the increased volume of passenger and express traffic. In November 1962 the company purchased the Taylor, Pearson & Carson building on the property next door, turning it into a combined service garage and company offices, while the existing terminal was renovated to provide better waiting room facilities, a new courier express area and an upgraded loading area. The project cost approximately $300,000.

Winnipeg, Manitoba – 1963

In contrast, Greyhound was in a tenant situation in Winnipeg as one of several companies renting depot space from Manitoba Bus Terminals Ltd., which was renting the building from Eaton's. Located at Graham and Hargrave Streets, the building was thirty years old and inadequate for the company's present needs.

In May 1963 Greyhound jumped ship and became a tenant paying an annual rent of $17,000 in a brand new $4.5 million development. Known as the "MA Centre", the property was owned by Oxford Leaseholds Ltd. and located at the corner of Portage Avenue and Colony Street in the heart of the business district.

Completed in 1964, this modern building featured an eight-storey office complex above the terminal, space for retail stores, a hotel, and parking for 300 cars. Able to accommodate a dozen loading buses at a time, the facility also featured a new Greyhound Travel Bureau facing Portage Avenue and drive-in express services, with room to expand for the next twenty-five years.

Secondary Depots

As a result of the new Trans-Canada Highway service, Greyhound's facilities in smaller communities were now handling increased passenger and express loads and had to be upgraded.

During 1964 new depots were completed in Kenora and Port Arthur, Ontario, and Princeton and Golden, British Columbia. Each of these new buildings included modern restaurants for the comfort of long-haul passengers and expanded courier express areas to accommodate the growing parcel express service.

Commission Agencies

As the sixties and seventies progressed, Greyhound continued to upgrade its facilities. In some smaller centres, Greyhound moved from company-owned depots to commission agencies, some of which were actually built by the company and leased to commission agents. For example, in Nelson, the company's historical heartland, the old depot on Baker Street, which contained a terminal, restaurant and ten-bus garage, was sold in 1968 to a commission agent who agreed to operate it in exchange for 10% commission on ticket sales and express.

Also in 1968, the company vacated its terminal located in a Penticton hotel, built a new depot on Nanaimo Avenue for $145,000, and promptly leased it to a commission agent. Politics were involved here, as an internal document related:

> As the Prime Minister of British Columbia, who is also the head of the Public Utilities

Commission, comes from this part of the Province, the Company must have a nominal bus depot of some sort in Penticton.

Other new commission depots opened in Kamloops in 1971, Sudbury in 1972, Grande Prairie and Medicine Hat in 1973 (replacing Greyhound's first company-built facility), and Cranbrook and Prince George in 1974. Greyhound also upgraded many other depots and began building centralized maintenance centres.

These upgrades included Edmonton, Vancouver, Kelowna, Whitehorse and North Bay in 1970, Winnipeg in 1973, and Red Deer, Lethbridge and Vernon in 1975. The first new maintenance centre was opened in Edmonton in 1970, accommodating the needs of both Greyhound and Coachways, and others were opened in Vancouver in 1971, in Sudbury in 1972 and in Penticton in 1974.

Calgary's Exercise in Patience

Perhaps the largest and most problematic facility issue of the sixties was the building of the long-awaited new Calgary depot. This depot was needed to replace the company's original terminal and office building on 7th Avenue.

Planning for the new terminal facility began in May 1968 when Greyhound's board empowered Borden to negotiate an agreement with a developer. Under the agreement, the developer would build a $10 million building on a site to be leased from the City of Calgary at 150 5th Avenue S.W. Greyhound would lease the main floor terminal for twenty-five years with a fifteen year option at 8% of the land cost and 10% of the construction costs annually, calculated to be $50,000 a year.

However, by November the plans had changed. Greyhound was now proposing to purchase the land outright and to try to find a developer interested in building a structure at a minimum cost of $5 million within a five-year period, as required by the city. An option to purchase the land was acquired, and in early 1969 Greyhound began negotiating with Cal-Mor Industries Ltd. to build a $15 million building that Greyhound would lease back at $56,000 per annum for the first twenty-five years.

These talks fell through and the company was forced to negotiate a relaxation of the city's building requirements. In May 1970 the company finally settled on a depot that it would build for approximately $700,000.

In the meantime the city's administration had changed. By November 1970 the costs had increased by $150,000 and the city was insisting on a parkade over the depot in addition to the 50-car underground parking lot already in the plans. Management was having second thoughts about the whole project, but decided to continue because the location was ideal for a bus depot and a comparable one could not be obtained without paying a premium price.

Construction finally got underway early in 1971. The Greyhound Building was sold to Alberta Government Telephones in January 1972 for $990,000, above its initial asking price of $950,000 back in August 1969. That same month the new depot was completed and opened by Alberta's Minister of Highways. Its features included underground passenger parking, cable television in the waiting area, dining room and cafeteria seating for 150, a package express section with its own entrance and parking, and an undercover bus concourse with loading capacity for up to thirteen buses at a time. Work began in 1975 to add a new maintenance and storage facility to the Calgary head office and garage at an estimated cost of $2.3 million.

Silversides Café operated by the Campbell family. Near London, Ontario, December 1997

Other developments in the late 70s and early 80s included new depots for Edmonton, London, Thunder Bay, Sudbury, Sault Ste. Marie and a new garage in Toronto.

Calgary Outgrown Again

The real estate market in western Canada was developing extremely quickly during the late seventies and early eighties, and property values in downtown Calgary were increasing. Greyhound's Calgary facilities had once again become outgrown, and in 1981 Greyhound decided to sell its valuable terminal property. The right offer would allow the company to select a good location and help pay the costs for a much needed new combined head office, garage and terminal complex.

Cadillac-Fairview, one of Canada's largest developers, made a particularly attractive offer and Greyhound's board voted to proceed with it in August 1981. Under the terms and subject to board approval, Cadillac Fairview would either purchase the property outright after receiving a city development permit, or lease it for ninety-nine years based on a 14.5% annual rental of the property's value plus escalation clauses for inflation.

Unfortunately, the Calgary real estate boom was starting to end. By early 1982 Cadillac-Fairview's board had declined to approve the agreement. Negotiations continued, developing alternate courses of action, but the development company needed more time. They got it, but for a price. Knight and his board required $250,000 for a non-refundable one-year option and a further $250,000 for Cadillac-Fairview to extend a second year.

Meanwhile, Greyhound began talks with a second developer, Trojan Properties, who had an option on a piece of land adjacent to Bow Trail at 9th Avenue and 14th Street S.W. The large site was ideal, located on the edge of the downtown core and convenient for

passengers but away from inner-city social problems and traffic congestion.

Trojan's offer was to purchase the property on its own and build the new facility for a total cost of roughly $30 million. The facility was intended to include 103,000 square feet of terminal space, almost double the 56,000 of the existing facility, and 57,000 square feet of office space compared with the cramped 22,850 currently used by head office.

Cadillac-Fairview and Trojan
In August 1982, facing gloomy economic forecasts, Greyhound's board had to make a decision. Cadillac-Fairview was not showing any signs of pursuing its option and Calgary development was slowing down. However, Greyhound was in dire need of a bigger facility. Accordingly, the board authorized its officers to purchase the Trojan property for approximately $15 million and gave the development company first right of refusal on the construction, if it could be performed for less than $15 million.

Cadillac-Fairview did renew its option, but early in 1983 it publicly announced it would abandon its redevelopment proposal. Although it was now apparent the existing terminal could not be sold and that financing costs of the new project would be high, the Greyhound board gave the go-ahead at the February 1983 board meeting to build the complex. Costs were

*Greyhound's new corporate headquarters
and depot adjacent to Calgary's core*

Breaking ground for the new Calgary terminal, October 1984. Left to right: Bill McKay, Trojan Properties; Ralph Klein, then mayor of Calgary; and Jim Knight

fixed at $15 million for construction and $700,000 for furniture and decorating.

However, because of delays due to the recession, Greyhound would not break ground until October 1984. Located on its own street at 877 Greyhound Way, the new facility was officially opened May 7, 1986 and is a Calgary landmark.

RENEWED COMMITMENT

Greyhound's next major phase of infrastructure investment took shape beginning in 1989 under Dick Huisman. As part of its customer service strategy, the company began a $14 million program of investment to clean up, refurbish, replace or relocate its major facilities.

These facility improvements were further driven by the federal government's announcement in October 1989 of significant cutbacks to VIA Rail service, especially in Western Canada. As roughly 36% of Greyhound's network paralleled VIA's routes, in January 1990 the company launched the new Greyhound Inter-City Express (ICE) Service. The service ran between key city-pairs, filing the gaps left by VIA, and was immensely popular, fuelling the need

for new and better facilities with intermodal connections to train, air and local transit.

Pacific Central Station

The Pacific Central Station in Vancouver, B.C. is Canada's crowning example of intermodalism in action. First built around 1945, the building was in a poor state of repair.

In 1992, following a change in terminal ownership, Greyhound, with partners VIA Rail and CN Rail, completely refurbished and repaired the facility. Greyhound's contribution was $3.5 million of the $6 million renovation project, with similar contributions from the other carriers. The work included seismic reconstruction and interior and exterior renovations.

The beautifully restored historic station was opened up to all transportation carriers, including a rail link to the Vancouver airport, making Pacific Central Station Canada's first, and very successful, intermodal terminal.

Winnipeg, Manitoba

The other arm of the infrastructure program was the development of new, separate cross-dock terminals and storefronts to support the company's courier express line of business. Cross-docks were built in Vancouver, Calgary, Edmonton and Winnipeg. The company opened storefronts in Regina, Saskatoon, Toronto and Vancouver and planned to open eight more in Vancouver, Calgary, Edmonton, Winnipeg and Metro Toronto by the end of the year. These storefronts were in addition to the 38 company depots and over 500 commissioned Greyhound agents across the country.

Before the cross-dock was installed in Winnipeg, the company used a nearby cross-dock operated by an industry partner. At Christmas time Greyhound personnel would process fifty to sixty 5-ton trucks a night through the tiny dock known as the "banana shed". It had few lights and no heat, and the temperature would plummet to -40C in the winter. Retired employee Lorne Anthony jokes that they had a "work or die policy – if you stopped, you'd freeze to death."

To keep up morale, staff bought a box of 150-watt light bulbs and changed the lights to "help make it warmer." At one point Anthony hung a brooder lamp on top of a crate, turned against the wall, to make a warm spot for people to thaw out.

Not long after the cross-docks were brought in it became clear that separating the courier express from the passenger business cut out the inherent synergies of the two businesses. By the mid 1990s the cross-docks had been shut down, and Winnipeg's courier express operation was moved to a new facility at Stevenson Road.

Prince Rupert, B.C.

In contrast to the long deliberations and two-steps-forward-one-step-back machinations sometimes experienced with Greyhound's major terminals are the thoughtful efforts and lightning raids to attain desirable properties in smaller Greyhound centres. One such example is Prince Rupert.

In early 1999 Dave Leach, then general manager for British Columbia, heard that a rental property in Prince Rupert had just been vacated by an airline that had shut down. Located at 112 6th Avenue, the property was at the end of the Prince Rupert Hotel across from a major mall. It was a perfect set-up, with booths and seating for passengers.

Upon hearing the news, Leach immediately drove from his office in Vancouver to Kamloops, then hopped a night bus to Prince Rupert. When he arrived, the hotel was just starting to sweep the floor, with plans to turn it into a nightclub. He convinced them to let Greyhound have the lease, and the company has been there ever since, creating significant business for the hotel.

Other terminal upgrades in the late 1990s included facilities in Kelowna, Kamloops and Vernon, as well as several agency locations.

Coquitlam, B.C.

Coquitlam is a special facility for Greyhound Canada. Previously, the company operated out of a depot in neighbouring New Westminster, both Vancouver satellites. Located in a poor part of town with awkward coach access and little customer parking, the tiny facility was not adequate. The company tried unsuccessfully for some years to find a replacement, until Dave Leach in his role as general manager, B.C. took a second look at the demographics. He realized that the smaller industries that use Greyhound's courier express products were moving further east in the Fraser Valley, away from the downtown Vancouver storefront.

Coquitlam was the solution to both problems. Greyhound bought a piece of land for a few million and sub-divided it for future sale while building a new depot with better access to its customers. The Vancouver cross-dock, a relic from the Ron Parker days, was converted to a garage and the existing garage was closed, generating savings. Coquitlam became the new courier express centre for the Vancouver area and the New Westminster facility was shut down.

The new depot first began operations on April 29, 2003, with a grand opening held on June 9. Shortly afterwards it received an Award for Accessibility from the Mayor's Committee for People with Disabilities, recognizing its design and functionality in removing barriers.

Windsor, Ontario

On December 20, 2001, the government of Ontario announced it would invest $3.25 billion over 10 years to develop the province's transit network, with a focus on public-private partnerships. Greyhound developed and submitted several proposals to the program. These included a joint proposal between

New Westminster, B.C. depot, late eighties. Replaced by the Coquitlam depot in April 2003

The Calgary terminal and headquarters

Greyhound and Transit Windsor to construct a new Windsor Terminal.

On November 1, 2002, the project was approved and the government announced it was investing $2 million in this intermodal project. Final site selection is underway, and the new facility will significantly improve intermodal accessibility, as well as helping to reduce congestion and pollution.

Toronto Intermodal Facility

The current Toronto bus terminal, located at Bay and Dundas, was first built in 1931, the same year as the opening of Maple Leaf Gardens. By 1987 however, it was acknowledged that the facility had become outdated and in need of major upgrades to make it a more modern and efficient facility. With no space to expand, various initiatives have been pursued over the years to find an alternative site. Greyhound is working with the Ontario Motor Coach Association (OMCA), fellow intercity carriers and other stakeholders to identify a more appropriate site for our Ontario hub, to enhance Greyhound's service and facility infrastructure in Southern Ontario.

Greyhound Canada continuously pursues infrastructure renewal and upgrade initiatives for its facilities. We are committed to facilities that achieve the multiple objectives of intermodal connectivity and alliances, operating requirements and accessibility needs, while being sensitive to environmental issues and operating costs.

CHAPTER NINE

GREYHOUND AIR

n 1993, the dream began for Greyhound to have an airline and bring intermodality to a whole new level. That year, Murray Sigler, former President of Canadian Airlines, visited Dick Huisman to discuss the possibility of creating a short haul airline in Western Canada, based on the highly successful Southwest Airlines model. Initially, Huisman refused to consider the idea, but later reopened the discussion.

Having completed overhauling Greyhound's facilities, fleet and approach to customer service, Huisman shared the general belief that the Canadian bus industry was mature and that double-digit growth was unlikely in the current environment. Greyhound continued to realize healthy profits, but bus travel had been declining since the early 1990s, because of competition from charter and discount airlines.

Huisman, himself a former executive of Canadian Pacific Airlines, had to consider where future growth opportunities lay.

Project Eagle

That fall, Huisman authorized Project Eagle, bringing together a small group of people to create the business plan for the airline. Led by Sigler, they were Kevin Lawless; Brent Statton from Canadian Pacific; and Terry Nord from WardAir. Lawless and Statton were charged with developing the market analysis and the revenue forecast, while Nord performed the operational development as well as investigating the regulatory and operating certificate requirements.

The group was installed in a small Calgary office on 6th Avenue in the Bow Valley Centre, where they worked in secrecy for almost six months.

The original concept was to build a Boeing 737 operation using the Southwest Airlines business model. This meant inexpensive fares, no frills, no interlining with other carriers, and service to secondary, less expensive airports if necessary. The target image was cheerful, young and vibrant.

Intermodality

While there were 78 airports in Canada, the bus industry served more than 3,000 points. Recognizing that passengers would need airport connections at both ends, the issue was to find a way to seamlessly link and feed to the airline using Greyhound's established network. The vision was to create intermodality at a whole new level without cannibalizing Greyhound's profitable bus operation.

Project Eagle's recommendation was to operate a semi-transcontinental airline, based in Winnipeg with short- and medium-haul spokes east and west. In order to mitigate the significant costs of airport fees, the group targetted under-served airports, such as Abbotsford (as an alternative to Vancouver), Kelowna, Kamloops, Calgary, Edmonton, Regina, Saskatoon, Hamilton (as an alternative to Toronto), London, Trenton, Kingston, etc.

Ultimately, the final list of cities was Vancouver, Calgary, Edmonton, Kelowna, Hamilton, Toronto, and Ottawa, all hubbed through Winnipeg.

The plan was ready to take to market in early 1994. Unfortunately, Canada was still feeling the effects of the recession, the travel industry was depressed and there was no money. The concept sat on the shelf until 1995 when discussion was renewed.

Regulatory Issues

At this time, Greyhound was 68.5% owned by The Dial Corp. of Phoenix, Arizona. This was a major barrier to the proposed airline, as the National Transportation Act, 1987 limited foreign ownership of Canadian airlines to 25%, which meant that Greyhound could not apply for an operating licence.

To get around this issue, it was suggested to contract the actual flying out to another company. Armed with legal advice that contracting out to a provider would not contravene the 25% rule, the hunt was on for an operator.

At the same time, Greyhound began developing a restructuring proposal to separate the bus business from the hotel and tour business carried on by subsidiary Brewster Transport. If successful, Greyhound's bus business would cease to be controlled by Dial and would become approximately 6% publicly held. If successful, this would bring Greyhound's U.S. ownership under the 25% limit.

Huisman was also able to convince Dial Corp. to fund the airline start-up, avoiding the need for an initial public offering (IPO).

Kelowna Flightcraft

The search for an operator in Canada with the right infrastructure was frustrating. Eventually, Greyhound identified Kelowna Flightcraft, an air charter and courier company based in Kelowna, B.C. with maintenance facilities in various cities including Hamilton, Ontario.

Serving an array of "private, commercial and military customers across Canada and around the world", and touted as "operating Canada's third largest aircraft fleet", Kelowna held a domestic licence and met all Canadian ownership and control-in-fact requirements to maintain its licence. Unfortunately, Kelowna Flightcraft was a 727 operator.

Boeing 727 vs. 737

Boeing 727 airplanes were a very different proposition than the 737 model. Greyhound had based its model on a 737 carrying 115 passengers, running on two engines and using two pilots. In contrast, the relatively old 727s provided by Kelowna carried 160 passengers, ran on three fuel-hungry engines, and required a crew of two pilots and a flight engineer. Additionally, the 727s were very noisy and needed "hush kits" to bring them up to Canadian regulations, which cost $2 million per airplane.

Accordingly, the original business case had to be revised to accommodate the change in aircraft. Since Terry Nord was no longer with Greyhound, it was Brent Statton's job to put the airline together using Kelowna Flightcraft.

The Agreement

On February 6, 1996, Greyhound signed an Air Charter Agreement with Kelowna Flightcraft Air Charter Ltd. of Kelowna, B.C.

The press release on February 11th announced the agreement "will provide the opportunity to link Greyhound's existing bus service with Kelowna Flightcraft's air network. Canadians will have the opportunity to travel across Canada through one low cost intermodal system using ground or air transportation, or a combination of both. The new air service, to be named Greyhound Air, will be operated by Kelowna Flightcraft using a fleet of up to six Boeing 727-100 [sic: in fact they were 200 series] aircraft.

"With Kelowna Flightcraft providing the airplanes and the flight operations on a cost plus basis, Greyhound Canada's share of total startup costs is expected to be less than $10 million, and it will have limited ongoing downside financial risk."

"Marking New Territory"

At the same time, Greyhound was developing groundbreaking creative for the advertising campaign. Greyhound's senior vice-president of marketing, John Munro, came up with a fantastic advertising campaign.

Prior to joining Greyhound in 1989, Munro had worked for Canadian Airlines International Ltd. and CP Air. Munro had serious misgivings about the likely success of the new airline and wanted to leave the company. He was convinced to stay on to build the campaign.

Because Greyhound's name was so firmly linked with bus transportation, Munro had to create an image that instantly told the reader Greyhound was in a new business. Working with ad agency Palmer Jarvis, Munro created an unforgettable image – a Greyhound dog lifting his leg on the tire of a competing aircraft, with the tag line, "We're marking new territory", followed by "Low fares without the fine print".

Launched in April 1996 at Easter, the shock ads were hugely successful with the public and achieved high retention even up to ten months after release. The ads were made using a retired racing greyhound from the Pacific Northwest called Ptolemy, marking the first time that a live dog was used in Greyhound advertising in Canada.

WE'RE MARKING NEW TERRITORY

GREYHOUND AIR.

1-800-661-TRIP(8747) Air Service operated by KELOWNA FLIGHTCRAFT

"We're Marking New Territory". Greyhound's cheeky ad campaign was an instant success

False Start

The plan was to launch the airline on May 12, 1996, with up to two flights each day linking Vancouver, Kelowna, Calgary, Edmonton, Winnipeg, Ottawa, Toronto and Hamilton, with Winnipeg as the hub. The launch was so successful that Greyhound received 50,000 phone calls the first week; five times the expected total of 10,000.

Unfortunately, immediately after the advertising launch, newcomer WestJet complained to the National Transportation Agency that Greyhound was operating illegally.

On April 12, 1996, Greyhound announced it had been advised by the National Transportation Agency (NTA) to "suspend the offering of low-priced inter-modal air/bus services to the Canadian travelling public". The NTA had ruled that Greyhound would have to hold a domestic licence in order to operate a "publicly available domestic air service". Greyhound's prior legal advice hadn't been as water-tight as hoped.

Scrambling, Greyhound and Kelowna immediately renegotiated their Air Charter Agreement, changing the "financial, operational and business relationships" effective April 22, 1996, and on April 24-25 they applied to have the decision reviewed, hoping the changes would satisfy the NTA's concerns.

Greyhound cited Kelowna's assumption of significant financial risk, while Kelowna's response indicated "it has already invested significant sums in the start-up of the passenger charter air service and that this investment was done in good faith with the belief that the arrangements between Kelowna and Greyhound would not offend the Agency or violate the NTA, 1987."

WestJet responded on April 30 to the NTA, stating there had not been a material change in the circumstances, and that Greyhound's "chartering aircraft for the purpose of operating a scheduled airline service is tantamount to leasing a licence". WestJet also tried unsuccessfully to obtain copies of Greyhound and Kelowna's responses and details on the amended arrangement.

On May 10, 1996, the NTA agreed that there had been a change in the facts and agreed to review its decision. It found, however, that "the essence of (the) proposed arrangement" had not changed and upheld its decision.

Greyhound had to refund almost 12,000 reservations while paying for the advertising campaign, the leased aircraft and the staff. It lobbied furiously to have the decision set aside.

Greyhound Canada Transportation Corp.

In the meantime, Dial Corp. of Phoenix, Arizona had approved Greyhound's restructuring plan.

On May 31, 1996, Greyhound Lines of Canada Ltd. was restructured from a bus transportation, courier and tourism entity with a U.S. parent company to become a bus transportation and courier company with no single, major shareholder or significant U.S. ownership. The company was split into two companies, Brewster and Greyhound Canada Transportation Corp. (GCTC). As of June 1, 1996, Greyhound Canada Transportation Corp. became 76% Canadian-owned, clearing the way for a CTA ruling.

CTA Overruled

On June 7, 1996, federal transport minister David Anderson set aside the CTA ruling and permitted Greyhound to piggyback on the licence of Kelowna Flightcraft, adding that Greyhound's restructuring satisfied domestic ownership requirements.

Transport Canada would go on to list Greyhound Air among its major accomplishments for 1996, counting the decision to let Greyhound fly among its efforts to "create a more efficient, commercially driv-

Greyhound Air ribbon cutting ceremony.
At right, Kevin Lawless. July 8, 1996

Launch of Greyhound Air. Liveried bus and plane on the tarmac. July 8, 1996

en, regionally responsive transportation system that is less dependent on the taxpayer's money".

Huisman was elated by the Minister's decision, and Greyhound began selling tickets the very next day, June 8, 1996. Even though the ad campaign had shut down, customer retention was high and sales were brisk.

Take Two

Greyhound Air's first flights took off on July 8, 1996. The mood was ebullient as passengers preparing to board the inaugural flights were greeted by magicians, clowns and other entertainers handing out chocolate dog bones and other promotional items. Greyhound described its new service as a "complete travel solution":

> Using an Intermodal Concept – "A Total Passenger Travel Network" Greyhound's concept is based on simplicity itself. Travelers are offered convenience, flexibility in one step, convenient daily schedules, less restriction, and the ability to travel throughout Central and Western Canada. Greyhound is as close as a passenger can get to door-to-door service: eight (8) flying markets and 1,100 communities served by bus allow travel anywhere between Ottawa and Vancouver.
> Up to twice daily flights will be offered from Vancouver, Kelowna, Calgary and Edmonton in the west through the Winnipeg hub to Ottawa, Toronto and Hamilton in the east. Air service commenced today in all markets except Kelowna, where the new service will take off on July 15, 1996.

Initial load factors were higher than expected, particularly for the Hamilton airport. Kelowna Flightcraft's staff of 80 pilots and 120 flight attendants performed very well and the onboard quality was high. Greyhound Air quickly built a reputation for excellent customer service.

The six Boeing 727-200 aircraft, logoed with the Greyhound dog on the tail, were highly visible and a favourite in the media. Greyhound Air was innovative as well, implementing the first electronic ticket system in Canada.

For the 24-day period July 8 to July 31, Greyhound Air achieved revenues of $5.3 million, based on an overall load factor of 69.5%, with air services sustaining a pre-tax operating loss of $1.3 million as a consequence of the short sales period.

Uphill Start

Unfortunately, the late start had been extremely costly. During three months of uncertainty Greyhound still had to pay for the airplanes, crews, advertising and legal costs, without an income stream. The total came to $17 million.

Then, when the CTA ruling was set aside, Greyhound Air had to pay for a second start-up campaign. Consumer uncertainty caused by the CTA-imposed delay meant that the campaign could not help but be less effective.

Most crucially, because it was unable to launch in May as planned, Greyhound Air had missed the all-important spring period, when most passengers plan their summer trips. By July it was too late to capture the summer market, leaving Greyhound Air woefully short on summer revenues to carry it through the money-losing winter months.

It was an uphill start from all angles. In the first five months of its operations the company recorded a $9.8 million pre-tax loss on revenues of $26.7 million.

Systemic Issues

As a discount airline, Greyhound Air promised to "provide cross-country flights at fares 50% below the going price". This pricing strategy automatically meant low margins and consequently intense pressure on Greyhound Air to control costs. However, this was impossible from the beginning.

Although Greyhound Air did not offer business class, hot meals or other luxuries, it had serious internal cost concerns directly related to its contract with Kelowna Flightcraft and the 727 aircraft itself.

The Kelowna Flightcraft agreement was a "cost plus" contract incorporating a guaranteed mark-up. Greyhound was responsible for all the costs but couldn't manage them down, while Kelowna Flightcraft was guaranteed a profit.

Secondly, the 727 aircraft posed a much more demanding cost scenario than the 737 on which Greyhound had originally based its airline business case. Taking into account the 727's greater capacity, higher labour costs (three pilots vs. two for the 737), the $2 million "hush kits" to muffle the three engines, and the simple fact of its greater age and resulting higher maintenance costs, the 727 aircraft's capital and operating costs were on average 40% higher than those for a 737.

These two factors drove up the seat mile cost substantially. In essence, the cost to produce the service was too high to break even.

This was compounded by other factors, such as Greyhound Air's overly generous, expensive frequent flyer program, and the fact that the airline did not have access to a computerized reservation system until April 1997, selling its tickets through the 1-800-661-TRIP (-8747) number and at bus terminals.

At the same time, Air Canada and the other carriers took aim at the new rival.

Nationals Take Aim

Greyhound Air operated a mixture of medium- and short-haul routes through its Winnipeg hub. Although its frequency was relatively low, its low-fare strategy was considered a threat by the major airlines, such as Air Canada, whose yields on domestic routes were affected by Greyhound's entry. Air Canada didn't wait long to react.

That fall, Air Canada and Canadian Airlines began matching Greyhound Air's fares on competing routes with economy seat sales. Even with good load factors, the deep discounting on Greyhound Air's already razor slim margins drove the price below the seat cost per mile. Greyhound Air didn't have deep enough pockets to make good the losses.

Years later, the Competition Tribunal would release a document prepared for Air Canada by an outside consultant. Dated January 1999, the document specifically cited low-cost rivals such as Greyhound Air, suggesting that Air Canada was "able to target new competitors and render them unprofitable by lowering fares and adding capacity" (Globe & Mail, February 6, 2003).

Spring 1997

Greyhound Air struggled through a terrible winter, facing mounting losses even as it grew its load factors. In December 1996, seeing the inevitable, John Munro resigned as senior vice president of marketing. Management placed all its attention on the airline, leaving the bus business to run itself.

In the first quarter of 1997, Greyhound posted a loss of $5.6 million compared to a profit of $2.5 million for the same period in 1996, despite achieving a load factor of 62.6% on the air service.

In April, Greyhound Air agreed to allow agents to book their flights on a commission basis, and by June 25% of bookings were coming through 2,400 participating agents.

That June, Greyhound announced its consolidated operating results for the second quarter and first six months ended April 30, 1997, incorporating the bus, courier and air transportation services.

For the second quarter, customarily a slow period for the airline industry, air service revenues totalled $19.7 million with an overall load factor of 64.2 percent. The pre-tax operating loss was $8.1 million. During this period Greyhound Air had been forced to cut frequency on weekends to try and reduce operating expenses. The pre-tax operating loss for the six-month period was $20.9 million.

Sadly, Greyhound Air never came close to making money until the summer of 1997. In its best quarter, ended July 31, 1997, it made a marginal $100,000 pre-tax operating profit on revenues of $34.5 million.

In August 1997, Greyhound Air's load factor reached 82% and 91% of surveyed consumers ranked Greyhound Air in the "excellent" category. As well, the airline had succeeded in attracting business customers, who made up roughly 39 percent of its passengers. Additionally, the intermodal bus and airline service connections were beginning to work, with 15-20% of passengers using Greyhound buses to connect to the airport.

However, Greyhound Air had been unable to achieve either the required yields or load margins in order to be profitable. As a result of the heavy losses, Greyhound was financially strapped. It had supported the airline with cash from its bus business, but reserves were now dangerously low and further operating losses were anticipated in the coming winter season. Greyhound needed a white knight.

Laidlaw Inc.

Greyhound began discussions with potential buyers in spring 1997. That summer, under newly appointed executive vice president and chief operating officer John Grainger, Laidlaw Inc. acquired Greyhound in a friendly takeover, holding 650,000 shares previously purchased at $3 each and offering a 53% premium on all outstanding stock. As a condition of the sale, Laidlaw Inc. required the shutdown of Greyhound Air.

On September 8, 1997, after fifteen months of operation and $30 million in losses, Greyhound announced it would shut down its Greyhound Air services at midnight on September 21 "as part of a takeover by Laidlaw Inc. of Burlington, Ontario". Using an arrangement with Canadian Airlines to honour tickets issued for Greyhound Air after September 21st, the shutdown was orderly and no passengers were stranded. Shortly afterwards, Grainger replaced Dick Huisman as President of Greyhound.

The CTA would have the last laugh, recounting the launch and demise of Greyhound Air in its 1997 Annual Report as "prior to the coming into force of the financial fitness requirements" necessary for a domestic airline.

Debates

Industry observers are divided on whether Greyhound Air, Canada's first discount airline, could have succeeded and become profitable, given enough time and money, despite the unfortunate double-launch caused by the regulatory issues.

WestJet, another low-cost airline modelled after Southwest Airlines and launched the same year as Greyhound Air, has been able to succeed, but its cost structure was better and avoided many of the pitfalls Greyhound Air experienced. WestJet chose short-haul routes not adequately served by the national airlines, making it less of a target. As well, Greyhound Air developed the test market for the previously underused Hamilton airport, which WestJet later adopted as its Ontario hub.

With a high-cost operation in a low-margin market, charging ticket prices often only one third of the fares levied by major carriers on the same routes, Greyhound Air has been compared to the short-lived People's Air. After strong initial success in the early 80s, People's Air was rendered nearly bankrupt by predatory pricing from the large U.S. carriers. It was acquired by Texas Air Corporation and merged with Continental Airlines in February 1987.

The experiment to build a truly intermodal system realizing synergies with Greyhound's existing bus operations had been a costly one. Greyhound Air helped pave the way for Canada's future discount airlines, but at tremendous cost to Greyhound's core business, putting its very survival at risk.

CHAPTER TEN

THE BUS IS BETTER

Over the last 75 years Greyhound Canada has revolutionized bus travel. Beginning in 1929 with four routes in B.C., Greyhound's innovative approach to quality passenger transportation continues to unite provinces and bring Canadians together.

Today Canada's premier intercity bus company, Greyhound Canada Transportation Corp. has come a long way from George Fay's 1920s sales trip to western Canada. Since its incorporation on November 30, 1929, Greyhound has grown quickly, adding routes, uniting provinces and bringing Canadians together. For decades the Greyhound name has been an international symbol for travelling in style, comfort and on-time reliability.

Throughout the years, Greyhound has continued to develop, providing customers with better service through coach improvements, top-notch training, increased schedule frequency and an ever-growing Canadian network.

Greyhound and its parent Laidlaw International are proud to count among their network acquisitions such historic names as Canadian Coachways, Gray Coach Lines, Gray Line Toronto, Maverick Coach Lines, Gray Line Vancouver, The Gray Line of Victoria, Voyageur Colonial Bus Lines, Gray Line Banff, Gray Line Ottawa, Grey Goose Bus Lines, and Penetang-Midland Coach Lines.

Statistics

Operating a fleet of 772 buses, today Greyhound daily logs an average 210,000 kilometres while carrying some 18,000 passengers and 21,000 parcels a day. Greyhound offers frequent service to 1,200 communities stretching from Vancouver Island to Montreal and beyond, using a network of over 100 facilities, 690 agencies, and interline partners in Quebec and the Maritimes. According to Dave Leach, senior vice president, "Greyhound is an essential lifeline between urban and rural Canada. We are committed to providing safe, affordable and convenient service."

Greyhound has revenues in excess of $330 million annually and in the past five years has enjoyed growth in all lines of business: +17% in passenger volumes, +29% in courier express and +26% in its travel and tour group. Referring to Greyhound's seventy-five years of service, Dave Leach, senior vice president, Canada says, "It is the passion we feel for what we do that makes it all worthwhile".

Partnership with MCI

Since 1937 Greyhound and Motor Coach Industries, originally of Winnipeg, Manitoba, foremost Canadian bus manufacturer and onetime Greyhound subsidiary, have worked together developing superior buses for Canada's demanding environment. Our top-of-the-line fleet includes such amenities as comfortable deep-pitch seating, videos, reading lights and washrooms, and a range of e-services are on the way.

World Leader

Greyhound is viewed as a world leader in intercity bus transportation. After reviewing bus operations throughout Europe and North America, the People's Republic of China's National Express Group selected Greyhound as the model for developing China's bus transportation network. On October 21, 2002 in Beijing the two companies signed a historic agreement highlighting Greyhound's best practices.

A veteran of the 1988 Calgary Winter Olympics as the official transportation provider, Greyhound is proud to have an active role in the 2010 Whistler Olympics transportation planning. The company also provides state-of-the-art campaign buses equipped with the latest in satellite technology and partnered with the National Post and Global TV's Decision Canada Tour, covering the June 28 federal election.

Environmentally Sound

Greyhound is proud to be part of the most environmentally-friendly mode of transportation. Transport Canada studies identify inter-city bus as by far the most fuel-efficient and least polluting mode of travel compared to trains, airlines and the personal automobile.

In the words of former Transport Minister David Collenette, "Bus is an environmentally friendly mode. Bus pollutes least of the passenger modes. It achieves the lowest cost consumption per passenger kilometre. This also means that it has the lowest level of greenhouse gas emissions of the passenger modes . . . Bus usage can ease highway congestion. Every full coach can get anywhere up to 55 people out of their cars."

With these advantages, Greyhound is proud to assist Canada in meeting its Kyoto commitments.

Intermodalism

Greyhound is a Canadian leader in promoting intermodality with the federal and provincial governments. Through such initiatives as the revitalization of Vancouver's historic Pacific Central Station in 1993 with partners VIA Rail and Canadian National Railway, and planned initiatives for other major cities, Greyhound focuses on building facilities that link multiple forms of transportation for the most effective, accessible passenger experience. Greyhound believes travellers should have access to fully integrated travel options.

Bringing the Goods to Our Customers–Greyhound Courier Express

Greyhound efficiently cross-utilizes its fleet to provide courier express and charter services using the same fleet. Beginning in 1992, the company added pup trailers to ship its courier express. Today its fleet of 93 pup trailers operates from B.C. to Quebec.

The company is about to implement state of the art web-based track-and-trace, bar coding and hand-held point-of-sale technology to its domestic and international courier express services.

Reputation for Safety

"Greyhound has the most demanding driver training program in the world", comments director of safety Lorraine Card. Hundreds of Greyhound drivers go on to achieve 20 to 35-year safety awards for remaining accident-free. Greyhound wins major safety awards both in Canada and the United States, including the 2003 Ontario Motor Coach Association Award for Driver Excellence.

The company is sharing its training program with the Motor Carrier Passenger Council of Canada to establish national operating standards and a driver certification program. This initiative will raise the profile of the industry, stabilize operator staffing through effective recruitment practices, and improve skill development industry-wide.

Preferred Employer

Recognized as a leader in employment equity, today Greyhound employs 2,094 unionized employees and 585 non-union employees. With an enviable employee retention record, Greyhound in partnership with the Amalgamated Transit Union (ATU) is committed to progressive labour relations, using interest-based bargaining to resolve disputes quickly and amiably.

The Freedom to Go

Greyhound is an accessibility leader. As early as 1959 Greyhound inaugurated reduced fares to visually disabled passengers, their escorts and service animals. A founding member of the Intercity Bus Code of Practice, Greyhound helped establish accessibility best practices in 1995, and is a member of Alberta's Advisory Committee on Barrier Free Transportation. "For our efforts, in 2001 the Canadian Foundation for Physically Disabled Persons awarded Greyhound the Corporate Award. That same year, National Transportation Week selected Greyhound to receive an Award of Achievement for our contributions to accessibility."

Today Greyhound provides wheelchair accessible coaches, seeing-eye/hearing-ear accommodation, and preferential senior and companion fares for the disabled community. "We are very proud of our record on accessibility", says Dave Leach. "In 2003 our new Coquitlam, B.C. terminal received an Accessibility Award from the city for eliminating barriers".

For commuters in the Greater Toronto Area, Greyhound offers freedom from rush-hour traffic and downtown parking. With over 120 schedules a day linking Toronto and the Golden Horseshoe Greyhound delivers a viable solution to gridlock.

For Youth, Greyhound continues to offer affordable student and companion fare products with regular service to Canadian universities. "Youth is a very important market for Greyhound", comments director of marketing Cheryl Heilman. "We believe students should be able to visit their families and experience Canada without going broke." As well, Greyhound offers seasonal fun such as ski trips to Whistler, B.C., the Bootlegger Survivor Road Trip and other innovative promotions such as the highly successful web-based Win a Year On Greyhound contest.

In 1997 the company launched its Travel Is Educational, Too! scholarship program that annually gives away up to $60,000 in scholarships, travel and other prizes to high school students graduating with an 80%+ average. Now in its eighth year, this spring the program received over 3,000 entries, and on May 11, fifty students across Canada were selected to receive prizes worth up to $3,400 in scholarships and free travel.

Go Greyhound

Greyhound's impressive successes over the years have kept pace with and indeed frequently anticipate changes in technology and consumer taste. With an integrated network of routes and facilities, strong leadership and a vibrant, committed workforce, this Canadian business icon will continue to say, "You're going places. Go Greyhound."

ACKNOWLEDGEMENTS

It is an honour to have been invited to write this book for Greyhound Canada's 75th anniversary.

I owe a great debt to Ted Hart, who wrote the first Greyhound history, *. . . and leave the driving to us*, and to Bob Borden, Lorne Frizzell, Grant Smith, Bill deWynter, Pat Williams, Jack Rajala, Ed Dunn, George Mermet, Bill Brown, Tom Kirkham and John and Keith Olson. Your memories, photographs and research preserved and illuminated Greyhound's first fifty years. I hope I have made these past twenty-five years just as accessible.

I also gratefully acknowledge the following Greyhound employees, alumni and industry members who contributed their memories, records, and photographs to the new portions of this book.

Norm Aitken, Lorne Anthony, Wanda Barg, Bill Betton, Lori Birce, Lorraine Card, Candice Cherry, Elena Chiappetta, Rob Galea, Cheryl Heilman, Dick Huisman, Fred Keeling, Walter Kiskunas, Kevin Lawless, Dave Leach, Cris Leonard, Ron Love, Pamela Malec, Paul Marino, Wayne McArthur, Al Mezzetta, Chris Michiels, John Munro, Cindy Newbergher, Bill Noddle, Pat Paras, Roger Pike, John Shamrock, Brad Shephard, Dennis Tillotson, Nancy Vacon, Ivan Wannamaker, and many others.

I especially thank every Greyhound driver. This book would not have been possible without you.

Eve Harris

Eve W. A. Harris
July 2004

Index

acquisition of, ...37, 83–86
competition with, ...67–68, 69–72
fleet of, ...132, 135, 138–39
spin-off of, ...99–100, 174
Broderick, Bill, ...21
Brown, Bill, ...21, 27, 109–11, 117, 118
Brown, Jerry, ...16, 17, 28, 65, 112, 125
Brown, R. E., ...78
Budd, R. W., ...33, 34
Buffington, Merrill, ...19
Bullock, James R., ...53, 54–55

C
Cadillac-Fairview, ...169
Cadotte, Raymond, ...105
Caesar, Orville S., ...9, 11, 19, 29, 30, 74, 166
Cafferky, Mike, ...102, 147
Cairns, Ivan R., ...53
Calgary and Eastern Bus Lines, ...63, 112
Calgary–Edmonton Highway, .59, 62–63, 67, 69
Callaghan, Cliff, ...147
Campbell, A. W., ...79
Canada Loves New York, ...56–57
Canada Pass, ...50, 83
Canada Steamship Lines (CSL), ...55, 96, 97, 98
Canadian Airlines, ...178
    See also Canadian Pacific Airlines
Canadian-American Trailways Ltd., ...32
Canadian Auto Workers Union (CAW),
    ....98–99, 103, 122
Canadian Bus Association, ...54, 158, 159
Canadian Coachways, Ltd.,
    ....67, 86–89, 116–17, 139
Canadian Greyhound Coaches (B.C.) Ltd., ...7
Canadian Greyhound Coaches Ltd., ...10, 32
Canadian Greyhound Coaches Ltd., Alberta,
    ....5–7, 61–62, 84, 163
Canadian Greyhound Coaches Ltd., B.C.,
    ....1, 5, 6, 61–62
Canadian Greyhound Lines Ltd.,
    ....10, 11, 18, 32, 77–78
Canadian National Railways (CN Rail),
    ....81, 162, 170
Canadian Pacific Airlines, ...173
    See also Canadian Airlines
Canadian Pacific Railway (CPR),
    ....18, 84, 85, 86, 99
Canadian Yelloway Lines, Ltd., ...6, 59, 61
Card, Lorraine, ...56, 58, 153, 157, 181

Carefree Tours, ...105
Cariboo Garage Ltd., ...74
Cariboo Greyhound Lines, ...72, 74
Cariboo Stages Ltd., ...72, 73
Carlson, Hank, ...126
Carscadden, George 57
Cascade Charter Service Ltd., ...101
Central Canadian Greyhound Lines Ltd.,
    ....7–9, 11–20, 65–66
Central Greyhound Lines, ...32
Chalmers, Norm, ...62
Chambers, L. C., ...28
Chatham Coach Lines (Cha-Co), ...93, 104–5
Checker Greyhound. See Prairie Coach Lines
Cherlenko, Bill, ...26
Circle Tours, ...3, 4, 65, 109
    See also Grand Circle Tours
Clark, Bill, ...109
Clark, C. T., ...74
Clark Transportation Company Ltd., ...68, 74
Cleary, Pat, ...109
Clermont, Garry, ...50, 52
coaches, ...50, 123–41, 127, 152, 154
    See also G.M. coaches; MCI coaches; pup
    trailers; Western Flyer
    dieselization of, ...132–33
    No. 25 ("Two-bits"), ...126, 152
    seats for, ...48, 123, 129, 140, 152, 158
    for tours, ...135, 139–40
Colebrook, R. F., ...71
Coles, Bud, ...101
College of the Rockies, ...99
Collins, Mickey, ...87
Collins, Percy and Jack. See Canadian
    Coachways, Ltd.
Colonial Coach Lines Ltd., ...82, 96
Columbia Icefield Snowmobile Tours, Ltd.,
    ....99, 138
community outreach, ...159–61
commuter services, ..57–58, 105–6, 154–55, 181
Confédération des syndicats nationaux (CSN), 97
Conti, Mickey, ...166
courier express. See express services
Cox, Clive, ...40, 42
Crawford, H. Noel, ...36
Crosby, Lou, ...71, 84, 85
cross-docks, ...49, 144, 145–46, 170, 171
cross-subsidization, ...87, 139, 146, 181
Cruickshank, Adam, ...5

185